WITHDRAWN

D1612077

The Religious Roots of the First Amendment

The Religious Roots of the First Amendment

Dissenting Protestants and the Separation of Church and State

NICHOLAS P. MILLER

OXFORD
UNIVERSITY PRESS

OXFORD
UNIVERSITY PRESS

Oxford University Press, Inc., publishes works that further
Oxford University's objective of excellence
in research, scholarship, and education.

Oxford   New York
Auckland   Cape Town   Dar es Salaam   Hong Kong   Karachi
Kuala Lumpur   Madrid   Melbourne   Mexico City   Nairobi
New Delhi   Shanghai   Taipei   Toronto

With offices in
Argentina   Austria   Brazil   Chile   Czech Republic   France   Greece
Guatemala   Hungary   Italy   Japan   Poland   Portugal   Singapore
South Korea   Switzerland   Thailand   Turkey   Ukraine   Vietnam

Published by Oxford University Press, Inc.
198 Madison Avenue, New York, New York 10016
www.oup.com

Oxford is a registered trademark of Oxford University Press

Library of Congress Cataloging-in-Publication Data
Miller, Nicholas Patrick.
The religious roots of the First Amendment : dissenting Protestants and the separation
of church and state / Nicholas P. Miller.
p. cm.
Includes bibliographical references (p.). and index.
ISBN 978–0–19–985836–1
1. Christianity and law.   2. Church history.   3. Christianity—Influence.
4. United States. Constitution. 1st Amendment.   5. Protestantism—History.   I. Title.
BR115.L28M55 2012
323.44′20973—dc23
2012000426

1 3 5 7 9 8 6 4 2
Printed in the United States of America
on acid-free paper

For Leanne,
who bears the present
so that I can hear the past;
Patrick, Kelli, & little Nicole,
whose pasts are so brief and short
that the lively present is all important,
but someday you will know why I wrote this,
I pray!

Contents

Foreword   *ix*

Acknowledgments   *xi*

Prologue   *xiii*

Introduction: Religion and American Disestablishment   1

1. The Monk and the Bard: From Luther's Protest to
   Milton's Protestant Vision   15

2. The Philosopher and the Enthusiast: The Collaboration of
   John Locke and William Penn   49

3. The Puritan Lawyer and the Baptist Preacher: Elisha Williams,
   Isaac Backus, and American Dissent   91

4. Revolutionary and Governor: William Livingston Opposes
   Anglican Control of King's College   114

5. Theologian and Politician: John Witherspoon and James Madison
   Make a National Principle   133

Epilogue: Back to the Future of Church and State   156

Appendix: Significant Works on Religious Freedom and
Early America   172

Notes   180

Bibliography   220

Index   233

Foreword

NICHOLAS MILLER'S ARGUMENT is that a long-standing and distinct religious tradition contributed much more directly to the religion clauses of the U.S. Constitution's First Amendment than historians have been ready to acknowledge. The standard picture has been that while religious motives were not entirely absent in the church-state considerations of America's colonial and early-national generations, pragmatic considerations were everywhere much more important. Miller does not question the presence of these pragmatic considerations.

After all, most of the colonies eventually came to include Presbyterians, Congregationalists, Episcopalians, and Baptists—not to speak of a diverse sprinkling of Catholics, Jews, Quakers, Mennonites, deists, Lutherans, German Reformed, and more—among their inhabitants. Given such a pluralism of religious adherence, and given the search for a polity that could enable a religiously pluralistic population to make common political cause, what was there to do but concede religious freedom and decree the separation of church and state?

Yes, says Miller, but such pragmatic thinking was far from the whole story. In a diligent search for precedents and careful attention to actual historical connections linking generation to generation, Miller has identified a skein of deep conviction about the free rights of conscience that stretches in a continuous line from the early days of the Protestant Reformation to the American founding era. The skein began when the first Protestants, in particular Martin Luther, proclaimed that individuals enjoyed an intrinsic right of private judgment when interpreting and applying the Christian Scriptures. Luther swiftly backed off from a full-scale defense of this right when his own biblical interpretations were challenged. But others did not. Through the sixteenth and seventeenth centuries, a surprising number of voices continued to insist on the right, including many long forgotten except by experts, but also some much better known like John Milton and William Penn.

In Miller's account, dissenting Protestants who objected in principle to the church establishments that almost all European Protestant regimes maintained were most insistent in making these claims. But because these dissenters were always successful enough at rooting their arguments in what Protestants of all sorts claimed for the authority of the Bible and in what they regularly affirmed about the competence of believers redeemed by following the message of the Bible, the dissenters' influence radiated well beyond the narrow confines of their separated churches.

One of the most controversial, but also best argued, sections in the pages that follow concerns John Locke. Miller contends that Locke put to use aspects of dissenting principles about the right of private judgment for scriptural interpretation when he promulgated his case for toleration in treatises that would carry great weight in colonial and revolutionary America. Whatever Locke may have actually believed about such matters, the arguments he offered to the public were a conduit between earlier dissenting defense of the right to private judgment and later American appeals to the same right.

For eighteenth-century America, Miller can show that defending this right figured prominently where it might be expected, as with the Baptist spokesman Isaac Backus. But he also shows its power among American religious figures whose own church traditions tended toward establishment, like the New England Congregationalist Elisha Williams, who was one of the first colonists to make full use of Locke, and the New Jersey Presbyterian John Witherspoon, the only clergyman to sign the Declaration of Independence.

In a carefully nuanced argument, Miller also explains why he thinks that James Madison's promotion of the First Amendment owed as much to dissenting Protestant convictions about the right of private judgment as to principles of the eighteenth-century Enlightenment or to the pragmatic necessities of constitution building in a religiously plural new nation.

If at first hearing, readers react with skepticism to Miller's account, they will be responding as I did when he first outlined this project to me. Through the care with which he assembled clear statements about the right of private judgment in the interpretation of Scripture and then the nuanced way he showed how the principle thus articulated worked its influence among figures well beyond the narrow circles of dissenting Protestantism, he made a believer out of me.

Readers who suspect that better history is required to adjudicate the frequently hackneyed debates between "accommodationists" and "separatists" today should be the first to give Miller a hearing. I am confident he will be as persuasive for such readers as he was with me.

Mark Noll is Francis A. McAnaney
Professor of History at the
University of Notre Dame

Acknowledgments

THIS PROJECT WAS relatively recently conceived and executed, but my interest in the subject matter of church, state, and theology has roots that go back to my days as an undergraduate. I owe special thanks to John McVay and Greg King, my theology professors at Pacific Union College, in Angwin, California, for awakening in me an understanding of the importance to a community of careful and faithful scholarship. I also owe to Harry Leonard of Newbold College, in England, an initial introduction into the discipline of history. To Vincent Blasi at the Columbia University Law School I owe thanks for introducing me to the intricacies of church/state law in his First Amendment Seminar.

I would like to thank both Andrews University and the University of Notre Dame for funding the studies and research that made this project, and my venture into the history profession, possible. I would like to acknowledge my professors at the University of Notre Dame who contributed to the development of my thinking both on the topic of religious freedom and on how to think seriously about it as a historian. Brad Gregory played an important role in causing me to confront some of the biases of my Protestant heritage and showing me that religious history projects are strengthened by cross-confessional dialogue. Special thanks goes to George Marsden, who early on put in extra time and effort to help this lawyer adjust to the nuance, texture, and context of historical thought and writing.

I owe an equal debt to Mark Noll, who has tried to complete that transformation by serving as main advisor, mentor, and guide on this work. I want to thank both men for their patience and kindness in sharing their excellence of scholarship, and for modeling how to accompany scholarly success with humility and a continued willingness to learn. I am grateful to Michael Zuckert for his special help in assisting me in wading through the thought and extensive literature of John Locke. I have also received helpful readings and comments on at least portions of my manuscript from Melissa Rogers of Wake Forest Divinity School, Andrea Luxton, Provost of Andrews University, Gary Wood, professor of political science at Andrews, and Katrina Blue, my able and persevering Graduate Assistant, who aided with the editing.

The readers for the Oxford Press, one of whom was Donald Drakeman, were extraordinarily helpful with their comments and critiques of the manuscript, and helped me fill in a great deal of the secondary literature, which is always a challenge when dealing with such a long period of time covering multiple geographic areas.

My colleagues and associates in the North American Religious Liberty Association, including James Standish, Alan Reinach, Barry Bussey, John Graz, Lincoln Steed, David Trim, and Greg Hamilton were helpful sounding boards and conversation partners in exploring the terrain of religious liberty and its development in conversations and writings over the last few years. Many of those interactions helped shape and guide the research and writing of this book.

Finally, thanks to my family. My parents, Tom and Vera Miller, early awakened in me a love for reading and learning, as well as a commitment to the importance of religious ideas and beliefs in order to both understand and appreciate the larger and smaller issues of life. Of course, the biggest thanks is due to my wife and children, who competed for my attention with this manuscript on weekends and evenings for a number of years. This book is fondly dedicated to them.

Prologue

IN COLONIAL AMERICA, there was no single model of church/state relations. Each of the thirteen colonies had both their own religious character and church/state arrangement. This condition makes any sweeping generalization about church and state in colonial America difficult. But one can group the America colonies into three segments with certain shared attributes: New England, centering in Massachusetts; the Middle Colonies, running from New York to Maryland; and the South, from Virginia south. A visitor to America in the mid-eighteenth century would have found dramatic differences in religious practices and church/state arrangements in the leading cities of these regions—Boston, Philadelphia, and Williamsburg—that reflected what was largely to be found in the surrounding regions.

A visitor who sailed into Boston harbor in the 1690s would soon find himself walking along cobblestoned streets with storefronts and church spires that would remind him of a traditional English port town.[1] It was not quite the oldest city in the British colonies—Boston had a heritage stretching back to about 1630, but Plymouth had been founded a decade sooner, and Jamestown more than two. But it was undoubtedly the intellectual center of the British colonies. It had the first school and college and was the largest city in the colonies for nearly a hundred years, until surpassed by Philadelphia in the early eighteenth century. Should our visitor enter a typical church door, he would find a largely white, English-speaking congregation, dressed plainly, often in dark clothing, singing metrical psalms unaccompanied by instrumental music, and listening patiently to lengthy sermons full of scriptural quotes and allusions.

While he might glimpse a Baptist or two and the occasional Quaker wandering through—and usually hustled along by religiously zealous town fathers—the religious and political scene was dominated by Puritans of the Independent, Congregational strain. A kind of separation of church and state existed, especially after the imperial Massachusetts charter of 1697. It was, however, a formal, institutional separation, rather than a practically meaningful divide. Ministers could not be magistrates, and vice versa. But the magistrates were expected to protect the interests and teachings of the church, and to carry out the punishments that the ministers found should be given to religious dissenters.

Before 1697, only church members in good standing could participate in politics, either as officials or voters. After 1697, voting was opened to non-members, but office holding, as a practical matter, continued to be limited to Congregationalists. Taxes were levied for the support of churches and their ministers, though this was done on a town-by-town basis, and not statewide. The only exception to this basic arrangement in New England was Rhode Island, founded by the maverick Roger Williams. His efforts, though, were destined for at least a century of obscurity and ill repute before his contribution to the story of freedom was recognized.

Despite their theocratic impulses, however, the American Puritans had developed distinct democratic processes within their churches. This democratic church governance was a feature of the Independent, Congregationalist strain of Puritanism that migrated to America. It stood in contrast to the Presbyterian polity of many of their British brethren. The Congregationalists took seriously Calvin's placement of the body of Christ in the body of believers, the gathered church. In these churches, pastors were appointed, and removed, by their congregations. Every member in good standing had a vote and a voice in major church decisions, including the appointment of elders and pastors. In an example of the power of the common man and woman in the pew, that doyen of eighteenth-century Puritan preachers Jonathon Edwards, after having attained national and international stature, found himself without a pulpit after his congregation ejected him in 1750 over a disagreement regarding baptism and church membership.

A connection has been seen between the American Puritans' church organization and their embrace of democratic processes in politics.[2] To be sure, the Puritans' form of democracy did not embrace a modern sense of personal or individual rights. Once chosen, rulers were expected to follow godly principles of truth and right and were not to be swayed by popular opinions or the so-called rights of conscience.[3] Erring conscience, in the Puritans' view, had no right to indulgence or protection. But a ruler's appointment was in the hands of the community. New England was thus the one region of colonial America that had a tradition of self-government by the mid-eighteenth century.

Most of the original New England colonies had been established with independent charters and operated with a great deal of autonomy. They were ruled by elected assemblies and internally chosen governors until they experienced a royal takeover toward the end of the seventeenth century. In a foreshadowing of the Revolutionary War, this takeover was resisted in various ways, at one point even with the use of force during the succession crisis of 1688, when it was unclear whether England had a king or not. By the beginning of the eighteenth century, New England had regained practical—if not total legal—control of its own affairs.

By contrast, colonies in the middle and southern regions were much more closely tied to the Crown. Royal governors, who were appointed by the king, usually oversaw these colonies. They generally possessed elected assemblies with largely advisory authority. Colonies without royal governors, such as Pennsylvania and Maryland, were operated by proprietors, who possessed royal-like authority over their colonies. In practice, they tended to give representative assemblies some authority, but it was limited and subject to modification, and even revocation, by the proprietor.

New England, on the other hand, by the eve of the American Revolution, had a heritage of more than a hundred years of relatively autonomous self-government. The town meeting had become a hallmark of New England's participatory democracy. It is unsurprising, then, that early opposition to restrictions on town hall meetings, set out in the Intolerable Acts of 1774, centered in New England. This region was also the scene of the first acts of revolutionary violence, including the Boston Massacre and the skirmishes at Lexington and Concord.

Democracy, though, is not the same as freedom of conscience. The former is merely a helpful condition, and not a guarantor, of religious freedom, as the Puritan hegemony in New England illustrates. Our visitor would have had to look southward for the colonial roots of liberty of conscience and disestablishment. Because it was the earliest English colony continuously settled, he might have turned far south to Virginia. This was home for many great leaders of the revolutionary period. Patrick Henry, James Madison, Thomas Jefferson, and George Washington were all famous Virginians. All of them spoke and wrote in different ways about the importance of freedom generally, and religious freedom in particular.

But a visitor to Williamsburg at the start of the eighteenth century, by which time it had replaced nearby Jamestown as the colonial capital, would have found few indications of either religious freedom or general equality.[4] The visitor would have enjoyed the broad, although often dusty, avenues as well as the spacious, even sophisticated, colonial homes, with backyards filled with fruit trees and English yews. The "Williamsburg" style of tasteful, upper-middle-class two-story homes with ornate white molding and lighted windows is renowned. By 1720 or so, churches themselves, formerly made of wood, were now solid brick structures that exuded a sense of permanence typical of an established church in a socially maturing society.

But if our visitor lingered, he would quickly discover a darker side to Williamsburg. He would encounter cramped, dark wooden cabins and huts, located down narrow alleys, for the slaves and servants—and a jail reserved for disturbers of the peace, ecclesiastical as well as political. It was not a society that valued equality as a core value. Rather, it was the colony where slavery had first entered the British-American colonies. The dark institution eventually spread throughout the colonies, but it remained most pervasive and apparently ineradicable at its entry point. Founded as an adventuring, commercial enterprise rather than a religious settlement, Virginia had early on developed an agrarian economy that was entwined with and apparently dependent on slave labor. In Williamsburg, as in larger Virginia, high commerce, wealth, and prestige lived side by side with scarcity, poverty, and chattel slavery in a manner not equaled in other regions.

Freedom of religion was also essentially foreign to early eighteenth-century Williamsburg. From its earliest days, colonial leaders had promoted an Anglican establishment, with the state-supported church doing its best to keep out and suppress its competitors. During its early history, Virginia did not persecute people for religious reasons to nearly the same extent as New England. Rather than religious pilgrims, fortune hunters primarily settled Virginia. Wealthy Virginia tobacco planters were largely content to ride in their plush carriages past the slave quarters to attend the plain, but substantial, Anglican chapel. Here, the parish priest, dependent on the landowners' tax moneys and support, commented little about what crops the gentry grew, how they treated their slaves, or how they spent their money. On the whole, Virginia squires did not display the religious enthusiasm to engage in widespread or systematic persecution of non-Anglicans.

Thus, dissenting religious groups, such as Baptists, Quakers, and later Methodists, worshiped on the edges of polite society. When they became too pervasive, however, as happened in the 1740s and 1750s, they did become the targets of harassment and even persecution. When Madison was a young man, he was inspired to the importance of religious freedom by the sight of Baptist ministers preaching from jail cells. It was not until after the American

Revolution that Virginia implemented meaningful guarantees of both religious freedom and disestablishment.

Many Virginians, whether Scotch-Irish Presbyterians, Baptists, or Enlightenment thinkers like James Madison, recognized that a better model of freedom existed in another state to the north. That state had for nearly a century in its colonial period embodied principles of religious freedom and disestablishment that reformers in Virginia hoped to emulate. That state was, of course, Pennsylvania. Its capital city, Philadelphia, had early become the touchstone, the shining example, of separating church and state and guaranteeing religious freedom for all.

Should our visitor have turned northward again and sailed to Philadelphia, he would have found a city unlike either Boston or Williamsburg.[5] It enjoyed a modern layout, like Williamsburg, and an English sensibility in its buildings and facades similar to that of Boston. Yet Philadelphia was distinct in its diverse population and vigorous activity. It was a vibrant and dynamic city, surpassing the populations of both Boston and New York—much older cities—by 1700 or so, at the end of only its first two decades of operation. William Penn had intended to create in Philadelphia a semirural, suburban atmosphere by creating large lots with room for gardens and orchards, so that businesses would be interspersed with fields and trees. But the great harbor, booming immigration, and lively economy made owners anxious to subdivide their lots. Soon there was a bustling commercial downtown crowded along the Delaware River.

The booming economic activity was matched by a blooming religious diversity. From its earliest days in the 1680s, Penn had made Pennsylvania a place welcome to virtually all religious peoples. Indeed, in his European travels he had specifically invited persecuted groups such as the Huguenots, Anabaptists, and even Catholics to settle in his new colony. Philadelphia soon had a multiplicity of places of worship and streets filled with Quakers rubbing shoulders with Huguenots who were bumping up against Baptists and even the occasional Jew and Anglican—the latter slightly appalled at the surrounding promiscuous religious diversity.

Pennsylvania was indeed the future of America. America did not become an image of Pennsylvania overnight, or even in a few years. But the example of Pennsylvania was important: it was cited as a stellar example of the successes of religious disestablishment by individuals as diverse as Thomas Jefferson, James Madison, the Virginia Baptists, and the Presbyterian New York lawyer and pamphleteer William Livingston. An example can only be effective, however, where its persuasive authority resonates with existing strands of thought or conviction. One of the most prominent themes in the intellectual life of colonial Pennsylvania was the right of private judgment in matters of biblical interpretation and religious choice.

The theological construct of private judgment, while most visibly articulated and lived in the dissenting Protestant strongholds of Pennsylvania and other middle colonies, had enough in common with the varieties of Protestant thought found throughout the colonies to allow religious disestablishment to become the persuasive paradigm of late colonial and early republican America. Even denominations such as Presbyterians, Methodists, and Anglicans, which in Europe adhered to the magisterial, state-church model of Protestantism, in America eventually accepted and even embraced disestablishment and the voluntary church model.

It is a historical truism to call America at its founding a culturally Protestant nation. But it is even more accurate to say that it was, or at least became, a dissenting Protestant nation. How and why the dissenting Protestant view of a separated church and state, always a minority position in England and the rest of Europe, and even in early colonial America, became the dominant position in the early republic is the subject of this book. It is the history of an idea, but one that is told through the lives and stories of those who conceived, shared, promoted, and implemented it.

The Religious Roots of the First Amendment

Religion and American Disestablishment

Restoring Religion to the Story of Religious Liberty

The argument of this book is quite simple. It is that Protestant commitments, at least as maintained by some dissenting Protestants,[1] to the right of private judgment in matters of biblical interpretation—a corollary of the Protestant doctrine of the priesthood of believers—led to a respect for individual conscience that propelled ideas of religious liberty and disestablishment in the early modern West. These religious commitments, in turn, were a central influence in the eventual disestablishment of religion in America during the colonial period and the early republic. This work describes a continuous strand of this religious thought—as well as the thinkers who spread it—from the early Protestant Reformation, across the European continent, through the English Reformation, Civil War, and Restoration, and into the American colonies and early republic.

This work aims to trace the connections between this keystone belief of Protestantism and the thought of those who promoted disestablishment in America. It first looks at the European background of these Protestant ideas and then explores the theological reasons given by leading political thinkers for disestablishing religion in colonial America. The goal is to identify religious and theological reasons for disestablishment that worked alongside other ideologies—Enlightenment and political—to disestablish religion in early America.

Religion has not been entirely overlooked in telling the story of the rise of religious tolerance and American disestablishment. Its role, however, has usually been limited to that of pragmatic response—either the response of self-preservation by minority religions or a political response to the realities of religious pluralism. It has often been assumed that religion made no principled, ideological contribution to this story. Indeed, the modern story of toleration has often been told in terms of the secularization of Western thought. "Toleration triumphed in the eighteenth century," it is often argued, "because reason triumphed over faith. It triumphed because religion lost its hold on people, and hence its importance as a historical phenomenon."[2]

Recently, however, several scholars have begun to acknowledge a substantive role for religion in the rise of toleration as well as in shaping certain aspects of the Enlightenment.[3] This project builds on these insights to trace the case of a particular Protestant teaching and its impact on religious disestablishment. I argue that religion *did* make an ideological contribution to religious disestablishment in eighteenth-century America in the form of a core Protestant principle—the right of private judgment in biblical interpretation.

That the right of private judgment in Bible study and interpretation is an important and central Protestant concept is not a new idea. The theme of a recent survey of Reformation history—*Christianity's Dangerous Idea,* by Alister McGrath—is that a basic, central, organizing idea of the Protestant revolution was the belief that all Christians had the duty to interpret the Bible for themselves. As McGrath puts it, "the idea that lay at the heart of the sixteenth-century Reformation ... was that the Bible is capable of being understood by all Christian believers—and that they all have the right to interpret it and to insist upon their perspectives being taken seriously."[4]

McGrath identifies this right of interpretation as an expression or outgrowth of Luther's "doctrine of the universal priesthood of believers." This doctrine not only meant that each believer could pray directly to Christ without a church-appointed priest but also gave "every Christian the right to interpret the Bible and to raise concerns about any aspect of the church's teaching or practice that appear to be inconsistent with the Bible."[5] McGrath argues that the related group of ideas surrounding the priesthood of believers—the perspicuity of the central teachings of Scripture, the supreme authority of Scripture, and the right to personal interpretation of Scripture—is a defining thread that runs through the story of Protestantism's engagement with Western society.[6]

McGrath's work is a general survey that deals with various aspects of Protestantism over five hundred years. Thus, he touches only very briefly on Protestantism in relation to church and state and makes no meaningful efforts to show how belief in the right of individual Bible interpretation affected church/state thought. The key role this principle played in disestablishing state churches in early America has generally been overlooked. In the rare instances where it has been acknowledged, its roots and development in Protestant doctrine and thought have not been well understood.[7]

The books closest in argument to this work are *Beyond Toleration: The Religious Origins of American Pluralism,* by Chris Beneke, and *Revolution within the Revolution: The First Amendment in Historical Context, 1612–1789,* by William Estep. Beneke notes the central role that the "right of private judgment" played in turning the culture of eighteenth-century America into one open to pluralism and disestablishment.[8] Beneke even identifies this principle with Protestants, but suggests that a policy of pragmatism was first given ideological, principled form by Enlightenment thinkers and the "radical political ideology known as liberalism."[9]

Estep's book traces toleration within Protestantism from its earliest days, but it focuses almost entirely on the Baptist contribution. He deals with theology, but the focus is on telling the stories of the men involved in the transmission of the general idea of toleration, not the theological makeup of the idea itself. He thus does not deal with the theological connections between apparently disparate groups and people like the Independent Milton, the Anglican Locke, the Quaker Penn, and the Puritan Elisha Williams. None of these men were Baptists, yet they were influenced by the same stream of thought of which the Baptists were a very visible example.

This work does its best to combine the positive virtues of both Beneke's and Estep's works, and then move beyond them to make clearer the role of religious ideas in forming our modern American conceptions of church and state. I take Beneke's recognition of an important theological idea and seek to trace the thread of that idea over the historical ground that Estep sets out, from the European Reformation into early America. Beneke and Estep provide important reality checks for this project. It would seem implausible that this work would be the first to note the role that the right of private judgment played in American disestablishment, and the first to argue that the roots of toleration lay deep in early Protestant thought.

These arguments would be highly questionable if no one else had seen evidence to support them. Beneke offers important support for my conclusion about the significance of the right of private judgment. Estep supports my contention that Protestantism itself was a meaningful vehicle for this idea in the centuries between the Reformation and the American founding. But I go beyond Beneke in showing that the principle itself grew from theological rather than secular Enlightenment roots. And I move beyond Estep's somewhat parochial focus on the Baptists as the primary, if not almost exclusive, vehicle for this idea.

This work does not argue that the explanation for disestablishment can be limited to religion or theology. Indeed, if disestablishment *was* connected only to purely religious arguments, it would collapse from internal incoherence. One would be relying exclusively on a theological principle for a civil rule that no civil rules can rely exclusively on revealed theology. The principle would devour itself. Thus, it is highly important, as many of the thinkers we look at recognize, that this religious principle could also be expressed and understood in terms of reason and philosophy.

The connections between disestablishment and enlightenment philosophy, as well as to the practical pressures of a growing religious pluralism in colonial America, are well documented.[10] But there are good reasons to believe that Enlightenment ideals and the pressures of religious pluralism are not the whole story. That pragmatism and utility played a role in causing religious people to embrace disestablishment does not mean that religious ideology itself—theology and doctrine—may not have also played a significant and important role.

Indeed, if religious belief is left out of the story of disestablishment, significant puzzles emerge. One is left with having to use largely elite, Enlightenment opinions to explain a widespread, popular phenomenon on which religion is highly influential. Disestablishment itself occurred, at least initially, almost exclusively at the state and local level, where religion was a much more important influence than Enlightenment thought. As one legal historian notes, "the American disestablishment occurred over a fifty to sixty year period, from 1774 to the early 1830s," and was "entirely a state-law affair," completely independent of the Revolution or the adoption of the Bill of Rights.[11]

One might quibble with this designation of the timing for disestablishment—most of the middle colonies had no established churches for decades prior to the Revolution, and only Massachusetts hung on to its establishment past 1818. In addition, the insistence that there was no federal connection seems overstated—state disestablishments clustered around the national events of the Revolutionary War and the passage of the federal constitution's First Amendment. But the larger point is correct. The credit for disestablishment cannot be given to a small, elite group of Enlightenment thinkers huddled in Philadelphia to draft a new national constitution.[12]

Disestablishment in America was a populist movement where religious, and not Enlightenment, influences predominated. "At the state level, where the work of disestablishment did take place, the vast number of those pushing for it were not doing so out of rationalism, secularism, or pragmatism. Rather, they were religious people who sought disestablishment for (as they saw it) biblical reasons."[13] Jefferson's preference for the skeptical, French Enlightenment was an elite phenomenon. The skeptical anti-clericalism of the French philosophers did not characterize the common man in the street in the American colonies. After the Bible, the most influential book in the colonies was not written by Rousseau, Voltaire, or Paine. Rather, it was undoubtedly John Fox's *Book of Martyrs*—an extended Protestant case history of the evils of centralized, oppressive religious authority with access to civil force.[14] At the local level, religious ideas were pervasive, deeply held, and profoundly influential.[15]

In probably the most thorough account of the development of church and state in colonial America, *The First Freedoms*, Thomas Curry shows how certain religious groups took the lead in moving various colonies toward disestablishment.[16] He notes the effects of the First Great Awakening in the 1740s in moving even the theocratic New England colonies toward a more moderate position. He also shows how the awakening deepened the existing commitment to pluralism and tolerance in the middle colonies, and how this evangelical attitude spilled over into the south, especially Virginia.[17] Curry does not, however, explore in detail the religious reasoning behind this move to disestablishment. And the question can be asked: was pluralism the cause or the effect of disestablishment?

A number of authors argue that pluralism was the cause.[18] They suggest that the pluralism produced by the Great Awakening or by diverse immigration patterns, rather than any theological views, explains this shift toward toleration. But, historically considered, in a number of instances a theological commitment to religious freedom actually preceded and caused the pluralistic conditions that are often cited as the pragmatic reasons for disestablishment. The most obvious examples of this process are Rhode Island and Pennsylvania, where the founders—Roger Williams and William Penn, respectively—at the outset created legal frameworks for their colonies based explicitly on their theological commitments to freedom of conscience and religious tolerance.[19]

New Jersey and Delaware were also influenced by William Penn and other Quakers and were places where the principle of tolerance preceded the growth of pluralism. New York is also a candidate for this category. Historically, New York possessed an established church—first Dutch Reformed, then Anglican. But in its early, New Netherlands phase, the colony had experienced a robust religious tolerance under Dutch rule. This tolerance led to a religious and ethnic diversity that prevented the later Anglican establishment from taking meaningful hold.[20]

A similar situation existed in the Carolinas. There, strong constitutional religious freedom clauses, likely drafted by John Locke, prevented the nominally established Anglican church from inhibiting the rise of a multiplicity of competing denominations. An early influx of Quakers and Baptists also provided principled political support, and agitators, for this nascent toleration.[21] Thus, in nearly half the original colonies, commitments to meaningful religious toleration, and at times full disestablishment, preceded the conditions of pluralism that are conventionally used to explain the rise of tolerance. This in itself should be reason to look closely at these religious ideas.

There is another reason to take religious beliefs seriously when considering disestablishment: those advocating for it did so. Taking theology seriously is to take the historical actors involved in disestablishment seriously. It is part of an attempt, as the intellectual historian Quentin Skinner has put it, "so far as possible, to see things their way."[22] They themselves acknowledged the role of pragmatism and a desire for social peace in arguing for religious tolerance. But they also wrote profusely about theological ideas—page after page—and insisted that at its core, religious tolerance, a philosophical precursor to full disestablishment, was not just useful, but theologically justified and even required.

To be sure, asserted reasons are not always the real reasons. People can use theological reasons to obscure other motives. But before one dismisses ostensible reasons, one must understand them, and have a basis to disregard them. It is an assumption of lawyers as well as historians that most people tell what they believe to be the truth most of the time. Even calculating liars will not be effective with their falsehoods unless they tell the truth most of the time. Religious reasons should be accepted as valid, as should any type of plausible reason, absent evidence for deceit or ulterior motive.

The study of religious beliefs in history is often viewed as part of the genre of the history of ideas, as set apart from social or cultural history. While this project will explore primarily religious ideas, it will do so in a way that supplements, rather than displaces, a typical cultural or social history. It looks at religious ideas in their social and political contexts and seeks to enrich, rather than replace, cultural and social histories that cover the same ground.

Method of Research

This project attempts to restore religious belief to the story of religious freedom and disestablishment in the United States. In writing about the growth of toleration in sixteenth-and seventeenth-century England, John Coffey identifies three major contributing factors—ideological, legal or political, and social.[23] Each factor, he argues, is important to the story, and no element should be ignored. Traditionally, the ideological strand has been given greatest emphasis, with the legal not far behind. But more recently, he notes, social dimensions have received greater attention.[24] This work attempts a more traditional, ideological focus, but with a twist—it takes religion and theology seriously as contributing to the shape of social and political ideas.

Leading thinkers and advocates for religious freedom and disestablishment are placed in their historical contexts. Ideas will not be viewed as flowing from brains floating free in a historical vacuum. The social factors that give texture to a religious work will be considered. But those religious ideas will not be reduced to the social and cultural factors that influenced them, as some modern theorists tend to.[25] Indeed, a meta-argument of this work is that a cultural history that takes religious beliefs seriously will have a greater explanatory value.

In the story of church and state, one explanatory role for religious ideas is that they help explain how elite, Enlightenment ideas were accepted at the popular level. This story reveals that dissenting Protestant religious ideals converged with Enlightenment ideas about the proper roles of church and state. More than this, it shows that the Enlightenment ideas of the elite thinkers were themselves influenced and shaped by religious insights. Thus, rather than a story that has a few, elite thinkers almost single-handedly changing the face of church and state, it becomes the more plausible story of cooperation between elite and popular thought.

Discovering the nature of popular thought, however, has always posed methodological challenges. The diaries, letters, and other records of common, ordinary people are widely distributed and not often maintained or catalogued. Thus, they are not reasonably accessible to the professional historian, absent extraordinary and time-consuming efforts. If the scope of the project expands beyond a small geographical area, or beyond a limited time frame, such labor intensive work becomes practically impossible. Given a large study covering the good part of three centuries, and thousands of miles, one must canvass more easily accessed elite records of the type that accurately reflect popular views and opinions.

What kind of records would these be? In short, statements of public persuasion, including sermons, legislative petitions, political speeches, or popularly circulated pamphlets. For these works of public advocacy to be effective, authors must argue from what they believe to be commonly held premises. While the ultimate point of the advocacy may be to change social policy or popular thought, the argumentation must be based on underlying, shared views, or it will be ineffective. No work of public advocacy can hope to be successful if its basic premises contradict those of its intended audience. Thus, public expressions of persons who might otherwise be considered elite thinkers will usually, if the thinker is effective, reflect popular mindsets and assumptions, especially in relation to religious beliefs that were foundational to communities in the early modern period.

In this way, this study of mostly elite thinkers also partakes of more popular cultural history. It focuses on key public statements from nine important thinkers on issues of church and state, as well as on a satellite of secondary documents and thinkers that shed light on the important terms and concepts in those main documents. I begin with the early Martin Luther and his formulation of the priesthood of believers and right of individual judgment of scripture, and trace the influence of these ideas to John Milton's mid-seventeenth-century England. Then, I look at three pairs: John Locke and William Penn, Elisha Williams and Isaac Backus, and John Witherspoon and James Madison, with an additional American figure, the New York lawyer William Livingston.

My focus is on the public representations of these figures rather than their private beliefs. I am not so much concerned with their actual theological convictions. Rather, I am interested in what their expressions reveal about ideas that found widespread, popular support. My argument is made not just from an abstract reading of these public documents but also by an examination of the social and political contexts in which they were written. These contexts will be enriched by looking at writings from secondary authors that informed or were influenced by those primary documents. The satellite of secondary authors and documents around each main thinker will provide some context for the community of ideas in which the main writers worked.

Criteria for choosing the main thinkers were that (1) they thought and wrote in theological terms, (2) they applied these theological categories to issues of church and state (3) in a sufficiently public, visible manner that they came to the attention of and in some way impacted those involved in key legal/legislative events in early America. Criteria for secondary thinkers and writers included (1) and (2). But the requirement of public, visible manner (3) was modified so that the secondary author's work was likely to have been seen by one or more of the primary authors. This procedure will help us understand how the primary author used his terms. It will also reveal whether the primary authors' ideas accurately reflected ideas already present in his culture and society, or if he modified those ideas in some way.

This work, though concerned with the history of a religious idea, includes the stories of men who helped develop this idea for their societies. It suggests that cultural or social explanations of historical events, especially those involving issues of religion, are more complete when religious beliefs are taken seriously.

Taking Religious Ideas Seriously

To take religious ideas seriously as a historical force runs against the grain of two major modern prejudices: the negative view of idea-driven history and the often skeptical view of religious history. Religious history has regained some respectability in recent years, through the work of writers like Barbara Diedendorf, Natalie Zemon Davis, Jonathon Butler, Patricia Bonomi, and others.[26] This respectability has often been gained, however, by forgoing meaningful discussion of religious belief, or at least by minimizing its importance. Religion is treated as something cultural or social rather than as consisting of ideas and beliefs. Thus, the new approach has tended to focus on ceremonies and ritual, community formation and individual experience, but not often on belief.[27] Theology continues, for the most part, to be sighted—like some endangered species—in the preserve of theology departments and seminaries.

The history of ideas, likewise, was sidelined as social and cultural history came into vogue. The abstraction of ideas from their cultural, geographic, and chronological contexts was considered to be sufficiently vacuous to make any study of ideas suspect. But recently, again, some historians have shown that ideas and beliefs do matter and that they often explain why people act as they do.

One historian of the seventeenth century not long ago noted that the great distance between our beliefs and those of the early moderns "has rendered so many seventeenth-century English perceptions incomprehensible to modern historians."[28] In a chapter entitled "Taking Contemporary Belief Seriously," he proposes that the first step in recovering an understanding of the times "will be the identification of contemporary belief." This is because if, in the "seventeenth century men killed, tortured and executed each other for political beliefs, that was because belief lay at the heart of the troubles."[29] Likewise, many people were willing to suffer, be deprived of livelihood, property, family, and even their lives for religious beliefs. In the face of martyrdom, it is hard to argue, as Brad Gregory has put it, that religious belief is really reducible to some sort of political, economic, or social interest. Not to take persons' *beliefs* seriously is not to take *them* seriously.[30]

The problem is directly relevant to this work's argument, as illustrated by the slighting of religious ideas in Anthony Gill's *Political Origins of Religious*

Liberty.[31] As the title indicates, Gill deals directly with the question of the rise of religious freedom; his conclusion is that political, pragmatic considerations were the primary movers in the emergence of religious freedom in America. While he does not entirely discount ideology or belief, he believes that most of the story can be told without reference to ideas or thinkers, religious or otherwise. As he puts it, rather than "grand intellectual debate," it was "three principal non-ideational factors [that] made politicians realize that religious establishment and other restrictions on religious minorities were not in their interest."[32]

The three factors that Gill identifies are (1) competition for immigrants, (2) pluralism in religion produced by immigration, and (3) trade desired among the colonies and with other nations.[33] These factors were certainly part of the story of how the American political system came to favor religious toleration and freedom. But it is hard to see how they tell a complete or adequate story if they are viewed as the primary factors. Factors (1) and (3), competition for immigrants and desire for trade, are going to be prominent factors whenever new lands are being settled. The second point, the pressure of religious pluralism, really seems to be dependent on the first and third points.

A weakness of Gill's conclusion is shown by the fact that his argument cannot distinguish among colonial Rhode Island, Massachusetts, or Virginia. All were new settlements whose leaders desired both more immigrants and favorable trade opportunities. Yet the church/state arrangements of these colonies differed dramatically for nearly 150 years.

The fact is, the religious ideologies prevalent in these colonies played a significant role in determining whether a colony was going to be open to religious pluralism and the religious tolerance that is a price of such pluralism. Those that were open to pluralism pursued immigration and trade opportunities in a manner that led to religious pluralism. Those that were not open to it pursued immigration and trade in a manner that discouraged such pluralism.

Perhaps an even more telling comparison lies between the British colonies in North America and the Spanish colonies in South America. The Latin American colonies had just as much incentive to promote immigration and trade for their colonies, and thus a motive to allow for religious pluralism. Yet, as Gill himself notes, "the coming of religious freedom to Latin America took a much longer route than it did in the United States."[34] Gill suggests that the reason for the difference is that Latin America began its colonial period with "a highly regulated religious monopoly inherited from colonial times."[35] Precisely—but this concession is merely to recognize that Gill's own pragmatic and political factors were relatively impotent in the face of a deeply entrenched ideological framework of religious monopoly that resisted such factors.

In his view, ideology was important, but apparently only in earlier "colonial times." But if it was important then, why was it so much less important a short while later? If ideology at one point constructed a system of centralized religion that worked against political and trade efficiency, at what point did that ideology stop operating? And why did it stop? It is not enough to say that the Spanish colonies had different political concerns from the mother country, since the very same thing was true of the English colonies and England. Yet old England had a more liberal approach to its colonial religious policy than Spain did. Was ideology relevant in the Old World only, and not in the New? That would be an interesting argument, but Gill does not make it.

Instead, Gill quotes with approval another historian who said "scratch an ideology and watch an interest bleed."[36] That is, he claims that most ideology is really interest or political consideration in disguise. Gill acknowledges that this statement has limits, and that religious beliefs do actually motivate. But, ultimately, his historical analysis finds the question of disentangling people's real beliefs from their self-interest too difficult. This is because historical actors are mostly dead, Gill notes, and not available for interviews. (One wonders, however, if live persons are more honest with interviewers than the dead are in their books, letters, journals, and diaries.)

He thus decides that the explanation for the growth of religious liberty can best be understood by looking at "policies on trade, economic growth, social conflict, and political survival."[37] Unsurprisingly, then, his book argues that the growth of religious liberty was largely decided by these factors. He helpfully identifies some important political incentives in relation to the regulation and deregulation of religion. But he ultimately cannot explain why some political actors acted perversely against these incentives, while others were more willing to rationally implement them. Why did Spain encumber its colonies with a "religious monopoly," thereby hampering its growth in immigration and trade? Why did England allow more religious flexibility in its colonies, thereby enhancing their social and economic viability?

Surely a good part of the answer lies in the very different religious outlooks of the two countries. But Gill gives no meaningful thought to the great religious gulf between the Spanish and British Americas, not to mention the less extreme, but still real, ideological and religious differences among Rhode Island, Massachusetts, and Virginia. In omitting these differences, he is overlooking a critical factor that operates intertwined with political factors. Gill argues that telling the story from a primarily political, policy perspective does not deny some role for ideology and religious beliefs. He simply views these as playing a secondary role that does not much influence the main story.

While this work tells the story from a primarily ideological point of view, it does not deny the role of politics, trade, and policy. It will reference these elements and show how even the most religious thinkers used these pragmatic points in their arguments for religious freedom. But it does contend that in the growth of religious freedom, ideas did matter, religious ones in particular, and that at times they mattered most. The argument is that political schemes and systems can in fact reflect the deepest values, commitments, and beliefs of a people, even when these core concerns and beliefs are inefficient or are in tension with rational political choice.

In opposition to Gill and a number of others, the following chapters argue that a study of the religious beliefs of those who pressed for religious liberty and disestablishment in colonial America can better explain the processes of disestablishment than an analysis considering only, or even primarily, political ideology, or pragmatic social, economic, and cultural reasons. I do not call for a return of theology as the queen of the sciences or of history; but I do propose that religious beliefs need to have a more meaningful place at the historical table.[38]

Outline of the Book

Six chapters plus an epilogue follow. After this introduction, chapter 1 provides background on the Reformation roots of "the right of private judgment" as a theological principle. It starts with Martin Luther and explores the influence of some of his early writings on subsequent thinkers, including the Anabaptists, Sebastian Castellio, and the English Baptists. It ends by exploring the place of these authors in John Milton's writings.

Chapter 2 examines how the minority, dissenting Protestant principle of religious liberty and disestablishment was popularized in early America by an unlikely partnership between a cerebral philosopher who never visited America, John Locke, and a Quaker enthusiast whose writings on religious liberty have not been given the attention they are due, William Penn. Locke and Penn appeared to inhabit two different social and religious worlds. Yet their lives intersected at key times that highlight the profound connections between their ideas on religious freedom. The influence of these two men on colonial America was significant, and will be explored at some length.

Chapter 3 moves across the Atlantic for a brief overview of the reception of "the right of private judgment" in America. The traction this principle enjoyed in colonial history is then shown in the works of two leaders at opposite ends of the New England social stratum. Elisha Williams, judge, preacher, orthodox president of Yale, and cousin of Jonathan Edwards, authored a landmark document defending the conscience rights of the "New Lights" against the colony's attempts to limit their preaching. On the other side of the social spectrum was Isaac Backus. Despite a lack of formal education, he became one of the most articulate Baptist preachers and a leading advocate for liberty of conscience. Despite different religious and philosophical commitments, both Williams and Backus drew on the stream of dissenting Protestant thought promoted by Locke and Penn.

Chapter 4 examines New York lawyer and political leader William Livingston, especially his involvement with the King's College controversy in the 1750s. At that time, Livingston opposed Anglican control of that college by publishing a series of articles that dealt with the question of church, state, and education. His writings illuminate the close relationship between certain Enlightenment ideas and those of dissenting Protestantism. This chapter builds a bridge from the time of the first Great Awakening to the revolutionary and founding period.

The final two figures, discussed in chapter 5, were centrally involved with the formation of America's first national government. One was a theologically sensitive politician, the other a politically astute theologian. James Madison, the politician of the pair, was trained by the theologian John Witherspoon. It is Madison, the primary drafter of the Bill of Rights and the First Amendment, who typically receives credit for nationalizing the principles of religious freedom. But as this chapter shows, Witherspoon and his fellow divines played the greater role in bringing the principle of religious liberty and disestablishment to the early American republic. Together, they exerted a crucial influence in defining American religion as following the course of dissenting rather than magisterial Protestantism.

Some may argue that my book shows the roots of American disestablishment, rather than of the First Amendment. These are indeed two different, if related and overlapping, things. Yet both the First Amendment and early American disestablishment were, in my opinion, symptoms and results of the same religious and social causes this book describes. Both the original passage and the incorporation of the First Amendment upon the states, when it came, reflected in good part the values of these original religious and social movements. Thus, these movements can be spoken of as the impetus behind both American disestablishment and the First Amendment, even though the latter caused only a small part of the former, at least for the first 150 years of the nation.

The book concludes with an epilogue reflecting on the importance of theology and religious belief in gaining a fuller understanding of religious liberty and disestablishment in America from the founding to the present day. During all of American history, the roles of church and state have been shaped by ideological commitments, whether secularist, Puritan–magisterial Protestant, or dissenting Protestant. Because many of our current disputes over church/state matters fail to distinguish between these differing ideological influences, opposing partisans often speak past, rather than to, each other. To assert that the founders were "Christian" does not answer whether they were more influenced by magisterial or dissenting Protestant ideals. Likewise, to call them Enlightenment thinkers or deists does not detail whether they were sympathetic with the skeptical Enlightenment of the French philosophes, or the more moderate forms of the Enlightenment found in England and Scotland that were much friendlier to religion.

By untangling these religious and ideological influences, this work hopes to make the current discussion more historically sensitive, and thus more productive. The culture wars will never go away; much like the poor, the zealots—both of the left and the right—we will always have with us. But we can hope to broaden and enrich an inclusive middle ground—a place where religion is not always the enemy of reason, and "religious" people of Enlightenment sensibilities can dialogue with "secularists" possessing spiritual impulses. I aim to illuminate more fully the religious map of our early republic, on which two groups once found common ground, defined in surprisingly large part by deeply religious thinkers from a dissenting strand of the Protestant Reformation.

I

The Monk and the Bard

FROM LUTHER'S PROTEST TO MILTON'S
PROTESTANT VISION

IN 1529 EMPEROR Charles V, fearing a new incursion into his empire by the Turks to the east, sought to consolidate power within his realm by patching up a recent rift with the Pope. As part of his efforts to return to the good graces of the papacy, he aimed to bring to an end the religious conflict and division that had roiled Europe over the previous decade since the Luther affair. In order to achieve an end to the new movement for reform, he called for a diet, or a meeting of the German princes, at the Great Cathedral in Speyer. The events at Speyer have, in fact and in myth, informed the psyche of Protestant self-image in relation to religious freedom. The very name "Protestant" derives from the formal "protest" lodged by the Lutheran princes at the Diet at Speyer. But the events there also revealed the conflicted, ambiguous relationship between the Protestant Reformation and religious freedom.[1] To understand Speyer is to begin to understand the paradoxical relationship of Protestantism to religious freedom.

The events at Speyer have been overshadowed in Protestant lore by Martin Luther's "Here I Stand" speech at the Diet of Worms about a decade earlier. But in many ways Speyer defined Protestantism as a movement more than Luther's virtuoso, but solo, performance at Worms. Speyer showed that the movement for reform was much more than the audacity of a single monk, or even the complaints of disenfranchised rabble-rousers. It revealed the reformers as having impressive political and social leadership gathered around an affirmative religious message—a principled theology that recast the traditional medieval relationships between the individual believer, the Bible, and the church and state.

The Diet at Speyer happened at a critical juncture in the progress of the Reformation. There had been an earlier meeting at Speyer in 1526 at which the forces of reform and those of the German empire had agreed on a temporary religious détente. This allowed Emperor Charles V to finish off a squabble with Pope Clement VII, which ended in Charles's troops sacking Rome in 1526. The pope narrowly evaded capture, scurrying to safety through a secret passage from the Vatican. But as the threat from the Turks in the East grew, Charles desired to unify his empire to face this renewed external challenge, and he recalled Germany's political and religious leaders to Speyer.[2]

Religious leaders and thinkers of the day sensed some crisis was approaching. The forces of reform had grown during the 1520s and had gained leaders among the German nobility. But the reforming movement was still in a fragile and vulnerable position. It seemed that a resolute effort by the empire could extinguish the movement before it caused further trouble. A series of unusual natural events in 1529 appeared as omens to many religiously sensitive minds. A great brightness burst on the January night sky—likely an appearance of the aurora borealis—causing Luther to exclaim "What that forebodes, God only knows." A few months later—as the Speyer Diet began to meet—earthquakes were rumored to have swallowed castles in Italy and split St. Mark's tower in Venice. Portents multiplied: astrologers declared that Saturn and Jupiter were ominously positioned in the heavens; the waters of the Elbe rolled with mysterious waves; "stones fell from the roofs of churches." Even the normally placid Philipp Melanchthon, Luther's phlegmatic theological ally, wrote "all these things excite me in no trifling degree."[3]

These unsettling events heightened the intensity of a scene already full of the drama of medieval pageantry. Emperor Charles had handpicked his brother, Duke Ferdinand, to chair the Speyer II showdown. Ferdinand entered the ancient city of Speyer amid the bustle and splendor of a troop of his armed cavalry, as did many of the other German princes in attendance. Philip of Hesse entered "to the sounds of trumpets and two hundred horsemen."[4] The opening services were held in the imposing Speyer Cathedral. Already five hundred years old, the cathedral was known as an architecturally unique edifice (four towers, two domes, the first all-encompassing gallery of its kind). It is, even today, the world's largest Romanesque church.[5]

The setting and events mirrored the grand determination of Ferdinand to crush the movement for reform and to restore unity—civil and spiritual—to his brother's realm. Yet as events unfolded, the religious détente of the first Diet was to be ended by the discord of the second. The only concession given the forces of reform was the allowance that Lutheran services could continue within existing Lutheran states. Catholic services could also be held within Lutheran territories. But no Lutheran services could be held within Catholic states. Here, the Edict of Worms's ban on Luther's teachings would be strictly enforced. Lutheranism would be allowed to spread no further.

The princes in the Lutheran minority were unwilling to accept the limited toleration offered by the Diet. In language often quoted by confessional Protestant historians, the minority princes declared, "Let us reject this decree. ... In matters of conscience the majority has no power." To express their opposition the princes—with the aid of Melanchthon—drew up a formal, written protest. It contained two main points. First, that as the matters concerned "the glory of God" and matters of "salvation," they had an obligation to follow "the commands of God ... each of us rendering him account for himself, without caring the least in the world about majority or minority."[6]

Second, that the Bible should be interpreted and taught not on the basis of the authority of the "holy Christian Church" but on the basis of comparing scripture with scripture. It was declared that "each text of the Holy Scriptures ought to be explained by other and clearer texts; and that this holy book is in all things necessary for the Christian, easy of understanding, and calculated to scatter darkness." They concluded by asserting: "if you do not yield to our request, we PROTEST ... before God ... that we neither consent nor adhere ... to the proposed decree, in any thing that is contrary to God, to his holy Word, to our right conscience, to the salvation of our souls, and to the last decree of Spires."[7]

From that time, within Germany, and eventually outside, the evangelical princes became known as Protestants.[8] Over time, this name became attached to the entire reform movement. Protestant writers came to link the name "Protestant" not only with the doctrine of justification by grace alone, but with the right of individual judgment in interpreting scripture and liberty of conscience. As one Protestant historian put it, "the principles contained in this celebrated Protest ... constitute the very essence of Protestantism. ... Protestantism sets the power of conscience above the magistrate and the authority of the word of God above the visible church."[9] Another wrote of the protest that it was "a document founded on the principle, that every man possessed the right of judging for himself in matters of religion, and that conscience was amenable to no authority but that of God."[10]

But the same Protestant historians often leave unmentioned a darker side of the Diet of Speyer. The Diet, including the Lutheran princes in attendance, condemned the Anabaptist movement, and called for its persecution. It decreed that rebaptizers should be punished, even with death if persistent in their errors.[11] While nobly championing their own "rights" to conscience and religious freedom, the Lutheran princes were apparently blind to any inconsistency in their attitudes and actions in condemning and persecuting the Anabaptists. As a direct result of these events, hundreds, even thousands, of Anabaptists died in the years following, at the hands of Catholics and Protestants.[12]

Speyer II can provide support both for those who view the Protestant Reformation as a continuation of essentially medieval ideas of religious coercion and for those who view it as the beginning of modern ideas of conscience and toleration. Which is the more accurate reading of history? Surely there is some truth to both views. Rarely do historical actors, especially those of the prominence of the German princes, fully escape the tug of the past, or fail to affect the unfolding future. But the apparent contradiction may be resolved if one understands the theological background of the princes. That background was laid in good part by Martin Luther, undoubtedly the greatest single theological influence on the minority princes at Speyer.

Luther did not attend Speyer II, but his closest theological associate, Melanchthon, was there. Further, the influence of Luther's writings and thought on the protesting princes is indisputable. Their political opposition only makes sense in the context of the influence of his religious reforms.[13] Indeed, the very language of their protest reflects some fundamental categories in Luther's thought. So did their treatment, unfortunately, of the Anabaptists. The puzzle of Speyer, and the larger paradox of Protestantism on religious freedom, is connected to the evolution of Luther's thought on the state's relationship with religion.

Church and State in the Medieval World: The Diet of Worms

Since Luther was also a creature of his day, we must know something about his world. On the eve of the Reformation, church and state were distinct entities, yet they were viewed as inseparable and organic parts of society as a whole. As one authority on the Middle Ages has put it, "the identification of the church with the whole of organized society is the fundamental feature which distinguishes the Middle Ages from earlier and later periods of history."[14] Church and state were indeed separate institutions. Yet the state was—under the theory of the two swords, civil and spiritual—meant to serve as the servant of the church in enforcing the church's religious rules and standards. Through the mechanism of infant baptism, virtually all citizens of the state were also citizens of the church. Church and state combined to oversee and enforce this civil and religious contractual relationship.[15]

It was a system with tensions and conflicts, as the interests of church and state often diverged. The pope and his bishops had enormous influence and persuasive powers, but they were hamstrung by their limited ability to wield force directly. They were, on the whole, dependent on kings and princes loyal to the church to carry out their decrees and to enforce their edicts. But such cooperation was often ad hoc, intermittent, and inconsistent. Lacking the means of consistent, direct coercion, the church had to resort to political and spiritual pressure to get civil rulers to act on its behalf. The church's persuasive powers, however, were significant. In a world where Christian belief held sway, the threat of excommunication or interdict persuaded many a civil ruler to carry out the wishes of the church.[16]

The tensions and limits of this system are well illustrated by the treatment of Luther at the Diet of Worms. Had the church had its way, there would have been no diet at Worms. A papal bull had already condemned Luther's teachings and excommunicated him. In the papacy's view, all that was left was for the heretic to be arrested and consigned to the rack or the flames. But the Elector Frederick, Luther's patron, was unwilling to hand over his star theologian without a formal hearing. He persuaded Emperor Charles V to hold a public hearing for Luther, and the Diet of Worms was convened in mid-April of 1521.[17]

That the Diet met of all, then, was something of a setback for Rome. It undercut the authority of the previous papal bulls against Luther. Still, it was a temporary defeat that could yet end in the condemnation and execution of Luther—hardly a victory from the reformer's view. Indeed, events initially unfolded much as the pope would have hoped. Luther was quickly questioned about the authorship of his books, which were assumed to be heretical. There was no room for arguing this point. Rather, the question was whether Luther would recant and reject his teachings. After a short delay, Luther made his memorable defense: "my conscience is captive to the Word of God. Thus I cannot and will not recant, for going against conscience is neither safe nor salutary. I can do no other, here I stand, God help me. Amen."[18]

Notwithstanding the enthusiasm of some modern interpreters, Luther did not view the conscience as an individual, independent, and unfettered moral center.[19] His conscience *was* bound and hemmed by something external; but not, as the medieval view would have it, by the pope or the church. Rather, his conscience was bound—"captive," as the English translation has it—by the word of God. But neither the emperor nor the church leaders could conceive of a claim to conscience outside the dual, cooperative sovereignty of the church and state. The line the church drew around the conscience with the spiritual sword the state would enforce with the civil sword.

Thus, Charles V condemned Luther as an unrepentant heretic in the Edict of Worms. The emperor ordered Luther's books and writings destroyed and his person arrested and turned over for appropriate punishment—execution.[20] At last the papacy had the civil mandate it had been seeking, or so it seemed. But Charles, unwilling to bear the ignominy of violating a promise of safe conduct, left open a small sliver of daylight—a twenty-day delay on the enforcement of the edict. Luther's allies arranged for the reformer to be "kidnapped" on the way home from the Diet. Some of Elector Frederick's horsemen whisked him away into hiding at Wartburg Castle, where he spent a productive year translating the Greek New Testament into the German vernacular.[21]

The story of Worms, with its second-guessing, yet ultimate affirmation, of papal condemnations, its responsiveness to papal requests—but with just enough delay to let the condemned heretic slip free—illustrates well the cooperative, conflicted, ambivalent, politically charged relationship between the medieval church and state. The church claimed to be the superior authority. But the superior sword of the state often made that claim theoretical only. Cooperation between the two was often inconsistent and slow, though often effective in the end.

The wheels of the medieval gods ground slowly yet exceedingly fine. Rare was the monk or priest who could oppose them without serious consequence. The medieval church and state agreed that the citizen's conscience was subject to the oversight of the church and state acting together. Luther's new teaching, as he expressed it at Worms, directly challenged this allied hegemony over conscience. It was a challenge produced by Luther's revised view of the proper relationship between believers and scriptural authority, and one he expressed in several of his earliest writings.

Early Luther on Church and State

Luther's ordeal at Worms took place about four years after the release of his ninety-five theses.[22] In the interim, he had thought deeply about the relationship between the church and civil rulers. In 1520 he published his most important work on the subject, the *Address to the Christian Nobility of the German Nation*. It was also the first of his polemics to be written in the German vernacular rather than the Latin of the church. It was a practical application of his theology meant to serve as a guide for civil leaders within society. At its core lay a teaching of the equality of all believers—the "priesthood of believers"— that had profound implications as to who should be able to read and interpret the Bible, as well as how church and society should be ordered.

Luther set out in this work his view on the proper role of the church in relation to the individual, scripture, and society. He believed that the church had wrongly erected three "walls of privilege" that prevented the correction of continuing abuses within the church.[23] The first wall was the assertion that spiritual authority was superior to that of civil. Thus, the church was not subject to secular jurisdiction in many temporal matters. The second wall was that the papacy alone had the right to authoritatively interpret scripture. Therefore, the pope could not be corrected by other persons. The third wall was that the pope alone could call councils. Thus, the pope could effectively control the church, and prevent any appeal from his decisions to the body of the church.

Luther attacked these walls of privilege by asserting the doctrine of the priesthood of all believers.

> To call popes, bishops, priests, monks, and nuns, the religious class, but princes, lords, artizans, and farm-workers the secular class, is a specious device invented by certain time-servers; ... For all Christians whatsoever really and truly belong to the religious class, and there is no difference among them except insofar as they do different work. ... The fact is that our baptism consecrates us all without exception, and makes us all priests. As St. Peter says, "You are a royal priesthood and a realm of priests" [1 Pet. 2.9], and Revelation, "Thou hast made us priests and kings by Thy blood" [Rev. 5:9.].[24]

Luther believed that all Christians have an equal spiritual status, though they may fulfill different spiritual offices. But those selected for such offices, such as pastor or bishop, act merely on behalf of the congregation, all of whom have, in principle, the same spiritual authority he does. He serves at the command and consent of the community, who can also dismiss him from his office should they desire.[25]

This doctrine, Luther believed, undercut all three walls of papal privilege. By putting all Christians on a similar plane, it nullified the claim of the church hierarchy that it was superior to secular rulers and rules, since these temporal authorities were properly exercising their own God-ordained civil offices. Luther opposed the church's claim of exemption from civil courts when its priests or bishops violated civil laws.[26]

Luther also asserted that while rulers had a spiritual appointment, the function and role of their offices were secular. "This government is spiritual in status, although it discharges a secular duty."[27] In other words, in affirming that all people, including popes and priests, were subject to the civil sword, he was not in this argument giving the state authority or jurisdiction in spiritual matters. In his treatise *Secular Authority: To What Extent It Should Be Obeyed*, written just three years later, Luther unpacked the implications of his priesthood-of-believers doctrine for the civil state, setting out his well-known "two kingdoms" theology.[28] He wrote:

> Worldly government has laws which extend no farther than to life and property and what is external upon earth. For over the soul God can and will let no one rule but Himself. Therefore, where temporal power presumes to prescribe laws for the soul, it encroaches upon God's government and only misleads and destroys the souls.[29]

In light of these separate jurisdictions, Luther argued that Christians had no need to obey a civil ruler who commanded religious belief or the giving up of heretical books. "Heresy," he wrote, "can never be prevented by force. That must be taken hold of in a different way, and must be opposed and dealt with otherwise than with the sword. Here God's Word must strive."[30] It was just this understanding of the civil ruler's role, or nonrole, in spiritual matters that animated the first point of the protesting princes at Speyer. As preaching the gospel had to do with matters of God and salvation, the civil ruler, or a vote of a majority of the princes, could not legitimately forbid it.

Luther's argument regarding the second wall was also critical to the princes' protest, especially its second point regarding scriptural authority. Luther's concept of a universal priesthood undermined that second wall, the papacy's claim to ultimate scriptural authority. Once the spiritual equality of all believers was granted, the primacy of the Holy See in interpreting scripture was undercut. As Luther put it:

> Each and all of us are priests ... why then should we not be entitled to taste or test, and to judge what is right or wrong in the faith? ... "He that is spiritual judges all things and is judged by none." ... We ought to ... test everything the Romanists do or leave undone. We ought to apply that understanding of the Scriptures which we possess as believers. ... Since God once spoke through an ass, why should He not come in our day and speak through a man of faith and even contradict the pope?[31]

By asserting the right of all believers to read the scriptures for themselves, Luther was not replacing a single pope with thousands and even millions of individual popes. Rather, he was moving the locus of scriptural authority within the church down from its apex, vested in the figure of the pope, and placing it at the base of the church structure, in the body of believers. Now all believers would have the opportunity and right to study scripture, and the body of believers would decide what doctrinal standards applied within the church. Neither the pope, nor a small group of experts, nor the civil magistrates should undertake this task for them.

This was the theory, anyway, though in practice Lutheranism and the other forms of magisterial Protestantism moved back toward a sort of unofficial magisterium of theologians and leading pastors who would decide what was orthodox. Still, this theory of populist scriptural interpretation was advocated by Anabaptists and other dissenters. It continued on as a critique within Protestantism, by dissenters who would complain about the "creedalism" and "popery" of the magisterial Protestant churches.

But at this early stage, Luther's commitment to remove the magistrate from spiritual matters and to give room for personal scriptural interpretation was not just theory. Events in 1522 showed his willingness to implement these revolutionary ideas. Leaving his Wartburg sanctuary, Luther returned to Wittenberg to confront his colleague, Andreas Karlstadt, and others who were advocating the forcible removal of images and the overturning of the mass by law and force. Luther agreed that the mass was wrong, even sinful. But he opposed the use of law or force to eradicate it. Rather than force, Luther would "preach it, teach it, write it," and allow God's word to work.[32]

Luther later moved away from these positions, especially after the Peasant's War of 1525, and eventually supported state oversight of church matters and the use of some civil force against certain types of heretics. This shift has caused some to overlook or disregard as mere rhetoric his earlier teachings on the inappropriateness of using force in religion. Thus, it is worth reviewing an extended quote from one of his Invocavit sermons, preached in 1522 on his return to Wittenberg to confront the radicals, to show how measured, reasoned, and clear his thought was on the topic at that time.[33]

He opened his series of Invocavit sermons by focusing on the individual responsibility all persons have to account for themselves to God after death. The opening lines of the first sermon summarized this personal duty memorably: "The summons of death comes to us all, and no one can die for another. Every one must fight his own battle with death by himself, alone. We can shout into another's ears, but every one must himself be prepared for the time of death, for I will not be with you then, nor you with me. Therefore every one must himself know and be armed with the chief things which concern a Christian."[34]

The next day, he spelled out the implications of this individual account-
ability to God for the role of the state in spiritual matters. It is an important
statement that deserves full quotation:

> The mass is an evil thing, and God is displeased with it ... it must be
> abolished. ... Yet Christian love should not employ harshness here
> nor force the matter. However, it should be preached and taught with
> tongue and pen that to hold mass in such a manner is sinful, and yet no
> one should be dragged away from it by the hair; *for it should be left to
> God, and his Word should be allowed to work alone, without our interfer-
> ence?* Why? Because is not in my power or hand to fashion the hearts
> of men as the potter molds the clay and fashion them at my pleasure.
> I can get no farther than their ears; their hearts I cannot reach. And
> since I cannot pour faith into their hearts, *I cannot, nor should I, force
> any one to have faith. That is God's work alone, who causes faith to live in
> the heart.* Therefore, we should give free course to the Word and not
> add our works to it. We have the right to speak, but not the power to
> act. We should preach the Word, but the results must be left solely to
> God's good pleasure.

Such enforced spiritual practices would be in vain: "forcing and com-
manding results in a mere mockery, an external show, a fool's play, man-made
ordinances, sham-saints, and hypocrites. For where the heart is not good,
I care nothing at all for the works." The reformers must first, he wrote, win the
hearts of the people. Even though the mass itself was a sin, he acknowledged,
he "would not make it an ordinance for them, nor urge a general law." Indeed,
he warned his supporters that if they did pass such a law, that he would "recant
everything that I have written and preached and I will not support you." "In
short," he concluded, "*I will preach it, teach it, write it, but I will constrain no
man by force, for faith must come freely without compulsion.*"[35]

This declaration was not mere rhetoric. At that time, it *would* have
been possible to do these things—abolish the mass and images by law in
Wittenberg—as the forces of reform controlled the town. Indeed, Karlstad
and others had begun to do some of these things, but Luther's sermons halted
their actions.[36]

Luther's early teachings help explain the stand of the Speyer princes. Their
refusal to submit on spiritual matters to either the emperor or a majority vote
of the princes themselves, as well as their commitment to the right of interpreting the scripture for themselves, directly echo Luther's early teachings on

these points. Thus, it is difficult to interpret the princes' protest as political rhetoric devoid of principled religious or ideological substance. But what about their willingness to persecute the Anabaptists? This seeming contradiction is also explained by Luther's developing thought on church and state.

Luther, the Peasants' War, and Seditious Heresy

Events of the mid-1520s caused Luther to expand his views on church and state to take into account the magistrate's role in dealing with heresy that manifested itself in seditious, or violent, conduct. The turmoil surrounding the Peasant's Revolt of 1524–25 and the controversy surrounding certain radical religious leaders associated with the revolt pushed Luther to a new emphasis on the importance of respect for civil authority. The revolt revealed that some ostensibly spiritual beliefs could have direct and immediate civil impact. The result of Luther's experiences in the revolts led to dire consequences for the Anabaptists.

The Peasant's Revolt began unfolding in the summer of 1524 in southwest Germany.[37] As the revolt spread, Luther wrote to distinguish his reforms from the populist demands of the peasants. In May 1525 he released a tract aimed at both the rulers and the peasants, pointing out the excesses and abuses of both sides and calling for restraint by the princes and submission by the peasants.[38] He outlined how the peasants' claims violated his interpretation of the gospel teachings. But he also insisted that the civil rulers should not punish the peasants for wrong beliefs, but only for sedition. "No ruler," he wrote, "ought to prevent anyone from teaching or believing what he pleases, whether gospel or lies. It is enough if he prevents the teaching of sedition and rebellion."[39]

A month later, after the peasants had engaged in even greater bloodshed, he wrote a tract whose title clearly revealed both its target and its polemical tone—*Against the Robbing and Murdering Hordes of Peasants*. In this pamphlet, he criticized the religious aspirations and leadership of the peasants, particularly fingering Thomas Muntzer and his brand of apocalyptic, revolutionary mysticism.[40] It was here that he first openly confronted ostensibly spiritual beliefs that were seditious, and thus (he reasoned) the legitimate target of the civil sword.

Luther has been often criticized for the extreme tone and content of *Against the Peasants* ("Let everyone who can, smite, slay and stab, secretly or openly, remembering that nothing can be more poisonous than a rebel").[41] Luther's tone was indeed newly harsh. But the revolt did not change the substance of his position toward the authoritative role of the magistrate in civil affairs. Luther had always, to that point, clearly rejected any use of force in opposing secular authorities.

The Peasants' Revolt confirmed in Luther's mind the connection between certain types of radical religion—especially of the mystical bent—and seditious, anarchic beliefs. In Luther's view, these mystical, seditious tendencies were associated with the Anabaptists, whom he came to view as continuing the work and tendencies of Thomas Muntzer and the *Schwärmer*, the demagogic, seditious, spiritualists.[42] As the modern-day heirs of the Anabaptists put it in the *Mennonite Encyclopedia*, "unfortunately, in Luther's mind the Anabaptist movement came more and more into the category of sedition, partly because of civil disturbances connected with the movement, partly because of radical utterances on the part of certain Anabaptists, and partly because of more or less biased reports. Consequently Luther was never able to recognize the quiet, purely religious Anabaptism."[43]

Indeed, this equation of the Reformation's spiritual left wing with peasant revolutionaries did remain fixed with Luther for the rest of his life. It explains, at least in part, his willingness to persecute the Anabaptists, despite his previous statements on the inappropriateness of using force against heresy. They were not, in his view, being persecuted for religious heresy. Rather, they were being punished for heresy that resulted in *civil* rebellion. Luther viewed the Anabaptists as the heirs of the Zwickau prophets, Thomas Munzter, and the spiritualist leaders of the Peasants' Revolt—gone underground, perhaps, but poised to resurface—and all the more deadly because of their deception in ostensibly preaching pacifism and nonviolence.[44]

Later, under the influence of Melanchthon and other traditionalists, Luther came to broaden his definition of sedition. It came to include those who advocated communal living as well as those who rejected the idea that Christians could be magistrates. Various Anabaptist groups held these views. But Luther never fully embraced Melanchthon's quick willingness to execute unrepentant heretics. He viewed the magistrates' role in spiritual affairs as a necessary but, it was to be hoped, temporary affair. At one point, he gave to the princes involved with church oversight the name "emergency bishops," indicating what he hoped was their provisional and temporary role in the church.[45] Toward the end of his life he again expressed misgivings about the intrusion of "princely power into the affairs of the church." He continued also to distinguish between the "heretic" and the "seditious heretic." The former could be banished, but only the latter could be executed.[46]

In dealing with the Anabaptists, the evangelical princes reflected Luther's view that the Anabaptists' beliefs, acts, and tendencies were genuinely seditious and not merely spiritually heretical. In this light, they were consistent in pro-claiming their rights of spiritual conscience, while censuring the Anabaptists for what they perceived to be that movement's anarchic and seditious teachings. Melanchthon had less patience than Luther for spiritual heresy and more willingness to use force against it. He would have supported the persecution of the Anabaptists even if they had not been seen as seditious. But at this stage, Luther was still the leading German theologian, and even Calvin had not yet come on the scene. Luther's interpretation in relation to the Anabaptists no doubt figured centrally in the insensitivity of the Protestant princes to that group.[47]

As Luther moved away from his earlier position on tolerance and began to accept the role of civil rulers in providing some religious oversight, he was urged on by Melanchthon. After Luther's death, Melanchthon's influence on church/state questions only increased. The civil magistrate's role in supporting and overseeing the church became the general rule in Lutheranism. As a result, Lutheranism matched the Reformed churches and the Catholics in the vigor with which it defended its legal status wherever it was the majority faith. But Luther's early views on church and state were not forgotten by everyone. They continued to exert an influence in some unexpected places, including the Anabaptists, whose persecution he had supported.

The Continuing Influence of Early Luther

Luther's approval of the persecution of the pacifist, evangelical Anabaptists is ironic, since they drew heavily on Luther's early views on church and state.[48] The evangelical Anabaptists were much closer than later Lutherans to Luther's early stated ideals on the civil magistrate's role in spiritual affairs. Central to the evangelical "Anabaptist view of government was their version of the two kingdoms' doctrine." As one Anabaptist historian has put it, the church/state position of the Anabaptists, "in its basic ingredients, was virtually identical with Martin Luther's."[49]

This was no coincidence, since many of the early Anabaptist leaders had been directly influenced by Luther's writings. Some had even identified as Lutherans before moving on to Anabaptism. Early Anabaptist leaders with connections to Luther or his works included Balthasar Hubmaier, who left the Catholic priesthood in part due to reading Luther's early works; William Reublin, who corresponded with Luther on church matters; John Denck, who moved from humanism to Lutheranism before becoming an Anabaptist; Michael Sattler, who associated with zealous Lutherans in 1523; and Pilgram Marpeck, whose spiritual awakening had also been via Lutheranism.[50]

These men used a logic very like Luther's to argue not only that the use of force was inappropriate against heretics but also that toleration should be extended to Jews and Muslims.[51] In 1524, Balthasar Hubmaier, shortly after studying Luther's writings, wrote one of the earliest Reformation statements on religious liberty. Entitled *Concerning Heretics and Those That Burn Them* (Von Ketzern und ihren Verbrennern), the work echoed Luther in arguing that heretics should be "overcome with holy knowledge" and the arguments of Holy Scripture. If they do not respond, he wrote, to "strong proofs or evangelical reasons, then let them be, and leave them to rage and be mad."[52]

Like Luther, Hubmaier acknowledged the right of the "secular power" to put to death "criminals who injure the bodies of the defenseless." But the godless who do not "injure body or soul" should be left unmolested.[53] He advocated religious freedom as a universal principle, arguing that it should be extended to both the "Turk or a heretic" who will not be won by "sword or fire but alone with patience and prayer." In a sad irony, Hubmaier himself was burned for heresy about three years later in Vienna.[54]

Hubmaier's beliefs in principled toleration, however, lived on within the Anabaptist movement. In 1527, the year prior to Hubmaier's death, other Anabaptist leaders, guided by Michael Sattler, set down their distinguishing list of seven beliefs at Schleitheim. The sixth, and longest, belief had to do with the civil sword and the inappropriateness of using it to enforce religious beliefs.[55]

Due to their small numbers and generally outlawed status, the Anabaptists have been generally considered to have had little direct intellectual influence within Europe. While their influence was likely modest, one commentator overstates the case in saying that the Anabaptist "espousal of [religious liberty] was stillborn."[56] Small though it was, the influence they did have was important. Both the Anabaptists and Luther's early writings had a disproportionately greater influence in the Netherlands than in other European countries. As early as 1521, five works of Luther had been published in Dutch. By 1524, the number had increased to a score or more. By 1530, there had been thirty printings of Luther's early works in the Netherlands, compared with three printings in England. The Anabaptists were the only organized Protestant movement in the Netherlands until the 1550s, when the Reformed churches became more active.[57]

Menno Simons, the great organizer of the Anabaptist wing eventually known as the Mennonites, worked and wrote in the Netherlands.[58] These two factors—the popularity of Luther's early writings and the success of Anabaptism in the Netherlands—may indeed be connected. Luther's early

thought, especially regarding the magistrate's lack of responsibility for dealing with heresy, dovetailed well with many of the main tenets of Anabaptism.
Simons himself said that Luther's writings played an important role in causing him to leave the Catholic priesthood to become a Protestant.[59]

The influences of early Lutheran and Anabaptist thought on Dutch
Protestants was one of the factors that helps explain the repute—or ill
repute—that the Netherlands developed in the sixteenth and seventeenth
centuries for its religious toleration. A number of persons prominent later
in this story had connections with the Netherlands, including William Penn
and John Locke, as well as the early English Baptists.

Yet it was probably the Anabaptist's example of suffering, more than their
ideas and writings, that influenced the developing case for toleration. Their
bloody experiences and patient endurance at the hands of civil and religious
authorities caused a number of other figures to reflect on the inherent injustice
of religious persecution and intolerance. These authors—disturbed especially
by the widespread cruelty toward Anabaptists—also picked up the threads
of Luther's early views on the priesthood of believers and the right of private
scriptural interpretation. With these, they began weaving a fuller tapestry of
thought about spiritual and civil freedom. This alternate view emerged as a
competing, if minority, vision dissenting from the model of coercion maintained within mainstream confessional Protestantism.

Sebastian Castellio: Spreading the Legacy of Early Luther

An early example of the expression of this alternate view came from the biblical scholar, translator, and author Sebastian Castellio. Originally a colleague
of John Calvin in Geneva, he fell out with Calvin over issues of free will and
the role of the magistrate in spiritual matters.[60] Moving to the University of
Basel, he engaged in open debate with Calvin in 1553 over Calvin's role in the
execution of the unorthodox physician Michael Servetus. Servetus was found
guilty of denying the Trinity and infant baptism and was sentenced to death,
with Calvin's approval, by the Geneva city government. Castellio responded
with his public, though anonymous, work *Concerning Heretics*.

Three things stood out in Castellio's exchange with Calvin. First, Castellio's
outrage regarding the cruel treatment of the Anabaptists was evident.[61]
Second was Castellio's extensive reliance on the early Luther in supporting
and validating his views on tolerance. Third was the connection Castellio
made between the importance of religious freedom and the right and duty of
personal scriptural interpretation. Castellio was an important and relatively

early link in the transmission of the legacy of early Luther to other dissenting thinkers throughout Europe.

For Castellio, the Anabaptists were the poster children for his argument that religious intolerance was evil. He mourned that in Germany alone the Anabaptists were subject to such severe persecution that "so much human blood has been poured out that if as many beasts had been killed men would lament." In lower Germany "men have been drowned, not one by one or two by two, but hundreds and thousands at one time and even whole shiploads."[62]

Castellio, however, did not have much to say about the beliefs of the Anabaptists. Rather, for his defense of the theory of freedom he relied on other, more mainstream and important Reformation figures. These included Luther, Erasmus, and Sebastian Franck. There was even a paragraph or two from Calvin himself, who in the first edition of his *Institutes* had written against using force in religious matters, either against heretics or even "Turks and the Saracens."[63]

But for Castellio, Luther was central. As one biographer of Castellio put it, "the German reformer most frequently mentioned in Castellio's writings was, without a doubt, Martin Luther." He relied, however, not on all of Luther. Rather, "above all," notes Roland Bainton, he "seems to have read the young Luther." Castellio quoted most extensively from Luther's 1523 work *On Secular Authority*, including this pointed passage: "When civil government undertakes to legislate for souls, then it encroaches upon the province of God and merely perverts and corrupts souls."[64]

Castellio could be criticized for handling Luther's views poorly in light of their evolution. But that would miss his main point. Castellio sought to capture a vital principle that he believed the earliest Protestants had defended and that flowed from basic Protestant commitments. He did not mean to prove that any particular leader or thinker always acted consistently with that principle. Castellio himself acknowledged that those he cited might have "afterwards written or acted in a different sense." But he believed that their early views were often purer expressions of Protestant's most important commitments, before they had became confused with political compromise or expediency.[65]

No mere collector of historical quotes, Castellio was a thoughtful theologian and expert Bible translator in his own right. His concern for toleration was closely connected with his view of the Bible and the right of individual interpretation. Once he found refuge in Basel after falling out with Calvin, he published two translations of the Bible: the first in Latin (1551), the second in French (1555).[66] The first he dedicated to Edward VI of England and the second to Henry II of France, using the occasion to urge both kings to exercise restraint and tolerance in regard to religious differences.

To both kings he wrote that the Bible revealed itself only to those who possessed the Holy Spirit and the requisite humility. In his dedication to King Edward, he wrote that because the Bible was in places difficult and obscure, God alone should be the judge of whether an individual was honestly reading and faithfully carrying out his or her own understanding of its teachings.[67] These basic questions of the spiritual nature of biblical interpretation and the obscurity of certain parts of scripture caused Castellio to emphasize the importance of allowing individuals to judge spiritual matters for themselves, and not to "judge one another, for with what measure we judge we shall be judged."[68]

These prefaces prefigured thinking that was more fully argued in his later works on toleration. For Castellio, both the Bible's clarity and its obscurity spoke to the need for toleration. Its clarity on central issues meant that all could read and understand themes central to salvation. This statement was akin to Luther's argument regarding the priesthood of all believers. But its obscurity on other points, a matter Luther was less prone to emphasize, meant that charity and forbearance should be exercised where there was disagreement. Judgment on spiritual motive usurped the prerogative of Christ at the final judgment.[69]

Castellio concluded his collection of quotations in *Concerning Heretics* with a short essay contrasting the children of flesh with those of the Spirit.[70] The difference? Those of the flesh visited judgment and persecution on those of the Spirit. To drive home his central point in defending personal and private judgment, he ended his work with this emphatic language: "JUDGE NOTHING BEFORE THE TIME, UNTIL THE LORD COME, WHO BOTH WILL BRING TO LIGHT THE HIDDEN THINGS OF DARKNESS, AND WILL MAKE MANIFEST THE COUNSELS OF THE HEART."[71]

Castellio's and Luther's experiences with Bible translation no doubt caused both men to see a similar connection between the right of judgment in biblical interpretation and freedom from civil interference. Lutheranism, for a variety of historical reasons, moved away from this emphasis. But Castellio, along with the Anabaptists, helped keep Luther's early emphasis alive. Castellio contributed to the survival of this alternative to the existing confessional communities—and in so doing maintained some of the earliest Protestant teachings that the Protestant states abandoned.

This minority view was based on both the words and the acts of the most influential of the first generation of the Protestant reformers. Although it was a minority view, it was viewed as sufficiently threatening by those in power to draw fierce replies, including responses by Calvin and Calvin's successor Theodore Beza, as well as from others throughout Europe. Castellio's work was quoted in France, Germany, and England and was even responded to by John Knox in Scotland.[72]

Castellio's work seems to have had the greatest impact in Holland and the Low Countries. By the 1560s and 1570s, rhetoric based on Castellio's views of toleration was widespread there. Most notably, it is to be found in the writings of a Catholic advocate for liberty, Dirck Volckertszoon Coornhert, who translated a number of Castellio's works into Dutch.[73] *On Heretics* was translated into Dutch twice in the seventeenth century and was read by religious liberty advocates through the end of the seventeenth century. Pierre Bayle, Huguenot scholar and refugee in the Netherlands in the 1680s, referred to Castellio in his work on toleration, *Compel Them to Come In*.[74]

Another refugee in the Netherlands who came into contact with Castellio's works was John Locke. His famous "Letter on Toleration," written during his time in Holland, and which we will deal with at some length in a later chapter, reflects many of the themes found in Castellio. Castellio himself was not widely read in England or America. But his works found a sympathetic audience among certain English dissenting leaders in the late sixteenth and seventeenth centuries. These English leaders, in turn, helped shape this alternate Protestant history and made it an alternate, if minority, Protestant view in England.

The British Connection: English Baptist Beginnings

The European reformation was channeled to America primarily via England. Even as late as the 1770s, nearly 85 percent of settlers in the American colonies were white and English speaking. Whatever religious conflicts and controversies existed on the continent, the form they took in America was primarily shaped by their evolution in England. This was certainly true of issues concerning toleration and religious freedom. Reference has already been made to certain English thinkers who encountered tolerationist thought while in the Netherlands. Early among these were English separatists who sought refuge in Holland from persecution by the state-sponsored church at home.[75]

Continental Anabaptists had little direct influence on the church in England. In the mid- to late sixteenth century, they occasionally immigrated to England as refugees, but as soon as their presence became known, they were either banished or burned. Their reputation as seditious fomenters responsible for the atrocities and outrages of the short-lived theocracy at Münster meant that "Anabaptist" was a term of opprobrium, often used to insult religious dissenters of all stripes.[76]

To be sure, the English church did have its share of dissenters. Whether in the reigns of Henry VIII, Edward VI, Mary, or Elizabeth I, the state-sponsored church always had its share of critics. The Puritans, starting in the reign of Elizabeth, worked from within the Anglican church to purify it by removing its "Romish" or "pagan" elements. But other groups, known as separatists, were intent on setting up their own competing churches made up of those willing to enter into a voluntary covenant of commitment to each other and to Christ. Termed Brownists, Barrowists, Separatists, or Seekers, depending on their origins and affiliations, these groups were a small but vocal presence that drew increasing attention from the state toward the end of the sixteenth century. Yet, despite their sufferings, these groups did not advocate for general toleration. Rather, they wanted the Queen to direct her intolerance at Catholics and the continued Catholic practices within the Church of England rather than at "godly Protestants."[77]

That emphasis changed, however, when some from these groups sought refuge overseas in Holland, by then already known for its toleration. Henry Barrow, a leading separatist in the 1580s, developed a following, who came to be known as the Barrowists.[78] By the early 1590s, most of the Barrowist leadership was in London prisons, where a number of them, including Henry, died. Those remaining realized that continuing in England meant imprisonment, or even death, and so chose exile in Holland. Arriving in 1593, they soon came into contact with a Dutch Mennonite group that influenced some of their leadership with ideas about infant baptism, free will, and religious toleration.[79] By 1597, an English visitor to Holland wrote back to London warning of "Englishe anabaptists" who believed that the "infants of the faythfull ought not to be baptized" and that "Maiestrates ought not to put malefactors to deathe."[80] By this time, these English Anabaptists were sending letters back to England promoting their views, causing at least one book to be written in opposition to them.

Later in 1608, another group of separatists led by John Smyth, a Cambridge-educated priest and university lecturer turned separatist, crossed the channel to Holland. Prior to traveling there, despite his separatist views, Smyth held quite conventional views of the duty of the civil magistrate. Just two or three years earlier in 1605, he wrote that "the Magistrate should cause all men to worship the true God, or else punish them with imprisonment, confiscation of goods, or death."[81]

But by the end of his first year in Holland, Smyth, became influenced by local Mennonites. He embraced adult baptism, and for a time he and his band of Baptists considered merging with the Mennonites. This idea was shelved for a variety of reasons, including a dispute over whether members of the church could serve as magistrates.[82] But the influence of Mennonites on the English Baptists was apparent in three areas: first, on the question of infant baptism; second, on the question of the universal efficacy of Christ's atonement, that is, they believed that Christ died generally for all;[83] and third, on the question of the civil magistrate's jurisdiction over spiritual matters.

The impact of this third issue is seen in a confession of faith John Smyth put together just before his death in 1612. In direct contrast to his 1605 statement, it called for the separation of the magistrate from religious affairs, based on the view that Christ was the king and judge (Smyth uses the phrase "lawgiver") of the conscience. In article 84, Smyth stated:

> That the magistrate is not by virtue of his office to meddle with religion, or matters of conscience, to force or compel men to this or that form of religion, or doctrine: but to leave Christian religion free, to every man's conscience, and to handle only civil transgressions (Rom. Xiii), injuries and wrongs of man against man, in murder, adultery, theft, etc., for Christ only is the king, and lawgiver of the church and conscience (James iv. 12).[84]

This remarkable early statement of church/state separation has been described as "one of the most complete statements of religious liberty of that generation."[85] Smyth died too soon to express a broader theological and theoretical grounding for the belief. This job was taken up, however, by his surviving colleagues, who also received guidance from Mennonites steeped in the earlier reformation writings on tolerance.

By this time, the Mennonites had themselves developed some scholarly expertise and resources on the question of toleration. Just prior to Smyth's death, in 1609, Mennonite historian Pieter Twisck published a compilation from over one thousand sources of historic statements in support of religious freedom. The lengthy title of the work speaks for itself, reading, in part, *Religion's Freedom, A Brief Chronological Description of the Freedom of Religion against the Coercion of Conscience, drawn from Many Various Books from the Time of Christ to the Year 1609; from which One Can See Clearly ... How One Should Treat Heretics; That the Steel Sword of the Worldly Governments Does Not Extend over Conscience to the Compulsion of Belief ...* [86]

A number of English separatist leaders had contact with Twisck, including the Pilgrims' minister and leader, John Robinson, who had a two-day conference with him in 1617 on religious toleration. (Interestingly, probably because of this contact, Robinson's Pilgrims, who eventually settled in Plymouth Colony, had a much more tolerant approach to religious issues, not requiring church membership for civil suffrage, unlike their Puritan neighbors in nearby Massachusetts.) Twisck's historical work provided the background for a number of statements and documents on religious liberty drafted by the English dissenters.[87]

Two of Smyth's most prominent associates in forming the English Baptist Church, Thomas Helwys and Leonard Busher, were also influenced by Twisck and the Mennonites. Around the time of Smyth's death, Helwys and a number of followers returned to England to establish the first English Baptist church. He soon wrote to the King of England about liberty of conscience. In 1612, sounding much like early Luther on the two kingdoms, Helwys penned "doth not the King knowe that the God of Gods, and Lord of Lords, ... hath reserved to himself the heavenly kingdom, ... and that with this kingdome, our lord the King has nothing to do ... but as a subject himself: and that Christ alone is King."

Helwys connected this two-kingdom motif with the Lutheran idea of all persons' duty as individuals before God to account for themselves and their religious choices. "Oh let the King judge, is it not most equall that men should chuse their religion themselves seeing they only must stand themselves before the judgment seat of God to answere for themselves, then it shalbe no cause for them to say, wee were commanded or compelled to be of this religion. ... For men's religion to God, is betwixt God and themselves; the King shall not answer for it, neither may the King be judge between God and man."[88] For his trouble and concern, Helyws was arrested and imprisoned in 1613. Despite a number of petitions in which he indicated a willingness to take an oath of loyalty to the king, he died in jail sometime before 1616.[89]

Within two years, the Baptist Leonard Busher also addressed a treatise on liberty of conscience to king and Parliament. Entitled "Religions Peace: Or a Plea for Liberty of Conscience," it was even more explicit about the connection between the free pursuit of truth and the importance of private judgment. One nineteenth-century historian observed of this work: "though not the first of the noble band who manfully claimed liberty of private judgment in divine things for himself and for all others, Busher's work remains to us as the *earliest treatise known to be extant* on this great theme."[90] This claim overlooks Castellio's works, and even those of the early Luther. That mistake is, however, forgivable if attention is limited to the English-speaking world.

Busher at times seemed to paraphrase Castellio on the issue of the king or magistrate not judging in place of Christ, but leaving religious choices to the individual. "And to judge men now for religion, is to judge afore the time, and also to sit in the judgment-seat of Christ, to whom it belongeth, yet not before the day appointed. How much less to kings and bishops?"[91]

Busher also echoed Luther's two kingdoms metaphor: "Kings and magistrates are to rule in temporal affairs by the swords of their temporal kingdoms, and bishops and ministers are to rule spiritual affairs by the word and Spirit of God, the sword of Christ's spiritual kingdom, and not to intermeddle one with another's authority, office, and function."[92] This principle in turn served as the basis for his extended argument that the king and Parliament should "therefore believe not such as counsel you to shed blood for [differences of] judgment in religion."[93]

Helwys and Busher may have used this language and drawn these metaphors based on their own, original creative review of the scriptures. But it is unlikely. Prior to their stay in Holland, the English separatists did not view the civil magistrate as being separate from spiritual matters. They certainly did not use language of personal judgment in religion or the two kingdoms metaphor. Suddenly, after contact with Mennonites and Twisck, in a country where Castellio's works were also known to be widespread, three of their leaders published prominent works echoing both Castellio and early Luther in language and metaphor. The reasonable explanation is that they encountered versions of Castellio and early Luther during their stay in Holland through their contact with the Mennonites.

That the English Baptists did not mention the Anabaptists or Castellio by name is easily explained by the British antipathy for all things Anabaptist, as well as by the absence of knowledge about Castellio in England. The English Baptists themselves differed with the Mennonites on a number of points, including the question of whether Christians could serve as civil magistrates. But we do not have to guess at the influence of early Luther on their thought. That influence was made clear in a plea to king and Parliament the Baptist leaders made just a few years later.

In 1620, about six years after Busher's plea, King James again called Parliament into session. Unfortunately, the king had not softened in his attitude toward religious dissent in response to Busher's writings. In his inaugural speech to Parliament, the king said: "The maintenance of religion stands in two points: 1. Persuasion, which must precede. 2. Compulsion, which must follow; for as ... no law of man can make a good Christian in heart, without inward grace. Yet it is not enough to a good cause, and let it go alone."[94] Such a public stand in favor of using force in religion required a response, or so the fledgling English Baptists believed. Thus, in 1620 the prominent Baptist John Murton responded with *An Humble Supplication to the King's Majesty*.

Murton, as a teenager, had been with Smyth and Helwys on their trip to Holland and had returned to London with Helwys in 1612. After Helwy's imprisonment and death, Murton became a prominent leader in the English Baptist cause and wrote a number of books on religious freedom and church and state.[95] Murton cited arguments—based in part on the model set down by Twisck—for toleration from the Bible, from civil leaders, and theologians.[96] The *Humble Supplication* contains the clearest, most logical exposition of the connection between the right of private scriptural interpretation and the freedom of conscience that had appeared in English up to that time. What the earlier Baptist works either implied or intimated about the connection between scripture and conscience is here set out with great clarity and force. In opening, the author acknowledges the divine authority of the king in civil matters but reminds the king of his own words, "that in matters of the worship of God, according to Paul's rule, *let every man be persuaded in his own mind.*"[97]

He then points out that Protestants agree that it is "high cruelty" for the "papists to constrain them" in religious practices. But is it not, he asks, the same "great cruelty" when Protestants do the same to other Protestants? The justification for such practice, he notes, rests on a claim to enforce the "true touchstone, the holy scriptures." Yet whose right is it to interpret these?

The rest of the work deals with this question. Its chapter headings reveal the flow of the argument. Chapter 1 is entitled "The rule of faith is the doctrine of the Holy Ghost contained in the sacred scriptures, and not any church, council, prince, or potentate, nor any mortal man whatsoever." In this chapter, Murton argues that many "learned Protestants" have claimed that "no church nor man whatsoever may be the judge, rule, or umpire, in matters of faith, but only the holy scriptures."[98]

And how are the scriptures meant to be interpreted? And who is meant to do the interpreting? The headings for chapters 2 and 3 leave no room for doubt. Chapter 2 reads: "The interpreter of this rule is the scriptures, and the Spirit of God in whomsoever."[99] Chapter 3 then identifies this interpreter directly: "That the Spirit of God, to understand and interpret the scriptures, is given to all and every particular person that fear and obey God, of what degree soever they be; and not the wicked."[100] These two chapters magnify the core of both Castellio's and Luther's argument regarding the role of scripture and the individual believer.

With Castellio, Murton acknowledges that the Bible is made up of both plain and obscure passages, and that the latter should be interpreted in light of the former. The Bible is plain enough that all believers can read and understand it, but it is also obscure in some places, so that all should exercise charity toward others. Certainly, the civil magistrate should play no role in enforcing it. Further, Murton acknowledges that the Holy Spirit must guide one in understanding scripture.

The Holy Spirit is given to each believer and is not necessarily, or even likely to be, possessed by the civil magistrate. With this in mind, who should interpret the Bible? "Hence it is most plain to whom the Spirit of God is given, even to every particular saint of God."[101] This is the basis—that the right to interpret scripture is given to every believer, and not to the elite, either in church or state—on which Murton builds his argument for civil tolerance. He goes on to appeal to the teachings of Christ, the church fathers, and the history of persecution of the saints by those in power.

The similarity of Murton's ideas to Luther's view on scriptural interpretation, the priesthood of all believers, and the limits of civil authority are not coincidental. In the section where Murton quotes significant church figures in support of his argument, Luther is given the most space.[102] The first citation is from Luther's early work on civil authority, a passage also used by Castellio in *Concerning Heretics*. Whether Murton got it from Castellio or directly from Luther, the point is that the English Baptists explicitly drew from the early Luther in constructing their church/state arguments.

Murton and Helwys and Busher composed their works around the same time and in places not far apart. Murton's explicit use of Luther indicates that Helwys and Busher, in using language and ideas similar to Luther's, were also familiar with his writings. But did this church/state thought inspired by the early Luther dwell only in the relative obscurity of Baptist house meetings or insular and sectarian letters and writings? There is good evidence that it extended far beyond.

First, these Baptist writings were drafted as public documents. The intended audience was the king and Parliament, not just other Baptists. Whether the king or members of Parliament read them is uncertain. But they were no doubt circulated as the equivalent of open letters to court officials, members of Parliament, and other public leaders. That these documents played this public role is indicated by the fact that some of them were reprinted several decades later, at times of renewed church/state controversy and turmoil.

Busher's *Religions Peace* was reprinted in 1646, the year of Parliament's final defeat of the king in the English Civil War. The year before, Parliament had abolished the episcopacy and voted to create a Presbyterian national church. Much was in flux in society, with further changes to church and state a distinct possibility. The Baptists sought to influence this critical moment by reissuing Busher's piece. About fifteen years later in 1662, two years after the restoration of King Charles II, they did the same with Murton's *Humble Supplication*. This was the same year that Parliament began passing new legislation requiring religious uniformity after the relatively tolerant years of Cromwell and the Protectorate.

The point is not that the Baptists were influential enough to change the course of English politics. Rather, it is that their views, their alternate readings of Protestant history, were part of the public discussion. When advocacy of liberty became more widespread in England in the 1640s—especially in 1644 with Milton's *Areopagitica* and Roger Williams's *Bloudy Tenet*—the earlier Baptist efforts influenced the kind of religious and theological argument these later authors used. Thus, in his *Bloudy Tenet,* Williams explicitly relied on Murton's *Humble Supplication*, quoting a lengthy section of it at the beginning of his own work.[103]

Many arguments for toleration appeared in mid-seventeenth-century Britain, but most of them repeated, with some variations, religious arguments the Baptists had been making already for decades.[104] As one historian of the period has noted, "secular arguments were made ... but fundamentally the case for toleration was biblical and theological."[105] Amid the various contentions, those that had the greatest impact dealt with the Lutheran two kingdom theme and the right of personal biblical interpretation. In particular, these two arguments were promoted most articulately by the prominent poet and seventeenth-century public intellectual John Milton.

Milton's Protestant Prism of History

Milton is of course best known for *Paradise Lost*, the epic poem about the fall of Lucifer, the creation of the world, and the fall of man. But he actually wrote more religious and political prose than poetry.[106] Indeed, he wrote his epic poem toward the end of his life—after his major political and religious prose writings had been completed. The poem tells a vivid, powerful story, conveying many of his political and religious ideas under cover of scintillating and colorful yet disciplined verse.

He was right to think that a poetic story might endure and have greater popular influence than his political prose works. Yet his prose also had an influence of its own. His defense of freedom of speech and the press, *Areopagitica*, is still read in law schools today. But his greatest contribution may have been a reviving of the Protestant story of the second Diet of Speyer and its implications for freedom of conscience.

In the public eye—because of his works ranging from arguments for liberalization of divorce laws, to defense of the press, to criticisms of the hierarchical episcopacy of the Anglican church—Milton became a spokesperson for the Commonwealth after the regicide of Charles I. In that capacity, Milton published a defense of the right of the people to rid themselves of tyrannical rulers. Other works followed, many of them concerned with the operations of church and state.

Over time, his thought moved to favor greater liberty, and also a greater equality in the church. He rejected not just episcopacy but also presbytery, or rule by a collection of elders, and came to favor a congregational, almost entirely democratic church governance. He also came to strongly oppose government rule in religious matters. Toward the end of the Commonwealth in 1559, out of frustration at Parliament's practice of intolerance and persecution, he published his fullest and most complete statement on church/state, *A Treatise of Civil Power in Ecclesiastical Causes*. It tracks so closely the arguments about scriptural interpretation and conscience of the Baptists Helwys and Busher that it would be a miracle of coincidence if there were no connection between them and Milton.

Some have proposed that Milton actually used the arguments of the Anglican scholar and apologist William Chillingworth, who in 1538 wrote the widely circulated work *The Religion of Protestants*.[107] There, Chillingworth developed and evolved the Protestant dictum "The Bible, I say, the Bible only, is the religion of Protestants." He defended the view that only the individual believer, and not the church hierarchy, has the right of interpreting the Bible. His strong view of the centrality of the Bible and the individual's access to it caused him to speak in terms of toleration within the church on minor matters. As one historian put it, the hermeneutical principles that Chillingworth shared with Milton caused Chillingworth to be set "clearly apart from either Anglican or conservative Puritan, [in] his insistence on the right of individual interpretation of Scripture, with its obvious corollary of latitude in the minor conclusions therefrom."[108]

Yet Chillingworth did not, either in theory or in practice, explore the consequences for civil religious liberty from this theological position. His famed work was silent on the treatment of religious dissenters by civil authorities. In his personal and political life, he was connected with Archbishop William Laud, who was his godfather.[109] At no time did he challenge or oppose

Laud's often heavy-handed attempts to impose uniformity on the Church of England. Indeed, during the revolution, he sided with the royalists and complained that the "rebels and traitors" breached the peace of church and state.[110] (Chillingworth came to an unfortunate end, dying of illness while held prisoner by parliamentary forces.)

Chillingworth may well have reinforced Milton's commitment to the individualism of Protestant biblical interpretation. But he provided no obvious impetus to make the connection—as the English Baptists did—between this belief and civil toleration of religious differences. The royalist Chillingworth did not share Milton's republican and libertarian views. Milton's ecclesiology—he supported the Independents—was, however, very similar to what the Baptists believed. Likewise, Milton also rejected infant baptism.[111] It is hard to imagine Milton, a learned bibliophile, knowing nothing about Baptist views on church organization, baptism, and religious liberty.

Indeed, there is more evidence that Milton knew the works of the English Baptists than that he had read Chillingworth. As did the Baptists' works, Chillingworth's works eventually went through multiple printings. But Chillingworth's second printing was not until 1664, well after Milton had composed his major church/state works.[112] Since there were no reported copies of works by either Chillingworth or the Baptists in Milton's library, the inference by scholars that he read Chillingworth is based on the similarity of language and argument.[113] The same criterion, however, supports the claim that Milton had read the Baptists, since his language and arguments resemble theirs even more than Chillingworth's.

There is even stronger evidence that Milton knew about Murton's *Humble Supplication* of 1620. During Roger Williams's visits to England, Milton had contact with the American dissenter. Both men studied at Cambridge from 1625 to 1628, and their continuing contacts over the years could well have stemmed from their time as students.[114] Williams wrote his most famous church/state work, *The Bloudy Tenet of Persecution, for Cause of Conscience*, while he was visiting England in 1644—the same year that Milton wrote *Areopagitica*. Milton personally recommended his printer to Williams at that time.[115] Williams, who had become a Baptist while in Rhode Island, opened his *Bloudy Tenet* with a lengthy selection from John Murton's 1620 *Humble Supplication*.[116]

This close contact between Milton and Williams at a time when they were both working on the topics of civil and religious freedom makes it likely that they had at least some familiarity with each others' ideas and works. Williams's contacts with Milton continued over the following decade. On a return visit in the early 1650s, Williams met regularly with Milton to instruct him in the

Dutch language. Thus, it seems likely that Milton was familiar with Murton's work, either through reading Williams, or even by reading Murton directly.[117]

Whatever the precise route of its influence, Milton's argument, especially its first and major half, tracks Murton very closely. Milton begins his *Treatise of Civil Power* by observing that "two things there be, which have been ever found working much mischief to the church of God and the advancement of the truth: force on one side restraining, and hire on the other side corrupting, the teachers thereof."[118] To deal with the first of these problems, the use of force in matters of religion, Milton proposes using arguments "drawn from the scripture only," although also paying attention to "protestant maxims."[119]

Of the four arguments that Milton used to advance his thesis, the two first were most fully developed. They were virtually identical to the first three arguments Murton advanced in his *Humble Supplication*: the centrality of scriptural authority; the right of each believer to interpret it; and the incapacity of the civil magistrate to interpret and enforce biblical maxims. In Milton's own words: "first, it cannot be denied, being the main foundation of our Protestant religion, that we of these ages, having no other divine rule or authority from without us ... but the holy scripture, and no other within us but the illumination of the Holy Spirit. ... It follows clearly that *no man or body of men in these times can be the infallible judges or determiners in matters of religion to any other men's consciences but their own.*"[120]

Thus far, he sounds somewhat like Chillingworth when the latter asserted that "the Bible, I say, the Bible only, is the religion of Protestants." But very quickly Milton moves beyond Chillingworth to join Murton and the Baptists in applying this principle to both the church *and* civil rulers. In doing so, Milton asserts that this view is not merely his own opinion, but is the consensus of "sound" Protestant thinkers: "With good cause, therefore, it is the general consent of all sound Protestant writers, that neither traditions, councils, nor canons of any visible church, much less edicts of any magistrate or civil session, but the *scripture only, can be the final judge or rule in matters of religion*, and that only in the conscience of every Christian to himself."[121]

Milton does not identify these "sound" Protestant writers. Rather, he references the historical incident that began this chapter, the protest of the German princes at the Diet of Speyer II, "which protestation made by the first public reformers of our religion against the imperial edicts of Charles the Fifth, imposing church traditions without scripture, gave first beginning to the name of Protestant; and with that name hath ever been received this doctrine, which prefers the scripture before the church, and acknowledges none but the scripture sole interpreter of itself to the conscience."[122]

Milton argues that Protestants, having denied the pope the final authority to interpret scripture, must also, to be consistent, deny this power to civil magistrates. If not, they would create a "civil papacy assuming unaccountable supremacy to themselves, not in civil only, but in ecclesiastical causes."[123] All church discipline, in Milton's view, belongs in the hands of the church. As a voluntary organization, the church's most extreme discipline should be "separation from the rest," excommunication or dis-fellowship, and never "corporal enforcement" or even "forfeiture of money."[124]

As his argument moves on, Milton explores the scriptural basis for his position. He stresses Paul's commendation of the noble Bereans, who "searched the scriptures daily" to determine if what Paul taught was true (Acts 17:11). He also cites Galatians ("let every man prove his own work"); 1 Corinthians ("The Spiritual man judgeth all things, but he himself is judged of no man"); James ("There is one lawgiver, who is able to save and destroy: Who are thou that judgest another"); and Romans ("Who are thou that judgest the servant of another? To his own lord he standeth or falleth").

Milton's second argument, that the civil magistrate has no right to use force in civil matters, is really a direct consequence of his first argument. "To judge" in spiritual matters, "as a civil magistrate he has no right. Christ hath a government of his own, sufficient of itself to all his ends and purposes in governing his church, but much different from that of the civil magistrate; ... principally ... that it governs not by outwards force." Milton argues that Christ's kingdom is essentially a spiritual kingdom, concerned with the development of internal virtues of the "inward man."[125]

This second argument forcefully restated Luther's two kingdoms doctrine. The heavenly kingdom dealt with the "inward man and his actions, which are all spiritual, and to outward force not liable." The "divine excellence of his spiritual kingdom" would be displayed when it was "able, without worldly force, to subdue all the powers and kingdoms of this world, which are upheld by outward force only."[126]

The internal nature of truth was a concept Milton developed more fully in subsequent writings. In his later work, *Christian Doctrine,* he explained more completely his idea of personally appropriated truth. He argued that scripture was "plain and perspicuous" in those things necessary to salvation, but that ultimately biblical interpretation depended on the aid of the Holy Spirit. Here he sounded almost Quaker-like in his view of the efficacy and importance of the "inner light." He pointed out that "even on the authority of Scripture itself, everything in Scripture is ultimately to be referred to the Spirit and the unwritten word." In sum, for

Milton, neither church nor society can be final authority on scripture for the individual.[127]

This understanding of the internal nature of conviction also helped shape Milton's third and fourth arguments in his *Treatise on Civil Power*. The third argument was that force in spiritual matters violated the fundamental spiritual teaching of individual "Christian liberty." Citing Galatians ("Where the Spirit of the Lord is, there is liberty"), Milton argued that civil force in spiritual matters was contrary to the personal freedom the gospel provided for. The fourth argument was really a response to proposed objections to Milton's arguments: that force in religion is needed to promote the glory of God; or that force in religion can promote a person's spiritual good; or that such force can be an effective warning to onlookers. He systematically responded to these, applying the principles he had set out in the three previous sections.

In closing, he asserted, "on these four scriptural reasons, as on a firm square, this truth, the right of Christian and evangelistic liberty will stand immovable." Really, these four reasons rested on the main foundation of the first two arguments, which restated the arguments of the English Baptists, especially Murton and Busher. But Milton's packaging is forceful and even unique. He is the prism, or lens, that takes the thought of early Luther, the story of the German princes of Speyer, the ideas of Castellio (whose writings are part of Milton's library), the arguments of the English Baptists, and the scriptural expressions of Chillingworth and focuses them into a single, whole, forceful package of a dissenting Protestant view of church and state.[128]

Milton's summation offers a Protestant story quite different from the story found in the confessional states of Europe. But his careful formulation gives a strong warrant that his story, as both ideology and history, was authentically Protestant. Milton took common Protestant beliefs about the authority of the Bible, united them with Luther's somewhat overlooked position on the equality of believers, and added the Baptist belief in a voluntary church communion. These elements combined to make a plausible and forceful statement of Protestant heritage, history, and belief.

But not even Milton's advocacy would carry the day in his England. His *Treatise* did not have the impact on Parliament he desired. Given the political exigencies of the time, it fell largely "upon deaf or hostile ears."[129] But now within one book—authored by the best known English writer of the seventeenth century after Shakespeare—lay a compelling synthesis of early Luther, the Protestant princes, Castellio, the Anabaptists, and the English Baptists. From the edges of English religious thought, these ideas had now moved much closer to the center.

To be sure, Milton did not produce a perfect statement on religious liberty or freedom of conscience. While drawing on the thought of Williams, Murton, and others, Milton still did not draw the circle of toleration as broadly as some of them had. He would not, for example, include Catholics or atheists.[130] He excluded Catholics for two reasons: because of their civil threat and because of their idolatrous nature. The first was a semidefensible position by Milton's reasoning. He cited the Catholic's earthly and civil allegiance to the papacy and the pope's orders for good Catholics to disobey and seek the overthrow of disobedient monarchs. Indeed, Catholic plots against the British throne, real and imagined, were sufficiently in the minds of his immediate readers for them to see a civil basis for restricting the role of Catholics in society.

His second reason for forbidding public Catholic worship was that its "idolatry" could not be carried out without giving offense to onlookers in public and to God in private. Earlier in the Commonwealth period, he had made similar arguments regarding the Quakers, Ranters, and other sectaries. Then he had argued that while the "civil sword" should not overthrow error, the regime should "not tolerate the free exercise of Religion, which shall be found absolutely contrary to sound Doctrine or the power of godliness."[131]

While Milton later moved away from this judgment regarding Quakers and other Protestant sects, he never let the "idolatrous" Catholics off the hook. This second reason for denying toleration to Catholics appears to violate Milton's own principles. What became of the right of private judgment in matters of scriptural teaching for Catholics? Milton was so convinced that they were violating scripture, intentionally and knowingly, that for him this principle could not apply to them. As he said, "we have no warrant to regard conscience which is not grounded on scripture."[132] So Milton's toleration appeared, at least in his application, to be limited to differences within a broad but biblically based Protestantism.

Yet despite these qualifications, Milton had given new life to certain Protestant ideas, which others applied more generously than he did. Milton had a pivotal role in shaping subsequent views of the history of the Reformation. "John Milton," wrote the British church historian A. G. Dickens, was a "fundamental re-interpreter of the Reformation who attained a truly prophetic dimension."[133] In commenting on Milton's *Treatise of Civil Power*, Dickens noted that Milton

> attacked the stifling menace of Presbyterian hegemony and identi-
> fied Protestantism with the individual's freedom to seek his own
> way to God. Milton's discussion of the Reformation was the most

original English contribution of his time … [as it] conceived of the Reformation as a continuous, unending process opposed to the mere erection of a new orthodoxy to replace the old. In this, Milton provided the Enlightenment with the germ of one of its great historiographic issues.

It does not challenge Milton's importance—only his originality—to note that the main arguments in his *Civil Treatise* were drawn from more obscure English Baptist writers. He did not so much create a new germ of Protestant thought. Rather, he watered, nurtured, and brought into the light a seedling that had been sprouting in the shadows for more than a century. He showed he knew this history by referring to a common, shared Protestant heritage emanating from Luther and the Second Diet of Speyer.

This reliance on a persistent, if overlooked, part of the Protestant heritage may have been part of a larger plan Milton was pursuing. It is at least possible that part of Milton's motivation in writing *A Treatise of Civil Power* was to make space for the later publication of his *Christian Doctrine*. The latter work contained "unorthodox" arguments regarding the nature of Christ and humanity. Thus, the argument might be made that in light of Milton's lack of orthodoxy in the *Christian Doctrine*, so also his contentions in the *Treatise* should be viewed as not fully Protestant.

But this effort to undermine Milton's position on church-and-state issues is not persuasive. Milton could not safely publish *Christian Doctrine* at a time when "heresy" would be punished by civil authorities. It may indeed have been the case that general concern about publishing *Christian Doctrine* lay behind what he wrote in his church/state treatise. But even if this supposition were true, to accomplish this larger goal, he needed first to argue from shared, common ground. And that is what he strove to do in his *Treatise*. For that purpose, he did not create or inject new teaching or doctrine into that work but drew on shared, historic Protestant principles. If Milton did want to move the conversation into "unorthodox" areas of Christian thought, he needed a foundational position based on historic, orthodox Protestant beliefs. The very "unorthodoxy" of his later published beliefs required that he adhere closely to what were widely perceived to be a genuine Protestant history in his preparatory work.

In that effort, he appears to have been successful, since there was not much immediate reaction to his work on civil power. Had he been trafficking in heresy or extreme arguments, one would have expected a negative reaction. There seems to have been none. Instead, encouraged by appreciative readers, he followed up this first work with another work the same year (1659) that addressed the other church/state problem identified in his original treatise—the problem of "hire on the other side corrupting the teachers thereof." Entitled *Considerations Touching the Likeliest Means to Remove Hirelings Out of the Church*, this second tract challenged the idea that the government should pay ministers or teachers of religion.[134]

Neither pamphlet produced the impact Milton hoped for. He had the misfortune to write them in a year overshadowed by more urgent events. That year, the protectorate collapsed, the army evicted the rump parliament, and a conflict-weary England concluded that experiments with republican forms of authority were too risky. Despite Milton's desperate arguments for a renewed effort at establishing a republican Commonwealth,[135] the royalists carried the day. By the next year, King Charles II ruled from the restored throne.[136]

The Restoration was a potential disaster for Milton. He had been a vociferous and articulate supporter of a republican government. But even more damning was the defense he had authored of the regicides who had killed the new king's father. Upon the ascension of Charles II, Milton was forced to go into immediate hiding. Here his age, blindness, literary reputation, and influential friends allowed him to escape the purge of the leading antiroyalists. Indeed, by the end of 1660 he had not only escaped death but, after only a brief prison stay, had received a royal pardon.[137]

Conclusion

To narrowly escape extended imprisonment or execution is better than the alternatives. But his reputation of antiroyalism did not make Milton's views on church and state popular. Instead, his church/state writings seem to have had little immediate impact in his native land. One can see, though, in the Act of Toleration of 1689 a belated recognition for at least some of the principles he advocated in his church/state works.

But in general, Milton's true influence lay not in England, but in the English colonies on the American seaboard. He set out the five core principles of religious freedom that would come to dominate the American church/state arrangement. These were "liberty of conscience, free exercise of religion, equality of a plurality of faiths before the law, separation of church and state and ... disestablishment of a national religion."[138] During Milton's day, various supporters of toleration advocated two or three of these points, but very few, outside Baptist circles, advocated all five, certainly no one of the stature of Milton.

His thought arrived in America in two forms: one in the extreme popularity of *Paradise Lost*, and the other in the strong influence his *Treatise on Civil Power* exerted on leaders directly responsible for shaping governments in America. Due in part to Milton's depiction of Protestant liberty, the Protestantism that became most influential in America was dissenting, rather than magisterial.

But how did this happen? Milton had synthesized the ideas of dissenting Protestantism in a powerful account of history and biblical teaching. He reminded the Protestant community how their very name came into existence because of the events at Speyer, and what that name should mean for issues of religious freedom. But this theory of Protestantism needed to be popularized and articulated in broader, more inclusive terms.

Milton's theories also needed real-world demonstration, something to show that they would actually work outside the library or the philosopher's parlor. Thanks in part to ideas of John Murton, Roger Williams had established his small colony on the same ideas Milton used to build his theory. But not even Williams was sure his struggling, infighting little patch of the American Northeast was a success. Most of his American colonial neighbors strongly believed that it was not.

How the dissenting stream of church/state principle received the broadening influence of one of the most sophisticated minds of the late seventeenth century, and how it was put into practice by one of the eras most passionate visionaries, is the topic of the next chapter.

2

The Philosopher and the Enthusiast

THE COLLABORATION OF JOHN LOCKE AND
WILLIAM PENN

Prologue: Their Intersecting Lives and Times

The English political theorist and philosopher John Locke, in exile in Holland, could see firsthand that 1685 was not a good year for religious freedom. That year, the streets of Amsterdam teemed with French Huguenot refugees fleeing the wrath of Louis XIV, the Catholic king of France. Louis had revoked what remained of the Edict of Nantes, the charter of toleration protecting the Huguenots, or French Protestants. The Edict's protections had deteriorated in its last decades, but for more than eighty years it had provided some semblance of religious toleration and peace to a country exhausted by several decades of religious wars.[1]

But now, overnight, French Protestant worship was banned, its churches ordered destroyed, its pastors exiled, and its members stripped of property and lands or worse. About two hundred thousand Huguenots fled France, many of them finding a haven in Holland. When Locke ventured out of hiding in Amsterdam, he walked the streets as a fellow refugee from religious and political persecution with this dispossessed group.[2]

To further darken the picture for Locke, King Charles II of England died that year, and his brother James II—an avowed Catholic—ascended the throne. While James proposed a policy of religious toleration, many viewed this as a short-term stratagem of convenience—to be jettisoned once Catholics regained control of English institutions. Many English people, including Locke and his politically powerful patrons, feared that under James the intolerance, persecutions, and even executions that had marked the reign of the last Catholic British monarch, Queen Mary, would be revived.

The revocation of the Edict had significance beyond France and England. The implications for religious freedom echoed through church sanctuaries, government corridors, and university halls across Europe. In hindsight, it may appear that the old world of monarchical privilege and absolutism was inexorably passing into a world of republican consent and individual rights. But these new theories were still very much in their infancy. To Locke and his contemporaries, their survival was precarious and uncertain. The revocation of the Edict and the accession of a Catholic king in England threatened, in many peoples' minds, to undo the tenuous 1648 peace of Westphalia and the relative détente it had brought to previously warring religious groups throughout much of Europe.

If religious toleration was going to continue to depend on royal whim and caprice—or the vagaries of royal succession—religious minorities nowhere were safe. A return to widespread and aggressive intolerance would jeopardize the peace of Westphalia, and perhaps plunge Europe back into destructive and fratricidal wars of religion. These events thus spurred the writing of several treatises on the nature and importance of religious toleration and even freedom in civil society. The most famous was Locke's *Letter Concerning Toleration*, the first draft of which was written that year from his exile in Amsterdam. Locke's *Letter* expressed, for his day, a remarkably robust view of religious freedom. As one scholar puts it, Locke's *Letter* was "the most influential statement of advanced religious toleration in the English-speaking world at this time."[3] But to truly understand the import of Locke's *Letter*— and its connection to the right of private judgment—we must consider the background of its drafting.

During his time in Holland, the question of toleration was not of merely academic interest to Locke. He was in Holland precisely because his views had placed him at odds with the power elites of his native land. While the evidence suggests that he avoided seditious activity himself, he had associated with those not so careful—including his patron, Lord Shaftsbury, who spent a portion of 1681 in the Tower of London. In 1683, Locke found it prudent to absent himself from England to a place beyond the reach of Charles II. His discretion was indeed the wiser part of valor, as several of his associates— including the Whig republican writer Algernon Sidney and the lords Essex and Salisbury—were soon executed in the Tower.[4]

When Charles II died, there was no hope for immediate improvement. Much of the political discontent had been driven by Charles's suspected Catholic sympathies. With his replacement, James II, being an open Catholic, these political concerns were only heightened. Within months of his accession, James had to suppress two major rebellions. Despite being far away geographically and having no real means to aid in the rebellions, Locke was accused of complicity—a probable falsehood fabricated by an unreliable accuser.[5] Nevertheless, a list of eighty-four dangerous Englishmen, alleged to have plotted against King James's life, along with a demand for their arrest and extradition, was sent to Holland—with Locke's name at the bottom.

Since the ruler of Holland, William of Orange, was the son-in-law of King James, there was ample reason to believe that Dutch authorities would cooperate with the English request. Locke was now not just an exile from England; he was a fugitive within Holland, forced to live in secrecy and hiding even in his land of exile.[6] It was at this time that an old but unlikely acquaintance, a former pupil from Locke's days at Oxford, came to his aid: William Penn, the Quaker and founder of Pennsylvania. Penn arranged with King James for Locke to be granted a pardon and permission to return to England.[7]

Locke, not entirely trusting the king, chose to remain in Holland for a time. There he stayed until the "glorious revolution" of William and Mary put a Protestant king on the English throne in 1688. At that point, his return to England was risk free. But the story of Penn's effort to arrange a pardon for Locke raises some intriguing questions. Why would a leader of the Quakers—a radical Protestant sect known for its commitment to egalitarianism—have influence with the last Catholic king of England, from a family known for its commitment to royal absolutism? What sort of relationship existed between Locke, the empiricist philosopher, and Penn, the enthusiastic visionary? And did the contact between these political thinkers have any influence on either's views of church and state?

As to the question of Penn's connection with the royal family, Penn's family had a history of connections with the Stuarts. Penn's father had a career in the navy that had begun as a captain under Charles I. While he had risen to admiral in the parliamentary navy, he had royalist sympathies that made him a key player in the restoration of King Charles II. The restored king knighted Admiral Penn upon his return to the throne.[8] Indeed, money that Charles II owed to Admiral Penn served as the basis for William Penn's request to Charles for land in America, which resulted in the colony of Pennsylvania.[9]

The younger Penn, even after becoming a Quaker, worked his family's contacts in high society to advance the cause of religious tolerance and to protect the interests of the Quakers. This support of religious toleration in England was actually an interest shared between the Stuarts and Penn. Both Charles and James Stuart knew that their sympathies with Catholicism would forever be a barrier to their political well-being in England. Their very survival could be in question if religious minorities—which the Catholics were in England—remained suppressed.

The Catholic-leaning Stuarts, therefore, had an interest in furthering the agitation of the Quakers and other religious dissenters for greater religious toleration, since this directly benefited Catholic interests in England. (For this reason, Quakers at times were accused of being Jesuits or secret Catholics.) For all these reasons, Penn could speak on behalf of religious dissenters to the royals, as shown by his appeal on Locke's behalf.[10]

But the question of Penn's connection with Locke—and its possible impact on either man's view of religious freedom—is at once more intriguing and ultimately more mysterious. In many ways, Locke, the philosopher, and Penn, the Quaker leader, inhabited two distinct worlds. Yet their backgrounds were quite similar. Both were products of relatively well-to-do upbringings and privileged education. Both were Oxford educated, with overlapping periods of residence at the university. Both had distinguished pedigrees. If anything, Penn had the more affluent heritage, being the son of a highly decorated admiral. Locke was the son of a moderately successful country lawyer and legal clerk. But after Oxford, they trod very different paths.

Locke ascended the heights of society, first as a physician to the aristocracy and a friend to the "Whiggish" political leadership, then as a political thinker and highly regarded philosopher. Penn threw his lot in at the opposite end of society, with the marginalized and widely despised Quakers. With his skills and background, he quickly became a spokesman and leader for the religious group. His identification as a Quaker, however, did not cause him to shed his "worldly" contacts. He often drew on these to gain protectors and to minimize the suffering of Friends like himself, or other dissenters, as in the case of Locke.

Locke was a Greek tutor during Penn's time as a student at Oxford. Penn would have quite likely studied with him, though there is no record of their interactions at that time. Moreover, during his exile in Holland, Locke resided with Benjamin Furley, a wealthy merchant and Quaker intellectual. Penn was also a frequent visitor to Furley's home, including at least one visit while Locke was in residence there in the late 1680s.[11] Locke also had in his library a number of Penn's works, including his most famous writings on religious freedom, *The Great Case of Liberty of Conscience*.[12] Drafted nearly two decades before Locke's famous *Letter on Toleration*, Penn's *Great Case* was a truly remarkable work that canvassed the realms of theology, philosophy, history, and law to make a wide-ranging argument for religious freedom.

Locke had access to Penn's work while working on his *Letter*. While his personal library in exile was very small, he prepared the *Letter* for publication while staying at Furley's house—which housed an extensive library of forty-four hundred volumes.[13] We know that this included Penn's important works, since Furley had translated Penn's works on religious freedom for the Dutch market.[14]

Locke's connection with the prominent Quakers Penn and Furley is a curious one. For most of his life, Locke was suspicious of what he termed "religious enthusiasm." To be sure, he did profess belief in God, miracles, and the authority of biblical revelation. He defended these beliefs vigorously in print.[15] But he also stressed the role of reason in assessing religious claims, whether miracles or claims of revelation. This caution did not mean that he only believed what reason could prove, but rather that he thought reason must be used to determine if a miracle or revealed truth really had the authority of God behind it. If it did, then it could be believed, even if it was beyond (although not contrary to) reason.[16]

This view put him at odds with religious enthusiasts, who claimed that God revealed truths directly to them, without external tools such as the Bible. Such claims made it very difficult for reason to be used to verify or test the basis of these revelations.[17] Quakers were among the most notorious "enthusiasts," claiming that they were led by an inner light that was as authoritative as scripture. Intemperate outbursts of prophesying, noisy invasion of church services, parading naked through the streets—these were the kind of "enthusiasms" associated with the Quakers.

Penn and Furley, though, belonged to the Quaker elites. Penn in particular, with his Oxford education, legal training, and theological study under leading dissenting theologians on the continent, wrote more from the position of dissenting Protestantism than as a disciple of George Fox, the founder of the Quakers. But Penn did bring Quaker sensibilities to his views of tolerance, especially when it came to the importance of the inner light in guiding each individual. His emphasis was similar in kind, if not in precise expression, to that of Locke, who viewed the subjective appropriation of spiritual truth as one of the central reasons that it could not be compelled. Penn had a truly significant influence on colonial America—he was directly responsible for the church/state arrangements in three separate colonies—Pennsylvania, New Jersey, and Delaware. But his thought on church and state has not received the attention given to some others, such as Roger Williams or Locke.

The story of Penn and Locke provides key insights into the early roots of American church/state thought. It reveals how strands of dissenting Protestant principles, both directly and through their shaping of moderate Enlightenment views, influenced American commitments to disestablishment. It was a paradigm embraced, as we shall see, as fully by many biblically committed, religious people as by advocates of the Enlightenment. And this common embrace came about, significantly, because many religious believers viewed this new church/state framework as more heavily indebted to Protestant religious ideas than to the Enlightenment.

Penn and Locke were not just passive conduits in the story. They played roles in passing along an even more robust version of religious freedom than some, like Milton, had espoused. They were also important in that they expressed the commitment to the right of private judgment in more fully civil, nonscriptural language. This secularizing of the language, however, was not perceived by many conservative religious observers to diminish or corrode the theological content of the ideas. Indeed, after the Puritans' failed attempts to establish a "godly commonwealth" during the British Civil War, even many religious people were cautious about building governments or basing a political philosophy entirely on scriptural foundations. While such people still looked to scripture, they also supported the same ideas in terms of natural law or natural theology and philosophy. They did not, however, consider the latter methods to be contrary to scriptural ideas, but rather an expression of them in the world of reason.

Since Penn was the first to write out his views on religious freedom, we begin with a look at Penn's background and church/state thought, especially in his preeminent work on religious liberty, *The Great Case of Liberty of Conscience* of 1670. We will see that Penn's arguments about human judgment prefigured those found in Locke's more famous *Letter on Toleration*. We will then look closely at Locke, his formative years, his contact with dissenting Protestant thought, and his developing ideas on human understanding, which provide the context for understanding his famous *Letter*. We will also look at the impact both these thinkers had in North America.

William Penn, the Educated Enthusiast

For many years in Philadelphia, it was unlawful to erect a building any higher than the statue of William Penn that stood atop Town Hall. This was an ironic role for a man who in life, as a practicing Quaker, believed that no human being deserved even the deference signified by removing one's hat. But Penn—born into a family of relative wealth, privilege, and power—was no ordinary Quaker.[18]

Most Americans know Penn as the founder of Pennsylvania. But many do not know that the colony was not named for William, but for his father, a well-connected admiral in the British navy. Born in 1644 in London, William the younger came from the union of a Presbyterian father and a Dutch Calvinist mother. Penn had dissent in his blood; the only question was which way that dissent would run. It eventually manifested itself in ways that surprised everyone around him.

Penn's well-to-do background allowed him a privileged education. He attended Christ Church at Oxford in 1660, the same year Locke served there as Greek lecturer and tutor.[19] Penn also had contact with John Owen, the well-known dissenting Puritan theologian who had developed some ideas concerning toleration and religious freedom. But about a year later, nonconformists, including Owen, were dismissed from the college. The circumstances of Penn's leaving Oxford are not fully known. It seems, however, that it may have been connected with his sympathies for the nonconformists, and that he left when they did.

Penn then went to Europe, such travels often part of finishing training for young English gentlemen. While in France, Penn's serious religious nature again was revealed by his decision to attend the Protestant Academy of Saumur. There he studied under Moise Amyraut, a leading dissenting Calvinist theologian who played a key role in promoting religious toleration in France. Amyraut, a lawyer turned theologian, was a highly influential Huguenot who modified Calvinist thought to argue for an unlimited atonement, that is, that Christ died for all, not just the elect. He still believed, though, in a particular election, that is, that ultimately God chose to save a certain group.[20]

While controversial in his day, Amyraut avoided excommunication or loss of his post. His theology, moreover, led him into broader views of religious tolerance.[21] In the 1650s, before Penn's arrival, he argued in his book *Christian Morality* that force could not be used to convince people of religious truth, but only persuasion and example.[22] Penn's later theological arguments on behalf of religious freedom bear the imprint of his time with Amyraut. Thus, Penn's Quakerism, at least in its church/state views, comes in good part from a dissenting Protestant mold.

After Penn returned to England, his father desired him to assist with the family business in Ireland. In preparation for that role, Penn studied law in London for a year, which put the finishing polish on his advocacy skills. After this, he went to Ireland to manage his father's estates, and there he came into contact with the Quakers. Impressed with their piety and apparently primitive Christianity, he soon joined the sect.

In choosing to become a Quaker, Penn appeared to give up a life of privilege and power—Quakers were ineligible to hold government office. The irony is that had he not become a Quaker, Penn's life story would likely be as unfamiliar today as the naval career of his father. Penn quickly assumed the role of advocate and champion for the oppressed Quakers. Due to his background and education, he had connections at the royal palace, at the courts, and in the boards of commerce. He used these connections to elevate the plight of the disenfranchised, often persecuted Quakers to new heights of visibility.

Penn and *The Great Case of Liberty of Conscience*

At times, Penn's advocacy work became, at least in his father's opinion, alarmingly hands on. Penn spent time in prison for personally violating restrictions prohibiting dissenting religious gatherings and preaching. In 1670, during one of these times in prison, Penn wrote *The Great Case of Liberty of Conscience*.[23] This work gave a full expression of his philosophy and theology of religious freedom. Its target was the newly passed Conventicle Act, which forbade nonconforming sects from gathering for worship and preaching. Penn used the opportunity to unleash the full range of his historical, theological, and legal training on the question of the proper roles of church and state. In it he combined dissenting Protestant thought, learned from both Owen and Amyraut, with the Quaker view of the centrality of personal experience in obtaining spiritual knowledge.

Though Penn wrote as a Quaker, the book did not defend unique Quaker doctrines or views. The title of the book, *The Great Case*, shows that it was a brief meant to persuade non-Quakers of the importance of liberty of conscience. As a good legal advocate, Penn knew that the strongest arguments are those that draw on assumptions, premises, and presuppositions shared with one's audience. This is what he did, showing that freedom of conscience flows from central Protestant theological commitments, as well as from views of natural philosophy and law also shared by the great Protestant thinkers. Thus, even his Quaker emphases on the importance of internal knowledge and spiritual light come with reference to scriptural texts, rather than to Quaker authors such as George Fox.

Penn divides his arguments in favor of religious liberty into the following basic categories: the nature and rights of God; the nature of Christianity; the teachings of the Bible; arguments from nature and reason; the nature of good government; and the witness of history. We will not explore the entire work, but concentrate on the portions that shed light on his affinities or differences with Locke, as well as on Penn's use of the idea of the right of private judgment.

Nature and Rights of God

Penn's first argument was a reversal of the usual modern claim for human rights. Rather than starting with his, or the Quaker's, inalienable right to worship, he started with God's right to man's worship. Rather than defending his own prerogatives, he chose to first defend God's. This, at least as a rhetorical matter, upped the ante for his opponents considerably. As Penn puts the argument in his heading: "Imposition, Restraint, and Persecution for Conscience-Sake, highly Invade the Divine Prerogative, and Divest the Almighty of a Right, due to none beside Himself."[24]

He gives five reasons for this right owed to God: (1) God alone is creator, (2) God alone is infallible, (3) God alone is king of conscience, (4) God works by grace alone, and (5) God alone is judge. The sum of these arguments is that only God has the knowledge, authority, and power to judge and rule in his spiritual kingdom. Any attempt on the part of man, argued Penn, to direct the worship or conscience of others invades these rights and prerogatives of God. It is a description of the right of private judgment from God's perspective. The believer has the right to private judgment because God alone has the right to judge a man and has not delegated that right to another.[25]

These arguments are theological, but not necessarily biblical. Penn scarcely used any Bible texts in setting these arguments forward. Rather, he relied on the reasoning of natural theology, from premises that persons of all faiths would view as universal and valid: there is a creator; he alone is omnipotent and all knowing; and he alone deserves worship, of which he alone will be the judge. Penn's list of basic truths about God are very nearly the same that Locke later accepts as being in the class of categorical "knowledge" rather than that of probabilistic "belief." Penn also prefigures Locke's appeal to God's property ownership rights in persons as creating duties in persons to worship God and to respect the worship choices of others.[26]

The Bible on Spiritual Knowledge, Authority, and Force

Penn's examination of the biblical teaching on worship and force also foreshadow Locke's wrestling with the problems of knowledge versus belief. Penn's choice of scriptures can be divided into three main categories: texts detailing limits on human knowledge, texts detailing limits on human spiritual authority, and texts describing appropriate Christian conduct or praxis in relation to power.[27]

Penn began with a rather obscure verse from the book of Job: "The Inspiration of the Almighty gives Understanding" (Job 32:8). Penn cited this text at least twice in his work, and it provided support to his basic argument regarding human understanding and epistemology. In Penn's words: "If no Man can believe before he understands, and no Man can understand before he is inspir'd of God," then it is unreasonable and inhuman to punish someone for not believing something.[28]

Penn then cited several other verses that emphasize the limits of human knowledge and the need to rely on God for true spiritual knowledge. "Woe unto them that take Counsel, but not of me" (Is 30:1). "Let the Wheat and the Tares grow together, until the end of the world," because, the implication is, the Christian cannot always tell one from the other (Mt 13:27). It is the "Spirit of Truth" that shall "lead you into all Truth" (Jn 16:8, 13).

The last group of texts represented a conclusion about how Christians should act—with meekness and the use of persuasion, given the first two premises. The three groups of texts work very like a syllogism. If only one with full spiritual knowledge has authority to judge, and humans lack full spiritual knowledge for others, then they cannot judge and coerce in spiritual matters. Thus, Jesus said that "the Princes of the Gentiles, exercise dominion over them ... but it shall not be so among you" (Mt 20:25). Jesus indicated there were different realms, Caesar's and God's, and that God's did not involve force (Lk 20:25; Lk 9:54–56).

It is, on the whole, a scripturally driven argument. But it uses scriptures that point out the role and importance of reason and understanding. For Penn, it was not a question of either reason or revelation, it was that revelation underscored the importance and role of reason in achieving meaningful belief. Again, he sets this out scripturally rather than exploring it philosophically, as Locke later did, but the argument is remarkably similar to Locke's in substance, as we shall see.

Nature and Reason

Penn then moved to the field of natural philosophy, invoking specifically the "Privilege of Nature and the Principle of Reason."[29] The former, he said, consists of arguments from universal human experiences, and the latter consists of truths from the world of logic. These arguments explicitly appeal to a system of natural rights and natural law or order.

He first referenced the universal sense of the equality of humanity, which he saw as a right existing in the order of nature. This was not an entirely obvious argument in Penn's time, since slavery still flourished in the British Empire. Perhaps that is why Penn dropped in the scriptural passage from Acts to lend support: "God has made of one blood all nations" (Ac 17:26). To legislate in spiritual matters is to set one's self over others and to violate this principle of equality of persons; it is to "invade their Right of Liberty, and so pervert the whole Order of Nature."[30] The language of rights, liberty, and nature used here in the service of religious liberty reminds one of Locke's similar use of such language twenty years later in his writings on government and toleration.

Penn then turned to the universal sense of God in humanity, which was perhaps a stronger argument in his day than in ours. If all can sense God, what business do some have to proscribe how others should relate to him? Such efforts, in effect, deny this universal God sense. Third, he asserted that persecution brings the "State of Nature to the State of War," destroying all natural affection. His conception here is obviously influenced by Thomas Hobbes, and he even acknowledges this by asserting that the state of war is "the great Leviathan of the Times." His use of Hobbes is obvious, yet limited, since he parts ways with Hobbes on the most important questions of personal liberty and the role of the state in religion. Still, it is an obvious engagement with the world of natural rights and reason, while asserting these faculties in a peculiarly Protestant manner.[31]

Penn then moves to "the noble Principle of Reason." He sets out eight logical fallacies of using force in religious matters. Most of them involve the idea that the use of force for religious purposes defeats the very purposes of religion and is thus incoherent and illogical. For instance, if religious belief is based on choice, and choice on understanding, and if understanding cannot be forced, how can belief be forced? Or if truth is based on reason, yet people choose to believe because of force, is not reason and real belief destroyed?

Next, Penn considers the nature, execution, and end of good government.[32] He proposes that the nature of good government is justice, and that religious force violates the principles of equality, fairness, and proportionality inherent in a just state. He then argues that the execution of government should be guided by prudence, by which he appears to mean regard for efficiency and practicality. He argues that religious laws interfere with the practical functioning of a state because they limit trade and commerce; they provoke disorder by creating religious dissenters; they give a bad example to foreign nations, that will enforce their own, perhaps non-Christian religious laws; and they reward nonbelief, since those who do not worship cannot run afoul of laws regulating worship.[33]

In this section, Penn shows that the biblical truths he has earlier outlined are also vindicated by logic. Once again, this broadens the base of his argument beyond scriptural authority, anticipating Locke's reliance on natural reasoning and philosophy. Because of Penn's biblical sections, however, it is more clearly seen that his natural philosophy is not at odds with his scriptural doctrine. Rather, they are alternate but complementary roads to the same end.

The theistic epistemology often identified with Locke,[34] which sees the worlds of reason and revelation as entirely complementary, was already developed in Penn two decades prior to Locke's major works on the topic. This is not to say that Locke got it from Penn, but that such a view was common currency in the stream of dissenting thought from which Penn, Locke, and eventually the American divines drew.

Like Milton, Murton, and the other dissenting Protestants, Penn emphasized the role of the individual believer in obtaining truth, and also God's role as being sole arbiter of conscience. Being a Quaker, Penn gave even greater attention to the internal experience of truth: the role of the Holy Spirit—the inner light—in bringing conviction. This move does not make truth relative, but it does make personal and subjective the experience and acceptance of truth.

Penn made explicit here what Locke later explained in his *Essay on Human Understanding*—the fact of the individual, personal human appropriation of spiritual truths. Penn did it from an explicitly biblical base. Locke came to a similar view of the human experience in relation to spiritual truth, but expressed it in philosophical terms.

Penn's American Influence

Better known than his theories are William Penn's practical contributions to American views of religious freedom in his founding of Pennsylvania. But in the modern era these efforts have generally been overshadowed by the attention paid to a better known advocate of religious freedom, Roger Williams. Some might consider this work notable in its omission, at least as a central figure, of Roger Williams. He has become something of an icon in relation to stereotypical understandings of the founding of religious freedom in this country. But that status is a relatively modern phenomenon.[35]

During his day, and for more than a century afterward, Williams was regarded by many in the New England church/state establishment as a sincere but misguided religious zealot, with poor religious and political judgment and even worse interpersonal skills. Others held more negative views of him, including that he was a schismatic heretic, as well as an accessory to libertines and infidels.[36] The reputed liberality of Rhode Island attracted some "notorious Delinkquents [looking to] avoid the stroake of Justice," and Williams himself acknowledged that indeed many of its inhabitants had become "wanton and too active."[37]

Williams worked hard to correct the mistaken impression that the cost of religious liberty was civil disorder and anarchy. His famous "ship of state" analogy—where the captain and crew could require civil peace, order, and duty of the passengers, while leaving their religious beliefs and practices untouched—became the model into which Rhode Island eventually grew.[38] But outside Rhode Island, his influence in America during his lifetime was minimal. When he was mentioned, it was generally as a negative example of the perils of hyperindividualism and rejection of duly constituted authority.[39]

The searchable database of all materials printed in America in the seventeenth century shows two mentions of his name during that century, one the article he published in dispute with the Quakers, the other a negative account by a Massachusetts chronicler in 1669 of his "lamentable apostasy."[40] Even into the mid-eighteenth century, references were very few and generally negative.

In a typical treatment, a 1749 chronicle of the British colonies recorded that the initial settlers of Rhode Island dissented from the received "Way of religious Worship" and were "by Degrees refined so much that all their Religion was almost vanished, afterwards it became a Receptacle of any People without Regard to Religion or social Worship; and their Modes of Civil Government were very variable and defective."[41]

It was not until the 1770s that Isaac Backus and other Baptists began to rehabilitate Williams's image as an early American supporter of religious freedom and civil liberties.[42] Perry Miller overstated it when he wrote that Williams "exerted little or no direct influence on the theorists of the Revolution and the Constitution."[43] This is to overlook the important influence Williams and his ideas had on men like John Milton, Henry Vane, and John Locke in the seventeenth century, and on Baptists like Isaac Backus and John Leland in the eighteenth. Still, his influence came from the margins, and in his own day he was scarcely the icon of religious freedom that he has become today.

But over time, Williams's reputation for founding the first state entirely separate from any church came to be increasingly recognized and celebrated. By the twentieth century, Williams had taken on an iconic status in relation to religious liberty that compared to that of Madison and Jefferson.[44] As the U.S. Supreme Court began grappling in earnest with issues of church and state in the 1940s and 1950s, they cited Roger Williams and his views with approval in at least ten cases dealing with church and state.[45]

William Penn, by contrast, has been virtually ignored by the Supreme Court on matters of church and state. The Court has cited Penn in approximately forty-two cases.[46] All but one, however, have to do with freedom of speech, criminal law and jury issues, and property disputes. In only a single case does the Court cite Penn's church/state arrangements in Pennsylvania as providing an example for understanding America's constitutional arrangement.

That case, ironically, is *Church of the Holy Trinity v. U.S.* (1892), in which the Court declared America to be a "Christian nation."[47] Penn was cited for including a mention of God in his 1701 Charter of Privileges, which secured the freedom of conscience in Pennsylvania.[48] The Court either overlooked or was unaware of the irony of citing arguably the most practically influential church/state separationist in American history for the proposition that America really is a Christian nation.

Both James Madison and the Virginia Baptists, in casting about for a historical example to support their arguments for complete religious disestablishment in Virginia, cited Pennsylvania—and not Rhode Island—as the important precedent.[49] Pennsylvania, from its earliest inception, enjoyed a broad and robust religious liberty. But just as important for the pragmatic American colonialists, it achieved a level of economic and social success unequaled in the surrounding colonies.

Very early on, Philadelphia surpassed Boston, and then New York, in size and economic importance.[50] By the 1720s, Philadelphia was considered the "Athens of North America" and the most "cosmopolitan city in the colonies."[51] This success was linked in the minds of onlookers to the freedoms, especially the religious liberty, its inhabitants enjoyed. This energetic freedom was witnessed by the delegates to the First and Second Continental Congresses, as well as the Federal Constitutional Convention, all held in Philadelphia. Pennsylvania, rather than Rhode Island, "was the primary model for the success of freedom of religion in the other states."[52]

Unlike the case of nearly all the other colonies, religious freedom was not a matter of development in Pennsylvania, but was part of its initial birthright. Pennsylvania's earliest laws contained a "Freedom of Conscience" provision that gave full and equal rights of citizens to all those who believed in "one almighty God" and forbade anyone from being taxed for religious purposes.[53] Pennsylvania did require all government officeholders to "believe in Jesus Christ." Thus, atheists were technically discriminated against in citizenship and non-Christians in holding public office. Practically speaking, though, the number of atheists and non-Christians was so small in early Pennsylvania as to be negligible. Furthermore, these religious exclusions were required by the British government to be in the colony's laws, and there is evidence that they were not actually enforced.[54] It was as robust a separation as could practically be achieved at that time and place.

Still, Penn's commitment to the separation of church and state should not be confused with the modern liberal goal of separating morality from the state. In his *Great Case* and in later writings to Parliament, Penn supported the magistrate's role in suppressing vice and moral behavior that threatened the civil community. The natural conscience, while needing enlightening on spiritual truths by God's spirit, could understand and be held accountable to fundamental moral dictates of nature. "There can be no pretense of conscience to be drunk, to whore, to be voluptuous, to game … these are sins against nature and against government, as well as against the written word of God. They lay the ax to the root of human society."[55]

These restrictions on morality, though, were viewed as part of the teachings of general revelation or the natural law, to which all humans, irrespective of their faith commitments, had access to. But on those beliefs about worship and ritual obtained by faith, whether through a holy book or the "inner light," Pennsylvanians had essentially complete freedom. Pennsylvania had this broad grant of religious freedom in the initial instance for basically one reason: William Penn's commitment to it. It was William Penn's personal sentiments that provided the preface to the initial 1682 "Freedom of Conscience" statute, which begins: "Almighty God, being only Lord of conscience, father of lights and spirits, and the author as well as the object of all divine knowledge, faith and worship, who can only enlighten the mind and persuade and convince the understandings of people. In due reverence to his sovereignty over the souls of mankind."[56]

Penn's practical influence on the colonial acceptance of a robust church/state separation through the success of the Pennsylvania model is hard to overstate. But Penn's theoretical contributions to the ideology of disestablishment were not as widely influential. Perhaps because of the liberal use of scripture among his philosophical and legal arguments, or because of his position within a marginalized sect, Penn's writings on toleration have not been widely used or appreciated by Americans, either of his day and our own. It took a thinker with a more philosophical mode of expression, writing from within a more mainstream religious perspective, to influence the popular mind. John Locke was that man, and to his story we now turn.

Locke, Freedom, and Knowledge: A Developing View

Admittedly, Penn and Locke make an unusual pair. Locke trembled with concern at the religious "enthusiast." Though he did not deny that God could impress truth directly on a person, he believed such incidents were rare. Even if such revelations occurred, Locke insisted that they should be judged by the Bible. Quakers would have reversed this order, choosing to judge scripture by experience.

But Locke's distinction between knowledge and belief, with the personal weighing of probabilities required by the latter, and the use of judgment in that weighing, opened up a similar, private, protected space in the life of the individual similar to that created by Penn's belief in the role of the Holy Spirit in leading individuals into truth. This is not to argue that Locke's epistemology was based on or even influenced by Penn (though some influence is possible, as we shall see) but to point out that Locke's epistemology was largely consistent with that held by certain dissenting Protestants.

Scholars have acknowledged that Locke's ideas on religious liberty were not largely original, and that they underwent substantive change from his earlier to later writings. As one recently summarized it, in matters of toleration "Locke was a debtor; and his position on the question of toleration underwent development (some would say, suffered a sea-change) during his writing life."[57] Locke's views on toleration have received much attention in recent years, but there is still need for "analysis of the changing ways in which he saw the issues of toleration over time, and the range of experiences which led him to modify his judgments about it so substantively."[58]

But what influences, and what change? Some influences are apparent: a learned, but religiously devout Puritan upbringing (his father was a country lawyer who served as a captain in the parliamentary army during the civil war); an education surrounded at Oxford by Independents such as Thomas Cole and John Owen, who would have extended freedom of worship to all "non-licentious trinitarians."[59] In his early writings, Locke would not go as far as Cole and Owen, but instead gave the magistrate power over "things indifferent" in matters of religion.[60] Within a few years, however, Locke expressed a view of religious freedom that was more expansive than what these men proposed.

Early Views on Church and State

Locke's early views, while progressive for the day, were tempered with some conservatism regarding the magistrate and religion. This is most clearly seen in his writings of the early 1660s, including the *Two Tracts of Government* (not to be confused with the much more widely known *Two Treatises of Government* written decades later), and his *Reflections upon the Roman Commonwealth*.

In the latter work, he lauded the Roman state's "enlightened" policy regarding religion, which he viewed as a tolerant Erastianism (the view that the state should be in charge of the church). The state supported and promoted merely two articles of belief: that gods existed, and that, most important, they were to be worshiped by people being "innocent, good, and just."[61] But apart from the simplicity of its creed, Locke believed that the key to the Roman state's benevolent toleration of religion was its semi-Erastian nature—that the national church was not overseen by church leaders or priests, but by the people and the senate. "The government of religion being in the hands of the state was a necessary cause of liberty of conscience."[62] Locke's early approval of a semi-Erastian church/state arrangement bore some resemblances to Hobbes's view, though Hobbes would have placed the oversight in the hands of the sovereign rather than the people. But Locke's position here stands in contrast to his later views on the magistrate's complete lack of jurisdiction over matters of religion.

These conservative sentiments were not just sentimental musings on ancient Rome. Locke expressed similar views in his *Two Tracts of Government*, published between 1660 and 1662. There he addressed the question "whether the civil magistrate may lawfully impose and determine the use of indifferent things in reference to religious worship?"[63] Locke answered this question with a resounding yes. "The supreme magistrate of every nation," he wrote, "what way soever created, must necessarily have an absolute and arbitrary power over all the indifferent actions of his people." His second tract echoed the same conclusion, opening with this question and answer: "Whether the civil magistrate may incorporate indifferent things into the ceremonies of divine worship and impose them on the people: Confirmed."[64]

In the *Two Tracts*, Locke took a position directly opposing what he published in his later works. In his earlier view, rather than the people delegating to the state certain limited and express rights while retaining the rest, he posited that the people retain only those rights God has expressly given to them. But where there is no duty expressed by God, and the matter is indifferent, then the rights to choose to act even in matters of worship are all given over to the state. As he put it:

> But the liberty God had naturally left us over our exterior, indifferent actions must and ought in all societies be resigned freely into the hands of the magistrate, and it is impossible there should be any supreme legislative power which hath not the full and unlimited disposure of all indifferent things, since if supreme it cannot be bounded by any superior authority of man and in things of indifferency God hath left us to ourselves.[65]

Notably absent from the *Two Tracts*, given Locke's later views, is any real anguish or argument over the line between those things that are required and those that are indifferent. His discussion assumes that the distinction between what is clear and what is indifferent is, well, clear. Problems of biblical interpretation and the inherently probabilistic nature of that belief do not concern him much. Indeed, he uses the problem of certainty as a reason that the legislator should be allowed to make the decision in those areas where we are uncertain of our own liberty or freedom.[66] It was only after 1670, when he began more fully contemplating the limits of human understanding—laying the groundwork for his famed *Essay*—that the concepts of uncertainty and probability begin more obviously to influence his view on tolerance.

Still, despite his early more conservative views, there were some indications of his future liberality on conscience. Locke was influenced, it is generally agreed, by Hobbes in some areas, for example on the existence of a state of nature and the social contract.[67] But Locke rejected, even at this early stage, Hobbes's extreme Erastianism, which would have disallowed any religion except that fully approved by the ruler. Further, in the short essay "Infallibility," written in 1661, Locke showed a grasp of the dissenting Protestant conviction concerning the freedom of the individual to interpret the Bible.

In that work, he asked: "Question: Whether it is necessary to grant that there be an Infallible Interpreter of Holy Scripture in the Church? Answer: Denied."[68] He started with the point that the authority to interpret laws was nearly equal to that of making them, since the interpreter could twist them to fit the meaning he desired. Applying this view to the Bible, Locke argued that both scripture and history showed that there was no earthly infallible interpreter of the scriptures. He acknowledged that there were mysteries in the Bible, which no man could interpret for another. Rather, each person must rely on the Holy Spirit for understanding. The Trinity was one such example.[69]

Those things, however, that relate directly to salvation are entirely perspicuous, for example duties to charity, justice, and benevolence. These require no interpreter. Finally, there are those things indifferent in the Bible, which require an interpreter, such as "what hair is too long," and it is here that the church can play a role in interpretation. But it is a "directive, not definitive," role, and the church members are safe in following even if the leaders err in these matters of indifference.

Locke continued to display his conservative side in dealing with religiously indifferent matters. But he ended the essay on a note that foreshadowed the direction his thinking would take when he explored the realm of human understanding. He pondered the difficulty of knowing where the role of individual understanding versus the role of church teaching begins and ends, as well as what role "reason" plays versus that of the "Holy Spirit" in interpretation. The more the Spirit is needed, the more will depend on individual illumination, and the less on reasoned community discourse or coercion. Yet as he acknowledged the dilemma, he also pointed toward a solution in his final sentence: "the interpretation of the Holy Bible derives much from learning, much from reason, and, lastly, much from the Holy Spirit illuminating the minds of men, but the most certain interpreter of Scripture is Scripture itself, and it alone is infallible."[70]

Locke here revealed a belief in the role of spiritual illumination in understanding some scripture. But other spiritual truths were more amenable to reason and discourse. These methods resulted in more objective kinds of religious knowledge that could be safely asserted by the church for the community. But his later studies in human understanding lessened this distinction and moved most religious beliefs into the realm of personal illumination and understanding. This shift brought him closer to the Protestant dissenters who proclaimed the central role of the Holy Spirit in applying spiritual truth from the Word. For them, and eventually for Locke, the magistrate could not rule even on matters indifferent. But it took Locke some time and thought to reach this position, and it is instructive to look at the influences on him during this journey.

Contacts with Protestant Dissenters

Locke's developing thought on knowledge and freedom developed during a time when he had contact with certain Protestant dissenters and their writings. Part of this influence came in the form of works by Sir Henry Vane, the younger,[71] and Vane's advisor and associate Henry Stubbe.[72] Locke knew Stubbe at Oxford, where Stubbe was both a student and librarian. Through Stubbe Locke became aware of Vane's writings and eventually became acquainted with the Vane family.[73] It was Henry Vane's brother Walter for whom Locke acted as secretary on a diplomatic mission to Cleves in the Rhineland in 1667. Locke and Stubbe corresponded on issues of religious toleration and discussed the views of Stubbe's mentor, Henry Vane.[74] Locke's contacts with Stubbe and Vane are significant for showing his exposure to the stream of dissenting church/state views kept alive in the Baptist tradition. Thus, these men deserve some close consideration.

Vane, son of a prominent member of the English gentry, had an eclectic and high-profile political career in both the American colonies and British

politics. As a teenager, the aristocratically bred and educated Vane underwent a profound spiritual crisis. The resulting religious experience led him to
diverge from his expected pathway of court office and preferment in England
and to sail away to the Puritan outpost in New England. Only twenty-three
years old when he arrived, he had such prestige and apparent administrative
ability that within eight months he was made governor of Massachusetts—
the top post in the colony.

An auspicious start to his administration was interrupted when he
chose sides in the contentious antinomian controversy involving Anne
Hutchinson and John Wheelwright. He advocated on behalf of Hutchinson
against the cautious, paternal, and at times authoritarian John Winthrop
and the established spiritual hierarchy. Unsurprisingly, the older, more
entrenched interests eventually won out. Vane left the colony, embarrassed,
frustrated, and unwilling to continue in a place that he believed violated
the consciences of believers. During his stay in New England, he developed connections with dissenting Protestant leaders, most notably Roger
Williams. He continued to maintain these relationships after he returned
to England.[75]

On his return to England, Vane entered the life of court and politics he
had previously abandoned. He obtained a government administrative post
and eventually becoming an influential member of Parliament.[76] But he held
to his earlier religious principles, and was willing to aid the cause of Protestant
nonconformists whenever possible. When Roger Williams came to obtain
a charter for Rhode Island in 1644, Vane helped him procure it. He aided
Williams again on his return to England in the 1650s.[77] In addition, Vane also
supported Williams's opposition to a national church and made speeches in
Parliament against state regulation of religious ideas. Williams made positive
references to Vane and one of Vane's parliamentary speeches in his 1644 work
on church and state: *The Bloudy Tenet of Religious Persecution*—the same
work that quoted the English Baptist John Murton.

In 1651, Vane published his first major work, a lengthy tract on liberty of
conscience. It was drafted in response to restrictions on freedom of speech,
worship, and publishing proposed by the Independent divines who had the
ear of Oliver Cromwell. Vane's work, entitled *Zeal Examined, or, A Discourse
for Liberty of Conscience*, is of interest to us for two reasons. First, it shows
familiarity with and uses many of the biblical arguments that the Baptists
had been making, including a focus on the right of private judgment. This is
not overly surprising, given Vane's acquaintance with Roger Williams and his
works, which frequently cited Baptist authors. Second, it handles questions

of religious knowledge and belief with sophistication, foreshadowing at least some of the approaches Locke later would take to these questions.

As to the first point, Vane joins the Baptists in pointing out the magistrate's inability to read the secrets of the heart or to determine what is spiritual truth. His first major argument concerns the nonexistence of any acknowledged "judge of Truth and Heresie." This is what Rome has a claim to, writes Vane. "Protestants," he asserts, "are justly broke off from them, because we did find that they did not teach right, and so did declare that there was no man, nor number of men whatsoever infallible in their determinations, and *that therefore Christians ought not to be lead by an implicit faith but to search the Scriptures, and be instructed from thence.*" Those Protestants who wish to impose their views "clearly declare, that they are but papists in principle, though they call themselves Protestant."[78]

He continues in this manner for many pages, using arguments found in the writings of the Baptists Helwys, Murton, and Smyth. He stresses the inability of a civil magistrate to be a "competent judge" in spiritual matters, and that to hold otherwise is to abandon a core difference with the "papists."[79] He does not mention the Baptists by name, probably for two reasons: first, the Baptists were not shy about writing for themselves, and at this time they had submitted their own pamphlets to Parliament. Second, Baptists were minority outsiders, often scorned, so citing them as authority might well have had a negative affect—the scriptural arguments stood very well on their own.

Then there are the parallels with Locke's later works. First, Vane agrees with Locke that knowledge of God's existence, and that he ought to be worshiped, is discoverable by the light of nature and reason.[80] He also says, as does Locke, that the way to worship God is found in the teachings of biblical revelation. In the absence of any infallible earthly judge, each individual must find these teachings. Vane also goes on to argue that the very nature of religious belief requires this kind of freedom. He argues that one must personally understand and appropriate spiritual truth, and that this is an essential part of true religious faith and belief.

To show this connection, Vane contrasts natural or civil knowledge with spiritual knowledge. He compares advice from a physician or lawyer with that from a minister. "A man may waive his own judgment in recovering his health or securing his estate," and rely on that of his "physicians or lawyers." But he "may not therefore waive his own light in matters of religion." Why? Because "a man is profited in his health or estate by the effect of another's skill … but in spiritual matters he is no further profited by the doctrine of another, than *he receives of it in the light of his own conscience*, and is made one with it by *inwards experience*."[81]

While using somewhat different language, this statement parallels Locke's later view that meaningful religious beliefs require understanding and assent. This view of the personal nature of spiritual truth lay at the foundation of both men's conviction about the basis of liberty of conscience. The process of appropriation was somewhat different for the two men. When Vane said "the light within us must be our Guide, to lead us into all that understanding of the Scripture, or other Truths, which are fitting for us to know," he was referring to the Holy Spirit.[82] Locke would have agreed with the need for internal assent, and also accepted a role for the Holy Spirit. But he would have identified the "light" more strongly with reason. The effect on the question of toleration, however, was the same—people had the right and duty to follow that internal light, whether the Spirit or reason or both, to discover and experience spiritual truths.

A final point of similarity with Locke is Vane's treatment of Catholics. He, like Locke, would not punish simple idolaters or heretics. But he does not extend toleration to "papists," because "they maintain the Jurisdiction of a foreign power over their consciences." This "foreign power" requires them, Vane argues, to break faith with heretics (i.e., to lie to Protestants) and to kill them if and when the Catholics gain the upper hand. Toleration does not extend to those who would destroy the very system of toleration. These are basically the reasons that Locke also gives for not tolerating Catholics.

Did Locke read Vane's work? While we have no record of it, we do know for certain that he was exposed to the substance of Vane's arguments. Locke was at Oxford when Vane wrote the work, and even then was interested in these matters, and he may well have read it at that time. A few years later Henry Stubbe, Locke's Oxford friend and colleague, wrote his own book on religious freedom. Stubbe's work mentioned Vane by name and discussed the substance of his views. We do know that Locke read Stubbe's work, as he wrote to Stubbe about it.

Entitled the *Essay in Defense of the Good Old Cause*, it carried the subtitle "A Vindication of the Honorable Sir Henry Vane."[83] In it, Stubbe repeated many of Vane's earlier arguments: that the magistracy had no power "to judge in spiritual matters";[84] that men could not rely on the "understanding and ability of others for spiritual truth";[85] that there is "no infallible judge to expound the scriptures," but that "the spirit of God in each saint is the sole Authentique Expositor of Scripture unto him that hath it"; and that "every one should follow his own judgment in matters of religion."[86] In short, it contained all of Vane's, and the Baptists', central biblical arguments about liberty of conscience, the limits on the civil magistrate, and the right of private judgment.

Locke's response to Stubbe's work was "broadly complimentary." He agreed that it would be "excellent for men of different persuasions" to "unite under the same government … and march to the same end of peace and mutual society though they take different ways to heaven."[87] Locke did warn Stubbe that Catholics should not be tolerated, because of their dispensing with oaths and willingness to break faith with "heretics."

It has been suggested, in light of Locke's continued conservatism on toleration for a few years, that his positive response to Stubbe was the expression of the collegial and deferential spirit of one college fellow to "a slightly more senior fellow" and not an endorsement of broad toleration itself.[88] The important point, though, is that Locke was early exposed, in a detailed and comprehensive manner, to the main biblical and religious arguments on toleration advanced by Vane, the Baptists, and other dissenting Protestants.

It would seem to be more than an accident, then, that when Locke fashioned his broader views on toleration, they bore distinct similarities to these dissenting Protestant arguments. At the least, this early exposure to these religious arguments influenced Locke to shape his own arguments in a manner that would find resonance within this growing dissenting Protestant stream. Whatever lay behind Locke's thinking, he was definitely moving toward the toleration promoted by this dissenting current by 1667.

It was then that he wrote—but did not publish—his *Essay Concerning Toleration* (not to be confused with the later *Letter Concerning Toleration*).[89] It is perhaps not a coincidence that it was in the same year that Locke associated with Henry Vane's brother, Sir Walter, on his trip to Cleves, Germany. (Henry was now dead, having been executed shortly after the Restoration for his part in the death of Charles I.)

Whether the broadening of Locke's views on toleration resulted from the trip itself, where he observed a number of different religions flourishing in mutual toleration, or from personal contact with the Vane family, or some other source cannot be proved. Both events likely had an effect.[90] Locke now clearly proposed a much more confined role for the magistrate in spiritual matters. He now limited the magistrate almost entirely to those matters touching on the common welfare. Nowhere does he suggest that the state should oversee even minimal religious beliefs of the church. But his scope for truly unrestricted religious belief and action is still somewhat narrower than his later formulation. He grants full toleration only to "purely speculative opinions and divine worship." Neither of these, he claims, have any impact or bearing on the world or other people.[91]

Then, harkening back to his earlier *Two Tracts* argument, he has a category of things, neither "good nor bad" but indifferent, that "concern society and men's conversations one with another." Locke is unclear in defining what is "indifferent" in matters of religious belief. On the one hand he appears to suggest that "in religious worship nothing is indifferent," thereby removing the magistrate from all things religious.[92] On the other hand he gives the magistrate power over some other matters he terms "indifferent," though it is not clear whether they are entirely civil.

His examples of matters indifferent include the raising of children, divorce, polygamy, the eating of foods, and the schedule of work and rest.[93] Many religious people, however, viewed standards for marriage and divorce, and days of rest and worship, as important religious questions. While Locke seems to have moved from protecting mere religious belief to including religious worship, he does not seem to have yet broadened his view to include religious practices more generally.

He also says that the magistrate could use force against particular religious groups that, because of their secrecy and close-knit affiliation, appeared to pose a potential threat to the state. They were not to be persecuted for their religious beliefs. Rather, their religion was a "ribbon" or a "badge" that identified them as potentially hostile. This was not directed especially against Catholics. He dealt with them directly as a species of seditious heresy, that is, as those with allegiances to a foreign civil power at war with England. Rather, in explaining the "badge" idea he gave as an example the Quakers, should they hypothetically become large enough to be dangerous to the state.[94]

In his *Letter* of 1689, Locke would drop all references to targeting religious groups on the basis of their religion being a badge. Furthermore, in that later letter he would make it clear that the magistrate had no role even in matters of "indifference" within religion. He would draw a brighter and clearer line between secular and religious matters. He later acknowledged that questions of days of worship and rest and questions of eating and drinking might indeed have religious significance. The magistrate should not legislate, Locke would eventually conclude, on these matters because of their status of being "indifferent."[95]

Human Understanding and Religious Beliefs

Locke did not express this broader view in print, however, for at least two decades. In the interim, he worked on his famed *Essay Concerning Human Understanding*. His evolving views on toleration can only be understood with some knowledge of this famous, complex work.[96] The *Essay* was provoked by a discussion he was having with some friends in 1671 on the topic of the relationship—as one present at the time described it—of "the principles of morality and reveal'd religion."[97] Locke scholars believe that the discussion had to do with the "basis of morality and its relation to natural and revealed religion."[98] Locke himself said that the discussion was "a subject very remote" from the topic of human understanding that became the theme of his book. It is not surprising that a book inspired by discussion of issues of church, state, and morality, though dealing with the somewhat different field of epistemology and knowledge, should provide some insights into those very issues.

For our purposes, it is impractical to even begin to summarize a work as voluminous and detailed as this one. But certain elements of it relate directly to our topic of private judgment, religious belief, and religious freedom.[99] The first is the emphasis that the *Essay* placed on personal judgment in relation to individual understanding. The *Essay* is famous for its rejection of innate ideas—positing instead the view of the human mind as tabula rasa, awaiting the imprint of sensations. This was a main point where Locke parted ways with Descartes. It left Locke necessarily with the view that humans must obtain ideas and notions from outside themselves, or as reflections on their own internal sensations. This meant that all persons must seek, find, and reflect individually for themselves.[100]

Locke viewed the world of knowledge as divided into at least two categories: knowledge and belief. Knowledge is that limited area of knowing where we can have certainty, because of our direct observation of the connections or disconnections concerning our observed "ideas" of the real world. This is a narrow area of understanding, dealing with mathematical proofs and observations of relation or identity, for example, white is not black, or gold is heavy, yellow, malleable, and does not burn.

Understanding that requires any sort of reasoning or reliance on evidence rather than direct observation or experience is classified as belief.[101] Most things we think we know fall into this second category, since they require some assessment of probabilities. This involves the exercise of individual judgment regarding the likely state of reality, given the probabilities.[102] In contrast to the way many moderns view it, he put both religious beliefs and beliefs about the natural world in this category. Indeed, he argued that moral truths could be known with greater certainty than most realities of the natural world.[103] Locke did not discount religious knowledge or revelation and accepted that it can provide the foundation for the most reliable types of belief. He argued, though, that we must use reason and probability to determine if what is claimed to be a divine revelation really *is* a divine revelation.[104]

For Locke, most religious beliefs, like most beliefs about life generally, fell squarely into the belief/probability category, where exercise of judgment is required. But he placed a belief or knowledge of the existence of God, along with his creatorship and our broad duty to worship and obey him, in the knowledge category. The details of the religious duties flowing from those truths, however, fell in the category of belief.[105]

Locke further believed that revelation could convey truths that were otherwise discoverable through reason, and vice versa.[106] Nothing can be revealed by revelation that is contrary to reason, because reason is the judge by which revelation is deemed authentic. It was not that reason needed to be able to validate or prove the truth of revelation, but revelation must not contradict reason. God was the author of the truths of reason and revelation, and could not contradict himself.[107] But most important, the use of reason in assessing the authenticity of divine revelation required the rational assessment of probabilities, along with the use of individual judgment to decide if each particular case of divine revelation was indeed authentic. One must assess, by reason, the legitimacy of an inspired document or person by examining their claims for supernatural indicia, such as the existence of miracle or prophecy.[108]

Locke's rejection of innate ideas and the important role for individual judgment assessing beliefs undercut the popular notion that each man's conscience reflected only those things that were true. This popular view allowed many mainstream Protestants to say with a straight face that they believed in liberty of conscience, but the state had the right to punish acts against conscience, or punish the one with the erring conscience, that is, punish the one who deliberately repudiated what conscience had revealed. Religious persecution was often justified on this basis. It was the position taken by the Puritan John Cotton in his debate with Roger Williams. This view assumed that everyone's conscience innately contained certain universal spiritual truths, and that the state, or state church, could hold persons accountable to these universal truths.

Locke's rejection of innate ideas and his promotion of a belief in the personal appropriation of truths meant that consciences would differ from person to person, depending on attentiveness, industry, access to revelation, and use of proper principles of reason.[109] Locke did not make truth purely subjective or relative. He did not deny universal morality or truth, but rather denied that universal morality was inherent in the human being. Locke argued that morality, even the existence of God, could be understood by the use of reason reflecting on the world.[110] His was a belief in the personal appropriation of truth to the understanding of each person. Belief was a matter of the understanding, not the will.

Some would cast Locke in the mold of a modern liberal whose commitment to toleration was based on a kind of epistemic skepticism. But this would not be a fair portrayal. First, while some skeptics of Locke's day did advocate for toleration, other skeptics viewed the individual difficulty of arriving at truth as all the more reason for the centralized state to enforce it. The political philosopher Andrew Murphy has pointed out that "Hobbes and the more general influence of Erastianism in English politics" took this precise path of using skepticism to argue for a religiously paternal civil authority.[111]

Further, Locke's view of the role of subjective judgment in religious matters was more akin to the subjectivity of the Baptists and Quakers than that of the true religious skeptic. Dissenting Protestants emphasized the importance of the Holy Spirit in bringing the conviction of spiritual truth to the soul. They believed that truth was not meant to be just an intellectual adherence, but an experience. So while it was truth that might be "known" in some objective sense, it did no good unless it was experienced and internalized by belief. This could only happen when it was voluntarily appropriated and acted on.

Locke's insistence on the "full persuasion of the mind" was thus not a concession to subjectivity or skepticism, but reflected a concern for the individual's experience of truth, and not just a simple knowing of it. Murphy has described well the link between Locke and the dissenting Protestant's view of conscience. For them, "conscience was a faculty of the understanding and not the will, it could not be coerced into believing one thing or another." On this, "Locke and Penn agreed."[112]

Based in part on these insights into the formation of knowledge and belief, Locke came to a stronger view of religious freedom by the 1680s. The political scientist and Locke scholar Douglas Casson has detailed the centrality and importance of the idea of the individual's exercise of probable judgment—the private judgments of individuals in assessing the world around them—in Locke's thinking on a wide range of topics, including economics, metaphysics, morality, politics, and toleration. Casson convincingly argues that it was in the formulation of the *Essay Concerning Human Understanding* that Locke came to sharpen his insights on private judgment in a manner that impacted his thought on a range of areas, especially that of religious toleration. No longer would he allow the magistrate involvement in things indifferent, or have a state-sponsored church with even a minimal theological creed.[113]

Mature Position: Locke's *Letter on Toleration*

We have a clear view of the shape of Locke's church/state thought at this point in his *Letter on Toleration*, published in 1689. Despite the philosophical nature of the treatise, scriptural texts and ideas still play an important role in it. As one scholar has noted, "like Milton, Locke is sure that reading of scripture is crucial and foundational."[114] Indeed, Locke begins his *Letter* by asserting that religious toleration is a fundamental teaching of Christ himself. On the first page Locke quotes the New Testament: "'The kings of the Gentiles exercise lordship over them,' said our Savior to his disciples, but ye shall not be so, Luke xxii. 25, 26."[115]

But Locke, unlike Milton (although like some of the dissenters from whom Milton drew, as well as Penn himself), extended his toleration beyond the "clear teachings" of scripture. Milton had viewed clear and central scriptural teaching as the bounds of conscience, although he allowed for diversity on a vast numbers of lesser issues. For Milton, the right of private interpretation ended where scripture was plain and needed no interpretation. But in his *Letter*, Locke's bounds of conscience have less to do with clear scriptural limits and more to do with the individual's need to personally comprehend religious duty. For Locke, this freedom of conscience must be respected, whatever the source of duty, whether from scripture or directly from God.

Later, Locke explicitly invoked the right of private judgment, stating that in matters of salvation "every man ... has the supreme and absolute authority of judging for himself."[116] But his focus became the conscience of the human being in understanding all spiritual truths, rather than just merely the words or reading of scripture itself. As he put it in his *Second Letter on Toleration*, "every own [sic] is judge for himself, what is right; and in matters of faith, and religious worship, another cannot judge for him."[117] The right to interpret scripture for oneself, rather than the foundation for all freedom, is merely one instance of the broader right of conscience held by all humans before God.

In a key line that reveals the importance of his theory of religious belief for toleration, Locke writes: "all the life and power of true religion consists in the inward and full persuasion of the mind; *and faith is not faith without believing*."[118] In Locke's sophisticated hands, as in Penn's, the right of private judgment of scriptural interpretation became, as it also had been with the earlier Baptists, a broader principle of the right of private judgment of religious duty and belief. In Locke's arguments, scriptural teaching supports both principles, and he treats them as related.

Locke seemed to grasp first the narrower principle of the right of private judgment in biblical interpretation, and this provided a base to move on to grasp the latter, broader principle of religious freedom. He early wrote on the right of private scriptural interpretation, then moved on to reject the role of the magistrate in scriptural matters of importance, and finally expanded that rejection to all matters of conscience.

One of Locke's main arguments regarding the impotence of civil power in spiritual matters echoed Luther's two kingdoms argument flowing from the priesthood of believers. Locke did not apparently have Luther's works in his library. But he did have Sebastian Castellio's book *On Heretics*, which quoted the relevant portions of Luther regarding the two kingdoms and the rights of conscience.[119] The Locke scholar Richard Ashcraft has noted Locke's reliance "upon a radical dichotomy between the two spheres of religion and civil interests" and that this view was supported by a "radical protestant appeal to the absoluteness of individual conscience as an essential component of 'Christian liberty.'"[120]

But Locke, going beyond Milton, supports these arguments with appeals to both scripture and nature. His main jurisdictional arguments are as follows: that the magistrate lacks jurisdiction over "the care of souls"; that "true and saving religion consists in the inwards persuasion of the mind" because it "is the nature of understanding, that it cannot be compelled to be belief of anything by outward force"; and that as there is one truth and way to heaven, it cannot be that men have a duty to follow their rulers, as most rulers disagree on truth.[121]

How did Locke move from the narrower right of private scriptural interpretation to the broader notion of the right of private judgment in spiritual matters generally? The movement strongly appears to be connected with his increasingly sophisticated views of human understanding, and the exercise of personal judgment required to accept most truths. This element of subjectivity was not a threat to religious faith; rather, it was a necessary basis of faith. As he notes in a follow-up to his original *Letter*, "where vision, knowledge, and certainty is, there faith is done away."[122]

Others have observed the connection between the advance in Locke's views of human understanding and his embrace of a more expansive religious toleration.[123] But the connection of Locke's thought in this regard with, and the parallels to, dissenting Protestant thought has not generally been seen. As I have already shown, this move from personal appropriation of belief to support for toleration is not unique or original with Locke. "Locke does not offer," writes Murphy, "new or unprecedented arguments for toleration."[124] The Baptists, as well as Vane and Stubbe, had already earlier argued for a broader toleration based on this private right of judgment in religious matters. It was an argument that embraced not just dissenting Christians, but Jews and Muslims. The Baptists had not generally spoken in terms of knowledge versus belief, certainty versus probability, and the distinguishing role of reason. But, as noted, their concept of the importance of the Holy Spirit in revealing truth through scripture to the individual believer brought them to a very similar epistemological stance. The Baptists had begun to call it soul liberty, but they used the language of reason and judgment that anticipated Locke's more philosophical framing.

For instance, in 1661, a Baptist by the name of John Sturgion wrote the recently enthroned Charles II, pleading for toleration for himself and his fellow believers. One of his main arguments was that it is "unreasonable" to deny men the "use of their reason in the choice of religion."[125] Sounding like Locke twenty years later, he wrote: "scripture, tradition, councils, and fathers, be the evidence in a question; *yet reason is the judge*." And if we "are to be persuaded, we must see that we be persuaded reasonably.... No man hath any efficacy or authority on the understanding of another, but by proposal and persuasion, and then a man is bound to assent according to the operation of the argument, and the strength of the persuasion."[126]

Both John Murton and Roger Williams had seen the logic of this connection of personal judgment, reason, and the personal conviction of religious truth. They had argued for a toleration that would encompass Catholics, Jews, and even Turks and other "pagans." In Locke's own time, Penn had clearly spelled out this connection between personal understanding of scripture and general liberty for all in his own work on religious freedom. Penn relied on not only a natural law and natural rights arguments but also the "force/understanding issue as part of a definition of what constitutes a rational being," which has become identified with Locke.[127] We know that Locke had access to Penn's major works on toleration, as well as those of other dissenters.

But the Quakers and the Baptists were of insufficient influence to make this broader notion stick. The Baptists did not have the breadth of philosophical background to express their concepts in terms that would appeal widely and endure. Penn did have the training and background to deal intelligently with the topic, but he was also writing from the margins of society as a Quaker. He had connections and influence to bring money and power to bear on behalf of himself and his friends, especially in the setting up of Pennsylvania. His substantive political and religious ideas, though, were sidelined, at least in Europe and England, as being part of his Quaker "enthusiasms."

Thus, Locke's unique contribution was not that he was the only one to express the universal principle of conscience and religious freedom in biblical terms or even in more broadly accessible terms of natural law and philosophical reasoning. Rather, his unique role was in doing so from a place of real influence in society, as part of a circle that included leading politicians and aristocrats, and as a member of the establishment Anglican church. His explorations of human belief and understanding were expressed in largely philosophical and natural terms that resonated with elite thinkers in a world that was looking for a way out of the sectarian violence of the British Civil War. His *Letter Concerning Toleration* provides "a synthesis of existing arguments in a highly effective, polemical form" that is the expression that is most remembered to this day.[128] But the fact of its durability should not obscure the truth that it embodied arguments made by many religious thinkers from the dissenting Protestant tradition of his time and earlier.

Locke and the Larger Religious World

Locke's teaching about (1) the subjective elements involved in understanding and the choice to believe, and (2) the resulting argument that thus conscience should not be forced represent, according to one political philosopher, the "two most important conceptual developments in the early modern emergence of toleration."[129] But as these were ideas he was transmitting rather than originating, he echoed, and by his influence, enhanced, what many Protestant divines in colonial America also believed. Certain recent scholarship argues that Locke had purely secular assumptions and aims, and that his goal was to "establish civil supremacy over religion."[130] But this was simply not the way he was read or understood by many, if not most, biblically conservative religious thinkers in colonial America.

The historian Steven Dworetz has done the most comprehensive, recent work on Locke and his influence on American colonial divines. He credits Locke with articulating a philosophy of human understanding and religious toleration that mirrored the "theistic liberalism" prevalent in the American colonies among the thinking classes.[131] Dworetz argues that one of the most important parts of this "theistic liberalism" was that it reconciled reason and revelation. Both Locke and the divines "tended to treat natural and revealed law as two consistent, complementary, and interdependent expressions of a single divine will."[132] Another central concept shared by Locke and the colonial divines—indeed, Dworetz identifies it as the "most important topic in this sermonology"—was the "belief in the prime necessity of individual judgment in the pursuit of salvation."[133]

As Dworetz puts it:

Theistic epistemology propels the doctrine of individual judgment into Lockean political theory. Each man must judge for himself, by the study of scripture, the content of God's law. But the law of nature for Locke and the clergy, is also the law of God. And if the "obligations of the law of nature" are "drawn closer" in civil society and constitute the basis of all legitimate "municipal laws, then individual judgment must extend from the religious to the political context. Thus, in the final political reckoning, *"the people shall be judge"* and, indeed, *"every man is judge for* himself."[134]

Here, Dworetz identifies Locke as assisting in the shift from the right of private judgment in religious matters to the right to decide about political matters in colonial America. But he does not argue, as I do in this work, that the doctrine influenced a shift in the legal climate relating to religious disestablishment. Rather, he argues that it was an important factor in causing religious Americans to support the Revolution, which is a separate argument.[135] In addition, he leaves unanswered the question whether the divines were directly influenced by Locke on these points or whether they shared a common heritage of religious thought. ("No one can say, 'influence' is impossible to prove.'")[136]

Other scholars have also noticed the similarity between Locke's thought and that of a certain strain of Protestantism. But contra Dworetz, Michael Zuckert argues that the Puritan divines were evidently influenced by Locke. The Puritans said one thing about toleration before Locke, and another thing afterward.[137] Still, Zuckert is open to the contribution of Protestant thought to American Lockean ideology. He asks whether "the convergence of Lockean political philosophy and Puritan political thought is all in one direction, or did Protestantism contribute something of its own?"[138] He acknowledges that the ministers, in their use of Locke, "do often add elements … of a loosely Christian character."

Zuckert notes that the Puritans made greater use of scriptural passages and argument, made greater emphasis on divine judgment, and emphasized the importance of religious foundations to sound politics. But ultimately, Zuckert thinks the clerical modifications were "shallow" and the Lockean doctrine was not "substantially Christianized" by their efforts. He thus concludes: "Puritan thought has been transformed, it has assimilated or been assimilated by Locke."[139]

Zuckert seems right about the shift in Puritan thought toward a more Lockean view on church and state. But he does not explore the question as to whether Locke's thought—with which Puritan thought became amalgamated— was itself shaped by other Protestant influences—not by those of the main

Puritan, Calvinist, or magisterial traditions, but by those of the dissenting tradition. Zuckert is aware that Locke's church/state thought is similar to that of the early Luther. He accepts that "this Lockeanization was a process made possible by a partial reversion to [Luther's] older doctrine of the Two Kingdoms."[140] Zuckert, though, does not claim any direct or immediate influence of Luther's ideas on Locke. He leaves the question open, apparently allowing that the convergence between Locke's thought and early Luther's teachings on the two kingdoms might be a sort of historical coincidence or accident.

But in light of the above history, this similarity does not seem to be a coincidence or accident at all. Rather, Locke had become familiar with a dissenting line of Protestantism that kept Luther's early thought on the two kingdoms alive. This is not to allege that Locke himself was a product of, or a believer in, the dissenting Protestant tradition. Rather, it is to say that Locke, in articulating his views on toleration, found a useful religious heritage and tradition to aid his popularization efforts. Locke may not have been a "true believer" in the broad range of dissenting Protestant ideals. But that would not prevent "true believers" from perceiving Locke as articulating the core or essence of that tradition in relation to church and state, albeit in more updated and widely accessible language and arguments.

Zuckert acknowledges that Locke's Protestant side was a necessary bridge between religious and Enlightenment thought. The important point is that Locke generally wrote in a style and manner that would attract rather than repel biblically committed religious thinkers. Even those skeptical of Locke's own religious commitments or orthodoxy, including Zuckert, accept that "echoes of Christian, or at least theological, themes are much stronger right on the surface of Locke's discussion" than with some other natural law and rights thinkers, for example the Lutheran Pufendorf.[141]

Given the evidence that shows the contact Locke had with the dissenting Protestant stream of thought, one can see that Zuckert's "Lockeanization" of the Puritans can perhaps better be understood another way: as one strand of Protestantism, Puritan, and Reformed thought giving way to, or melding with, another strand, that of dissenting Anabaptist and Baptist thought, at least on the topic of conscience and society. As we have seen, Locke himself did not originate the important premises of "theistic liberalism," such as a belief in the consistency of special and natural revelation and the rights of conscience and belief. Rather, these fundamental ideas were advanced by certain dissenting religious thinkers writing well before Locke.

A prime example of this "theistic liberalism" is Penn's *Great Case for Liberty of Conscience*, written two decades prior to Locke's works on understanding and toleration, as noted earlier. The content of Penn's work foreshadows Locke's epistemology of both reason and revelation, including the personal appropriation of spiritual truths, and an emphasis on the necessity of personal judgment in religious matters. Penn's work also speaks in terms of the "Order of Nature" and the "Right of liberty," using arguments from the realms of nature, reason, and logic that foreshadow Locke's more famous works on these topics.

The similarity seems more than coincidence. Not only did Locke have access to Penn's works when he drafted his *Letter on Toleration*, but he participated in active discussion with leading Quaker thinkers during his time in Amsterdam.[142] While in Holland, Locke participated in a largely Quaker conversational circle known as "the Lantern." From his visits there, Locke gained a "greater appreciation of Quaker thought and life, including its large degree of support for toleration."[143] At this time, Locke was actively thinking about epistemology in relation to Quaker thought. Marshall records that Locke's "journals show that he read Quaker works in these years and was attempting to find ways to accommodate Quaker accounts of the indwelling spirit with the status of Scripture."[144]

The degree to which Locke, in constructing his own epistemology in relation to religious freedom, was influenced by dissenting Protestant thought in general may never be entirely ascertained. It seems fair to say, as one scholar has put it, that "Locke himself was rooted in the Dutch [Mennonite] arguments for toleration."[145] But for the purposes of this work, it is not necessary to prove that Locke copied or depended on the views of the Mennonites, Penn, the Quakers, or other religious dissenters. Rather, Penn's writings (along with Milton, Limborch, and Vane, as well as Castellio, and the early Luther himself),[146] show what other devoutly religious thinkers were writing in relation to epistemology and religious freedom prior to Locke—writings of which Locke was well aware. In light of this, Locke, like Milton, is better understood as a lens magnifying and focusing existing currents of thought, rather than creating new foundations for religious toleration.

The historian John Marshall contests the view that Locke was influenced by or shaped his arguments in light of dissenting Protestant thought. In a number of works, Marshall has argued that the modern notions of toleration have their roots in an early Enlightenment group of thinkers who created a republic of letters in the late seventeenth century. He argues that this movement was not meaningfully aided by religious currents of thought, but indeed was largely in opposition to biblical religious thought.[147] Marshall provides a fine-grained and detailed overview of Locke's thought and development, as well as the larger community of toleration of the seventeenth century. His works are so voluminous and detailed that a point-by-point analysis is impracticable here, but a few things can be said in response to this claim.

One of the problems with Marshall's argument is that he overlooks or minimizes the stream of dissenting Protestant tradition I have discussed so far. This would especially include the English Baptists, who were writing strong works supporting a vigorous toleration a half century before Marshall's "early Enlightenment" takes shape.[148] He acknowledges, but similarly attempts to marginalize, Milton's work in the area of religious freedom and disestablishment. He focuses on Milton's allegedly unorthodox and Arminian views as somehow disqualifying his church/state views as an expression of legitimate Protestantism. But he fails to acknowledge Milton's use of the Baptist Murton's argument about the private right of scriptural interpretation and the degree to which Milton's arguments anticipate Locke's right of judgment arguments.[149]

Marshall almost entirely ignores Henry Vane and his assistant, Henry Stubbe, despite Stubbe's direct contacts with Locke regarding Vane's scriptural arguments for toleration. In his early book on Locke, Marshall does acknowledge Stubbe's contact with Locke but makes no mention of Vane or his work, with which Locke was familiar. This is a key oversight, because it undermines Marshall's thesis that all meaningful influences on Locke for toleration were "unorthodox" or deviant from historic Protestant thought.

Furthermore, Marshall also must minimize the religious and theological commitments of the figures he identifies with his "republic of letters." He attempts this by labeling them as either biblically liberal or unorthodox, for example, as Arminians, latitudinarians, Arians, socinians, Quakers, or Anabaptists. The problem with this argument is twofold. First, there were some basically "orthodox" believers, as measured by then-contemporary majoritarian standards in the Protestant West, among the tolerationists, such as Roger Williams, Henry Vane, Henry Stubbe, and even John Milton, whose more daring views were not revealed until after his death.[150]

But to "secularize" all religious thinkers that were defined by their contemporaries as "unorthodox" is to fall into the same trap in which the majority was caught in Locke's day: to define "orthodoxy" by majority vote and make those outside the majority view unrepresentative of genuine Protestantism. Marshall's argument becomes something of a tautology. If orthodoxy is what the majority believes, and the majority believes in intolerance, then anyone who believes in liberty of conscience must, by definition, be unorthodox.

Marshall's argument is perhaps not quite this wooden or simplistic. He does often find in his heroes of toleration some genuine divergence from historic

Protestant views on central issues such as anthropology, or Christology, or the Trinity. But he also counts among his outsiders more general categories like "Arminians" and "latitudinarians." But there were biblically conservative and biblically liberal Arminians. Many if not most Arminians, especially of the Dutch variety that most concerns Marshall, would have considered themselves to be just as "orthodox" as their Calvinist counterparts. Some latitudinarians would have taken the same position. To define away major parts of the Protestant tradition as somehow not really "Protestant" is to "prove" that Protestantism did not help produce toleration by clever definition rather than by genuine historical evidence and analysis.

Marshall also overlooks the fact that many of those even obviously outside the pale of traditional Protestant orthodoxy crafted their arguments on toleration to appeal to those still within it. To persuade outsiders of a position, it was necessary to use arguments that they would find coherent and persuasive. Milton, despite his unorthodox leanings in certain areas of Christology and anthropology, grounded his arguments for toleration on what he and others believed to be central Protestant historic events and beliefs, including commitments to scripture. Locke, as we have seen, operated in much the same way.

Many of Marshall's circle of "early Enlightenment" figures would be genuinely surprised to find themselves classed as primarily secular rather than religious thinkers. Pierre Bayle, Hugo Grotius, Jean Le Clerc, Gilbert Burnet, Isaac Papin, Philip van Limborch, Benjamin Furley, Charles Le Cene, even Locke himself, certainly viewed themselves as religious, even theological thinkers, writing in an ongoing stream of religious traditions. A number of them, including Limborch, Bayle, and Le Clerc, were professors of theology first and political writers second.[151] Limborch himself, a remonstrant, had Mennonite roots and continued to associate closely with Mennonite and Quaker thinkers. His writings on toleration reflected these influences. His influence on Locke in turn is made apparent by the fact that Locke dedicated his *Letter on Toleration* to Limborch.[152] Le Cene, Papin, and Burnet were Protestant ministers, though Papin later became a Catholic (not a particularly "Enlightenment" thing to do) and Burnet became bishop of Salisbury and an influential church historian.[153]

Marshall writes that this "republic of letters" coalesced in the 1680s and 1690s. It is interesting to note, then, that the same arguments he points to as being central to this "early Enlightenment" group of writers were found at least a decade earlier, as we have seen, in the writings of William Penn. Again, Penn is an important test case, as he gives us a reading of the climate of dissenting religious thought on toleration prior to the time that Locke, and Marshall's "republic of letters," was active.

An examination of orthodox but dissenting English preachers and leaders of Locke's era shows that they read him as an orthodox religious thinker, rather than a devotee of reason. As one scholar notes, within the first two decades of the eighteenth century, the "essential distinction of the Nonconformists was their refusal to allow any civil or religious authority to exercise power over the individual's conscience, or for that matter, to exercise any power 'derogatory to the honour of our great Master, the sole legislator in his own kingdom.'"[154] Whether it was the Baptists, Congregationalists, or Presbyterians, English orthodox dissenting bodies all shared a common ideology regarding church and state. It was based on their view of the individual's access directly to scriptures and their author, Jesus Christ, who alone was the "Lord of conscience."

James Bradley, the historian of British nonconformity, noted that the "two defining principles of English non-conformity and British dissent, generally [were]: (1) the right of private judgment (Christ as sole Lord of conscience) and (2) the spiritual and voluntary nature of the church."[155] In expressing these ideas, Bradley notes, Locke was held in high esteem, and cited with much frequency by dissenting Protestants, who frequently referred to him as the "immortal Locke."[156]

The "vast majority of eighteenth-century Dissenters, as well as a number of English churchmen and many American divines, looked back with gratitude to Locke … as the exemplar of tolerationist views."[157] Isaac Watts, the evangelical hymn writer, wrote of Locke's "admirable" *Letter* and how it transported him "into a new region of thought. … There was no room to doubt in the midst of sun-beams. … [It] taught me to allow all men the same freedom to choose their religion, as I claim to choose my own."[158] From across the Atlantic, churchmen such as Charles Chauncy and John Henry Livingston, respectively father of the Reformed Dutch Church in America and president of Queen's College (now Rutgers), acknowledged their debt to Locke in leading them to embrace religious freedom.[159]

Locke's Influence on American Views of Toleration

The influence of Locke on American divines persisted, and even increased, well into the eighteenth century. One scholar who reviewed the sermons of the revolutionary period states:

> Had ministers been the only spokesmen of the American cause, had Jefferson, the Adamses, and Otis never appeared in print, the political

thought of the Revolution would have followed along almost exactly the same line—with perhaps a little more mention of God, but certainly no less of John Locke.[160]

Dworetz states that "most Americans before and after 1763 'absorbed' Lockean political ideas *with* the gospel." It was not that all Americans read Locke but that "many of their religious leaders had read, understood, and sympathized with Locke, and had been preaching the fundamentals of Lockean political theory—thereby establishing the substantive Lockean connection—for many years before Parliament tried its hand at tax reform." Colonial "New Englanders," Dworetz adds, "tended to take their ministers seriously."[161]

Indeed, colonial pulpits rang with both affirmations of Lockean natural rights philosophy and also of the right of private judgment of scripture. The following statements from sermons between the 1750s to the 1770s well illustrate the point.

> All men have a "right as moral agents and accountable creatures to think and act for themselves in things that relate to their own eternal salvation." Every Protestant "according to his abilities should search the scriptures and judge whether the things which his minister delivers according to this rule." Each individual has a "natural, unalienable right to think and see for himself"; for "as every man must answer for himself at the great and last day, so every one ought to be left at liberty to judge for himself here." "Christian liberty" means that "every Christian has and must have a right to judge for himself the true sense and meaning of all gospel truths." As a prerequisite for moral agency and salvation, it is "not only the right but the duty of men to defend liberty." To renounce "liberty of private judgment in matters of religion" would "destroy the foundations of all religion" and "must therefore be a violation of the law of nature."[162]

Many other, virtually identical statements occur in numerous colonial sermons.[163] Locke's influence on the colonial divines is undeniable.

Baptists show that the source of this principle was more than just Locke. Historically, of course, the Baptists were in the forefront of urging disestablishment on the basis of the right of private judgment in biblical interpretation, as we have already seen. This advocacy continued in colonial America, as I will show in some detail when I examine the work of Isaac Backus later.

But the Baptists had a much more ambivalent, and sometimes hostile, attitude toward Locke's philosophy of natural rights. The Baptists, at times, found that the British government provided a shelter and protection for them against the excesses of the Puritan majority. It was not entirely clear that an independent America would be better for Baptist minorities. They were, thus, very cautious about the rights language used to stoke the fires of revolution, and leery of Locke because of this. But they were very committed to notions of private judgment in matters of religion.

Baptists stand as evidence that the strand of disestablishment thought existed prior to Locke and his writings. Locke may indeed have influenced Puritan thought in this regard. But his thought had the resonance it did because of the shared connections both parties had with the dissenting Protestant heritage.[164] (I will examine an example of this resonance between Locke and dissenting protestants when I explore in some depth the Baptist leader Isaac Backus.)

Of course, there is the matter of Locke's direct legal influence in the American colonies. He appears to have counseled William Penn on the framing of the very religiously liberal Pennsylvania constitution.[165] He also played a role in the drafting of the constitutions of the Carolina colonies. Lord Ashley, Locke's employer and sponsor, was one of the patentees of the Carolina district in the Americas. Locke, as his principal advisor and assistant, had a hand in helping administer and manage the settlement of the new colony.[166]

In 1669, Locke assisted in drafting the constitution of the Carolina colony, though his hand was not sole or entirely free. Certain paragraphs of the original draft of the constitution are in Locke's own handwriting. It is unlikely, given Locke's stature and reputation, that he was merely playing a clerical role in writing what had actually been dictated by Lord Shaftsbury.[167] But he also had to respond to and balance the wishes of eight lords and proprietors of Carolina. We know that certain provisions were included to which he was opposed. But the imprint of some of his ideas can be seen on the document, especially in the clauses relating to religion.

In relation to church and state, the constitution required that all inhabitants believe in God and in his public worship. This was consonant with Locke's view that a belief in God and worship were a fundamental truth of reason, and a basis of contracts within society, and indeed to the contract of society. We know, however, that Locke objected to another clause that established the Anglican church as the only one "allowed to received public maintenance."[168]

Locke was able to ameliorate this official establishment by other provisions, for which he does appear to have been responsible, that extended significant religious freedom to all other religions. The constitution allowed that Native Americans, Jews, and "other dissenters from the purity of the Christian religion" might be granted freedom of worship, with no civil disability or private interference or molestation. Believers of all religions, Christian or otherwise, including Catholics, would have these rights as long as they organized in groups of seven, agreed to worship God publicly, according to some reasonable ritual, and avoided sedition.[169]

Despite these regulatory requirements, the religious freedom extended was truly remarkable. It was broader than that of any other colony at the time, with the exception of Rhode Island. Pennsylvania had very broad religious freedom protections, but even there, officeholders had to profess belief in the divinity of Christ. Carolina had an officially established church, but the reality was that the Anglicans put few resources or personnel into the Carolina colony. Thus, a multiplicity of sects flourished. Early on, a number of Quakers moved to the new colony, and were active in limiting the powers of the established church and maintaining freedom for all religious groups. While there were a number of dynamics that help explain the relative tolerance of the Carolina colony, certainly a major starting point was the broad principles of religious liberty that Locke placed in the constitutive documents.

Conclusion

In beginning my research for this book, I had no real sense of how prominent a role Locke would play in it. Although familiar with his *Two Treatises of Government* and his *Letter on Toleration*, I had no idea how many connections I would find between Locke and dissenting Protestants of various stripes, or that so much influence would run both ways. Because of this, I rather backed my way into a heated historical controversy over the influence and role of Locke in the American founding. Over the last half century, the historical consensus seems to have swung from viewing Locke's role as central and massive to marginal and trivial, and then back toward a more sensible assessment that he was one among a number of quite important influences.[170]

This book is not meant to assess Locke's place in America's founding generally. Rather, I am interested in Locke for his role in articulating a public philosophy of religious liberty that resonated with the religious values of dissenting Protestants on both sides of the Atlantic. Historians are now beginning to recognize that arguments over whether republicanism or liberalism was more responsible for the American founding overlook the fact that the two systems were then neither fully developed nor viewed as exclusive and competing. As one historian has put it, "for most of English and American history liberal and republican conceptions of liberty, far from being at odds with one another, go hand in hand."[171]

But, given what has been shown above, what are often thought of as liberal, or republican, or Enlightenment notions of liberty and freedom would seem to be products of, or at least meaningfully influenced by, dissenting Protestant thought. It is hard to see how ideas of religious disestablishment, religious liberty, or even a government limited by individual rights can really be traced to Renaissance Italy or a classical republican tradition. Certainly, Bernard Bailyn and others have shown that there was some influence of classical thought on the founders. But Bailyn acknowledges that the appeal to classical thought was often a kind of rhetorical "window dressing."[172] And writers that he cites as examples of Enlightenment influence, such as Hugo Grotius and John Locke, can be equally understood as dissenting Protestant thinkers.[173]

In light of the material above about Penn and Locke, it is apparent that the predominate church/state philosophy of America in its colonial and early republic phases—rather than being the "Machiavellian moment," as posited by J. G. A. Pocock[174]—was really the "early Luther moment."[175] And it was so in good part because of Locke's ability to articulate theories of church, state, and toleration that resonated with the theology of conservative, dissenting Protestants of colonial America.

Still, Carolina aside, Locke was more the theorist of religious freedom for America than the implementer of such freedoms. The American colonists had developed a deeply pragmatic outlook on the hardscrabble, colonial frontier. If the only available church/state models were the New England establishments and the southern quasi-establishments, all the elegant theory in the world would likely not have pushed them into the flurry of disestablishment that took place in the colonies between 1776 and the early 1800s. It was the flourishing, commercially successful colonies in the mid-Atlantic region, with their crown jewel Pennsylvania and its capital, that provided the evidence that disestablishment would not produce anarchy but rather could provide the framework for a robust social and commercial success.

But without Locke's finely articulated thought, with its firm theological foundations, the movement for disestablishment would have had no central core principles and message. It would have relied merely on example, and would have been subject to collapse if the Pennsylvania economy experienced a downturn. It would also have met with resistance in strongly religious communities that might have objected to a revised social structure for purely economic interests, if they had viewed it as in conflict with basic moral principles. The example comes to mind of slavery, which did infiltrate many communities because of its perceived economic value. But it was ultimately ejected from many communities, and then the whole country, because it came to be seen for the moral evil it was.

Similarly, if disestablishment had been viewed as a commercial advantage, but a moral failing, it would have been resisted and rolled back during times of religious revival. But the opposite is true, as the First Great Awakening led to a broader support for disestablishment, and the Second Great Awakening did not fully end before all states had disestablished religion. The positive correlation between religious revival and disestablishment in mid-eighteenth- to mid-nineteenth-century America was connected with the compelling way Locke articulated the philosophical and political expression of what were perceived to be Protestant theological principles.

An enthusiast, activist, and builder *and* a thinker, philosopher, and theologian were required for the dissenting Protestant view of church/state religions to prevail in America. While we are unsure of the precise nature of any interactions Locke and Penn may have had at Oxford and then in Holland, we do know that they undertook a final and most enduring collaboration in America—through the force of their ideas and the power of the examples of their projects. The powerful combination of ideas found in books and in the governments in Pennsylvania and the Carolinas helped prepare the American political, social, and religious framework to embrace disestablishment as eagerly as the European forms of Protestantism embraced state religion.

This cooperation took place, though, by proxy. It unfolded through people who were influenced by these ideas and models and added to them their own meanings. To this unfolding story on the ground in colonial America we now turn.

3

The Puritan Lawyer and the Baptist Preacher

ELISHA WILLIAMS, ISAAC BACKUS, AND AMERICAN DISSENT

Prologue: The Right of Private Judgment in America

That the right of private judgment was a key part of the growing American colonial consciousness is well established. As one scholar recently wrote of this period, "by the late 1730s, hardly anyone denied the 'right of private judgment' or the value of toleration."[1] Of course, what was meant by "toleration" varied from colony to colony. Still, the principle had become widespread, if not universally accepted. More controversial was the question of whether the right of private judgment was a construct of pragmatic and Enlightenment thought, or whether it also expressed a core Protestant theological value.[2]

Was the notion of disestablishment and the growth of voluntary religion a product of core Protestant thought, an imposition of at least vaguely antireligious Enlightenment thought, or some combination of the two?[3] Were Locke and his "liberal" allies Enlightenment corrupters of genuine Protestant thought, or did they draw on historic, if dissenting, Protestant principles to contribute to the organic evolution of Protestant thought?[4] These questions are not merely the concern of modern interpreters. They were raised almost as soon as the colonists began citing and using the phrase itself.

One answer at the time came in 1730 from the South Carolina Presbyterian minister Hugh Fisher. In Fisher's view, the right of private judgment was surely just a cover under which "Arians" or even "Atheists" could hide their corrosive beliefs.[5] It was a liberal idea of the Enlightenment, he asserted, rather than a true Christian principle. Fisher was responding to Josiah Smith, another Presbyterian pastor and fellow South Carolinian. Smith had invoked the right of private judgment to oppose a move by the local Presbyterian churches to require subscription to the Westminster Confession as a creedal statement.[6]

Smith, a Harvard graduate ordained in Boston by Cotton Mather in 1726, was a pastor near Charleston. He opposed a proposal by the local Presbytery to require the creedal affirmation of all pastors. To support his opposition he wrote a series of pamphlets, one entitled *Human Impositions Proved Unscriptural, or, the Divine Right of Private Judgment* and another *The Divine Right of Private Judgment Vindicated.*[7] In his writings, Smith acknowledged that his opponent associated private judgment with the supremacy of reason over all authority, including revelation.[8] But Smith insisted that this was a mischaracterization of the right. The right was not a rejection of scripture but "a right of judging according to Scripture."[9] Or, as he put it elsewhere, it was not a "right of judging contrary to Scriptures; but of bringing every Doctrine to the Test of Scriptures."[10] As a biblical example and support of his position, he several times invoked the Bereans, who, as recorded in the book of Acts, compared the apostle Paul's teachings with the scriptures.[11]

Given the history I have treated thus far, Smith, in asserting the religious roots of private judgment, had the better of the argument. While the right of private judgment played a role in both Enlightenment and Protestant thought, it originated in the West as a Protestant religious idea that was only later borrowed and modified by Enlightenment thinkers. In the American colonies it was invoked first by religiously orthodox leaders rather than Enlightenment figures.

Indeed, the first appeal to the "right of private judgment" printed in America was made by Cotton Mather, the notable Puritan divine.[12] Writing more than twenty years before Smith, Mather identified private judgment as a central principle of Protestantism. Mather, a Puritan bulwark against the skeptical Enlightenment, invoked this right in a sermon preached in 1718.

Interestingly, as Milton had done in his writing on liberty of conscience, Mather referenced the 1529 protest of the Protestant princes at the Diet of Speyer. He noted that the very name "PROTESTANTS" came from this protest related to scripture and the right of private interpretation. There were "two glorious positions" in that "protestation," Mather argued. The first was that the "sacred SCRIPTURES are the rule, and a sufficient one, for faith and worship and manners unto the people of God." The second was related: "there are plain scriptures enow to explain the obscure ones, and every Christian has the right for explaining for himself." The only way of escaping church tyranny—whether in Rome or in the separated churches who clung to the spirit of imposition—he concluded, was by "asserting the right of private judgment" in relation to scripture.[13]

Protestant ministers were not the only ones who claimed that private judgment was religious in its roots. British political thinkers acknowledged their debt to religious thinkers and pastors for the concept. John Trenchard and Thomas Gordon, British Whigs, best known for authoring the *Independent Whig* and *Cato's Letters*, discussed the religious roots of the right of private judgment. Writing at about the same time as Mather, but a world away, they acknowledged the Protestant, religious roots of the idea of the right of private judgment. "Here in England," they asked, "why are we free, why Protestants; but because we are guided by Reason, and judge for ourselves?"[14]

Trenchard and Gordon do not claim to originate this right of private judgment. Rather, in asserting it, they appeal to the "concurrence of the best and wisest of our own Clergy, who acknowledge and contend that we are not to take the Almighty's Meaning at second-hand, nor receive that for his Will which we ourselves do not find to be so."[15] Here they acknowledge that they were drawing on, for political use, a term that is already widely understood and accepted in the religious world.

The very titles of their essays underscored the religious basis of the principle they were describing. These include "Of the Explication of Scripture," "Of Creeds and Confessions of Faith," and "Of the Clearness of Scripture." These foundational essays upheld the right and duty of individual scripture study against the imposition of creeds.[16] Their arguments regarding civil protection for private judgment and reason rested on this foundation of private biblical interpretation, the perspicuity of scripture, and the rejection of creedal authority.[17] Though Trenchard and Gordon had secular political goals in mind in their writings, they bore witness to the Protestant foundation of the right of private judgment.

Cotton Mather and Josiah Smith, as Protestant clergymen, illustrated the *Independent Whig*'s claim that the right of private judgment concept was rooted in the Protestant religious world. Later, however, the principle did begin to take on an Enlightenment, secular hue in some circles. But when the principle first became popular in America, the testimony of both religious leaders and Enlightenment thinkers concurred that it arose out of Protestant theology. Both groups specifically identified those relevant religious beliefs as *sola scriptura*, the perspicuity of scripture, and the interpretation of scripture by the individual believer.

Only later, in the 1750s and 1760s, did the right become more frequently associated with Enlightenment thought. A good example of this

Enlightenment use is that of Jonathon Mayhew, a notable Massachusetts minister who began preaching in the 1740s. John Adams called Mayhew one of the half dozen most important articulators of revolutionary ideas.[18] Mayhew, however, was controversial for his religious views by the time of his ordination in 1747. He was thought to hold Arian or possibly even deistic convictions. Students of Mayhew are correct in saying that he joined together evangelical and Enlightenment thought, with the result often reflecting more of the latter than the former.

In 1748, Mayhew published a sermon entitled *The Right and Duty of Private Judgment*.[19] In that sermon, Mayhew argued in a manner that showed the principle of private judgment operating in both a religious and an Enlightenment manner. He explained this principle of "freedom of thought and inquiry in religious matters," but did so in a decidedly Enlightenment manner.[20] At the center of Mayhew's scheme was the "exerting of our own reason in weighing arguments and evidences." The picture was of autonomous reason, sitting in judgment on all doctrines of "natural and revealed religion."[21] But Mayhew, even with his Enlightenment bent, grounded the basis of private judgment in scriptural teaching. The foundation of his argument for private judgment was the words of Christ in Luke: "Ye hypocrites, ye can discern the face of the sky—and why, even of yourselves judge ye not what is right?"[22]

Despite the existence of a certain secular branching of the idea, illustrated by Mayhew, theologically and biblically conservative thinkers also continued to invoke the right of private judgment throughout the eighteenth century. Two important examples of that tradition come from different ends of the social spectrum in New England. Elisha Williams and Isaac Backus were important for bridging the period from the earlier part of the eighteenth century to around the time of the American Revolution. Indeed, Backus was publicly active up to the time of the Constitution. A close look at their most important works on the topic of religious liberty can provide insights into how these disparate, yet biblically serious, religious thinkers viewed the right of private judgment. Their works show that the strongly Protestant content of this principle continued to play a vital role in America up to the constitutional period and beyond.

Elisha Williams was a Congregationalist and a defender of New England society. He nonetheless advocated for the right of private judgment in opposing the persecution of "new light" preachers during the time of the Great Awakening in Connecticut. Isaac Backus was one of the converts of the "new light" preachers whom Williams defended. Backus soon himself became an effective Baptist preacher and man of public affairs. To compare the thought of Backus and Williams is to see how the right of private judgment remained central to the Baptist tradition, even as it gained a foothold among the Baptists' historic Puritan opponents.

Elisha Williams, the Orthodox Puritan Lawyer

The "River gods" was the name given to a series of imposing aristocratic leaders in the towns along the Connecticut River in western Massachusetts during the eighteenth century.[23] Elisha Williams, born about 1694, was a prominent member of one of the "River god" families. He was part of a long line of eminent ministers, military men, and magistrates in the region and was a cousin of the Puritan divine Jonathan Edwards. His eventual role as dissenter from the decrees of the established order, then, was less a parish squabble and more akin to the drama of a Wagnerian opera—a battle among the gods of New England, with serious, colony-wide political careers and influences at stake.

Unlike his brothers and cousins, Elisha Williams did not follow the traditional Williams path to the pulpit.[24] While he studied theology as a youth, he took up teaching and avoided taking a pulpit. At one point, he studied law in preparation for a legal career, but he ended up using his legal training as a state assemblyman and a judge rather than a practicing lawyer. When he was twenty-five or twenty-six, he underwent a deeper conversion experience and decided to enter the ministry after all.

He then worked as a pastor for three or four years before becoming rector of Yale College. Because the previous head of Yale had tried to take the college down an Anglican, Arminian-friendly road, the trustees were anxious to reestablish a Reformed orthodoxy. Elisha more than met these expectations. In an opening sermon, he reaffirmed Calvin's teachings on utter depravity, election, predestination, and irresistible grace. He did so, though, in a way that showed he was open to understanding these doctrines in the context of insights provided by contemporary thinkers like John Locke.

Elisha's Seasonable Plea for the Liberty of Conscience

At the time of the First Great Awakening in the 1740s, Elisha's openness to the advancing nature of truth placed him at the center of the controversy between the religious enthusiasm of the "new lights" and the establishment defended by traditional "old lights." By this time, Elisha had terminated his successful stint at Yale in order to recover his health and to pursue a career in

Connecticut politics. Shortly thereafter, despite losing a race for governor, he was made a judge on the Superior Court and later became Speaker of the Connecticut Assembly.

In 1742, the Assembly passed a bill that placed stiff restrictions on itinerant preachers and also made it difficult even for recognized preachers to speak outside their own parishes. While Elisha was opposed to some of the excesses of the Awakening, he nonetheless supported what he thought was "agreeable to true Principles of Calvinism." Since he was not opposed to appropriate enthusiasm in religion, he was counted as an ally of the "new lights."

Elisha spoke against the new law in the assembly and in public. His stand came at a cost. He was aware of the risks but stated his intent to "act his own Principles, let Man make what Use of it they please, and he would serve Mankind as well as he could, so far as they would let him."[25] In 1743, the Assembly removed him from his judgeship, and shortly afterward he also lost his appointment as justice of the peace. While his political fortunes later rebounded, he lived in political limbo for some time. But he refused to either back down or remain silent on his politically unpopular position regarding religious liberty. The next year, he published his *Seasonable Plea for The Liberty of Conscience*, an exposition from reason and scripture of the principles of religious liberty in the context of the anti-itinerancy law.

A Seasonable Plea: Overview

In a short introduction, Elisha introduced what was his, and our, recurring theme: that as the "Sacred Scriptures are the *alone Rule of Faith and Practice* to a Christian … every Christian has a *Right of judging for himself* what he is to believe and practice." It was thus "perfectly inconsistent with any Power in the civil Magistrate to make any penal Laws in Matters of Religion."[26] Protestants, he noted, were agreed in the profession of this principle, but too many had departed from it in practice. He then launched into a philosophical and religious discourse to defend these two propositions.

The Origin and Ends of Civil Government
Whereas Penn had begun with the spiritual and divine, the nature and rights of God's kingdom, Elisha began with the temporal and earthly, the rights and limits of civil kingdoms. He provided first an overview of the origins and ends of civil government. His argument was based, by his own references, on the work of John Locke. He started with the equality people have in the state of nature, at least by the time they attain the age of reason. Reason was the basis

of understanding, free choice, and action and was thus, in Elisha's view, the basis of natural freedom. This very reason confirmed that all are born with equal rights to liberty and property.

But these rights to liberty and property could not be well preserved in the state of nature. Governments were instituted to preserve and protect these rights. The state drew its power from the people, and its legitimate end was the preservation of persons, liberties, and estates. Given these ends of government, Elisha moves on to discuss what liberty or power persons give up to the civil government to allow it to accomplish its ends.[27] The two primary sacrifices, he writes, are the *power* of the individual to do "whatever he judgeth fit" to preserve his person and property, and the *freedom* from societal laws that protect the persons and properties of others.

Rights Retained by the Individual

Elisha then comes to his main concern, the liberties and rights that people *retain* on entering civil society. He begins with the general rule that no more natural liberty or power is given up than is necessary for the preservation of persons and property.[28] Thus, persons retain all their natural liberties that have no relation to the ends of society. They can read Locke, or Milton, or the Bible, and the state has no business interfering.

Second, he states that persons retain the right of judging in matters of religion. This is a right based on the nature of humanity, which is that of a rational being, capable of knowing his or her Maker, and accountable to that Maker. As faith and religious practice depend on individual judgment, logically that faith cannot depend on the will of another human. Humanity's reason was a critical point for Elisha's argument. As he put it:

> This *Right of judging every one for himself in Matters of Religion* results from the Nature of Man, and is so inseparably connected therewith, that a Man can no more part with it than he can with his *Power of Thinking* ... —A man may alienate some Branches of his Property and give up his Rights in them to others; but he cannot transfer the *Rights of Conscience*, unless he could destroy his rational and moral Powers, or substitute some other to be judged for him at the Tribunal of God.[29]

Thus, Elisha took an approach that was opposite, though complementary, to Penn's. Rather than beginning with God's power and privileges, Elisha started his argument with the essence of the nature of man as God created him. But like Penn, in drawing on the nature of man and his relation to God,

Elisha did not base his reasoning explicitly on biblical authority. Rather, it was an argument from reason, an argument of natural theology.

Some have contended that this use of natural theology made Elisha more a disciple of Locke and the Enlightenment than Protestantism. But we know that Penn used the same kinds of natural rights arguments before Locke and that the distinction between Protestant and Enlightenment thought on this topic was not terribly clear. Elisha himself obviously believed that natural rights arguments were not in opposition to biblical ones, as he next turns to the Bible as an additional, second argument to support his thesis that religious matters were issues of private concern.

The Bible and the Right of Private Judgment

Elisha next appeals to the "truth, that the *Sacred Scriptures* are the alone Rule of Faith and Practice to every individual Christian." He begins an extended biblical survey that defends the same points he made in his previous argument from reason and nature. In so doing, he traces arguments strikingly similar to those of Locke and Penn about spiritual epistemology, authority, and the limits of human spiritual power and oversight. But where Penn started with texts regarding Christians being taught directly of God, and receiving truth directly from the Spirit, Elisha starts with texts asserting the basic Protestant doctrine of biblical supremacy in religious matters. He quotes 2 Tim. 3:15–16— scripture is "given by inspiration from God, and is profitable for Doctrine, for Reproof, for Correction, for Instruction in Righteousness"—and John. 20:31: "these things are written that ye might believe that Jesus is the Christ ... and that believing ye might have Life through his name."[30]

Having asserted biblical supremacy, Elisha moves on to the right of every person to "read, inquire and impartially judge" the meaning of scripture for himself. No person or group, whether pope, priest, bishop, pastor, counsel, or civil body, could be the final authority on biblical matters for the individual. If any earthly authority were the final arbiter of biblical matters, that authority would replace the scriptures as the final authority.[31]

This conclusion meant that believers had the duty to check pastors and teachers by the Word. Elisha cited Paul's commendation of the Bereans for their willingness to test his teachings against the Hebrew scriptures (Acts 17:11). He also quoted Paul as saying "I speak as to wise Men, judge ye what I say" (1 Cor 10:15). This deference to scripture alone, Elisha argued, defined the core of the biblical rule of faith and practice. If one accepted the primacy of human authority, effectively some person or persons would become the rule of faith and practice. The Bible is the tool, he asserted, by which Christ rules the church. Any other rule denies Christ the right to be "King in his own Kingdom."[32]

At this point, Elisha began to echo William Penn's arguments about the "rights of God." It brought him to a similar final point regarding civil power: it has no jurisdiction in religious matters—both because it has nowhere been affirmatively granted such jurisdiction *and* because of the existing jurisdiction over spiritual matters claimed by God and Christ. In his view, just as an Englishman is subject to the laws of England, and not of France or Spain, so the Christian is subject to the laws of God and Christ in religious matters, and not to human laws. He quoted scripture on this point: "No man can serve two masters" (Mt 6:24).[33]

Limits of Earthly Civil Power

Elisha then set out "corollaries" of these principles from reason and scripture. The first is that the civil authority has no power to "make or ordain Articles of Faith, Creeds, Forms of Worship or Church Government." These matters have no relationship to the legitimate ends of civil society, and they invade the rights of Christ.[34] And if the state has no business running the church itself, it certainly has no right to "establish any Religion," for example, religious beliefs, or rules, or kinds of worship, on penalty of civil law.

To accept that human authorities might so legislate is to confer on them the attribute of infallibility. Rather than a single pope, those who accept civil rule by use of religious standards create literally hundreds of popes. Each state and each government is now a final religious authority within its own jurisdiction. But if they err, then what they enforce is no longer the Bible, but human authority. Enforcement of human spiritual authority plainly violates the biblical rule of faith and practice. In setting out this argument, Elisha expressed a rather sophisticated view of Bible reading and interpretation. He noted that, as the Bible was not written as a coherent, self-executing legal code, for the legislature to "enforce" the Bible, it would first have to interpret the Bible. Thus, what the legislature would implement will not be the Bible itself, but the legislature's view or understanding of what the Bible teaches.[35]

This difference between "the Bible" and "the Bible as understood" was an important basis of Elisha's view of liberty. Thus, his commitment to religious liberty rested in part, as Penn's and Locke's did, on personal epistemological abilities and limits in spiritual matters. Again, it was not a denial of truth but the acceptance that spiritual truth must be internalized to be effective. This can only happen if truths about God are understood and accepted by the believer.

The Meaning of "Establishment of Religion"

In his discussion of civil rule, Elisha provides insights into what "religious establishment" meant in the mid-eighteenth century. Today, some insist that a religious establishment referred only to the creation of a national or state church. But Elisha uses the term more broadly. An establishment of religion for him meant state efforts to enforce any standard, practice, or rule based on the scriptures rather than on the legitimate civil ends of government. Such ends could include morality and virtue, insofar as they affected society as a whole, but laws with exclusively or primarily religious purposes were not appropriate.[36]

But at the same time, he was far from being a modern American constitutionalist. He allowed that the state, while it could not legislate on issues of religion, could recommend or encourage ("Approbation" or "Recommendation" were the terms Elisha used) certain religious beliefs and practices. He also saw no conflict between his argument against establishment and the civil enforcement of agreements between pastors and their religious societies for financial support.[37] He supported, in other words, enforcement of a tax on members of a church to support a pastor, whether or not an individual member voted for or agreed with the theology of that pastor.

While this church tax practice differed from a general assessment in support of religion, it contained enough of an entanglement of church and state to fail to pass modern constitutional muster. It illustrates that while the general principle of the right of private judgment was filtering into the larger Protestant community, it initially received a narrower application than it had in the dissenting communities from which it originated.

The Extent and Limits of Ecclesiastical Authority

As to ecclesiastical rulers, Elisha says that Christ has limited their authority to persuasive teaching.[38] This limit was shown by Christ's last instructions to his disciples: he instructed them to go into all the world, "teaching them to observe all things that I have commanded you" (Mt 28:20). The church, as a voluntary society, has the authority to require only those things of its members that Christ required of them through the Bible.

This provision limits the church in at least two ways: first, it cannot use civil force in applying those requirements; it is limited to spiritual disciplines. Second, it cannot enforce matters not required by the Bible itself. Elisha allows that certain things that are left unspecified in the Bible, such as the time and place of religious meetings, must be decided in some way, and this he leaves in the hands of the local congregation to determine, by majority vote. But even here, if the minority disagrees strongly with the result, civil force is disallowed. The minority can withdraw from the community and worship as they feel conscientiously compelled to do.[39]

At the heart of Christian liberty, Elisha argued, is a prohibition against men assuming power over others in spiritual matters. This could be done by either creating rules beyond those set down by Christ or enforcing them in a manner other than prescribed by Christ, that is, teaching and persuasion. Elisha quoted Matthew 23:8–10: "call no Man Your Father upon Earth, for one is your Father which is in Heaven: Neither be ye called Masters, for one is your Master even Christ." Earthly rulers simply lacked the jurisdiction to legislate in spiritual matters. When earthly rulers made that attempt, it was simply "Tyranny."[40]

Finally, Elisha appealed to the rights of Englishmen, both under the Magna Carta and the Act of Toleration. The Connecticut charter, Elisha reminded his readers, was subject to the Act of Toleration, and the anti-itinerancy law could thus jeopardize their colonial status. But this, he noted, was a relatively small matter, given the fact that the right of private judgment and religious liberty was not conferred by the Magna Carta or Act of Toleration, but rather came from God. And all those who infringed on it would find at the last judgment, he warned, that "Christ will be King in his own Kingdom."[41]

Elisha's views on church and state were not the majority opinion in the New England of his day. Still, since he continued to be a respected religious and community leader, it is apparent that the principle of the right of private judgment had gained a foothold in New England. This happened not only through the growth of the Baptists, but also through the infiltration of dissenting Protestant views into the opinions of otherwise traditional Congregationalists.

Importantly, for my argument, Williams read both Locke and dissenting Protestants seamlessly. For him, Locke's arguments were compatible with scripture and indeed represented the same ideas, if formulated and conceived in more modern and philosophical language. That scripture and Locke were in harmony, at least on the issue of toleration, is a view of Locke that was also found on the opposite end of the New England social spectrum, as we shall now see.

Isaac Backus, Self-Made Dissenter

Unlike Elisha Williams, Isaac Backus did not have the benefit of university training. He was a self-taught, yet remarkably effective, advocate for religious liberty.[42] He was born into a relatively comfortable Connecticut family in

1724, with a father who served in the state Assembly. But at the age of sixteen, Isaac's father died. His mother now had to raise eleven children on her own. Isaac was needed all the more in the fields of the family farm, and college was out of the question.

Although the family had been dutiful members of the standing order, Backus's religious commitment had been, by his later accounting, shallow and careless. But the time of crisis in the Backus family coincided with the outbreak of the Great Awakening and the preaching of George Whitefield in 1740. Because of that preaching, Isaac's grieving mother was reawakened with a new and deeper conversion experience, and shortly thereafter so was Isaac.

Soon Backus was involved in his first religious controversy, when he and his fellow "new light" enthusiasts began to object to the halfway covenant. This measure was an arrangement in the Congregational church whereby those with no profession of conversion could obtain a certain kind of church membership that allowed them to have their children baptized. Defeated in their attempts to reform this system, Backus and other "new lights" withdrew to begin their own congregation on "purer" principles, allowing as members only those who were converted. But Backus and his friends found that by separating, they had entered uncharted and perilous legal waters.

The New England establishment had, grudgingly, granted a certain level of toleration to recognized religious groups, such as Anglicans, Quakers, and Baptists. But these exceptions were carefully restricted. They did not apply to those merely seeking a "purer form" of the established church. Backus and his friends had effectively declared revolution against the existing order; as a consequence, many of them were fined and imprisoned.

Thus began Backus's first of many experiences in opposing the state enforcement of religious orthodoxy. It was a journey that took him from the established church to the separatists, and eventually, by 1751, into the Baptist Church. It was during his time as a Baptist minister that he wrote and spoke most widely on issues of religious freedom. Backus's first substantial work on liberty of conscience appeared in 1770, when he objected to the excommunication of a family who objected to infant baptism from the Standing Church in Berwick, Connecticut.

The title of his work, *A Seasonable Plea for Liberty of Conscience*, suggests that Backus was familiar with Elisha Williams's earlier work of the same name.[43] The title may have been meant to tweak the social establishment that claimed to honor religious liberty by borrowing from one of their prominent thinkers. It was here that Backus first favorably cited Locke on the proper role of the civil magistrate, mentioning the *Letter on Toleration* by name.[44]

While Backus's *Seasonable Plea* contained the core of his philosophy on religious liberty, it did not set out any real detail. Three years later, Backus had an
opportunity to expand on this foundation, which led to a complete statement
on the role of church and state and a full exposition of his theory of the two
governments.[45] The occasion had to do with the Baptists' ongoing struggle
against the New England system of religious taxes.

Some background is needed to understand this 1773 work. By the late
1760s, the scattered Baptist churches had organized into an association to
pressure the New England states to exempt their denomination from taxes.
Massachusetts continued to allow general taxation by cities and towns in support of local congregations of the majority church, which was almost always
Congregationalist. The association, after appointing Backus "Agent for the
Baptists in New England," tasked him with seeking remedies for tax griev-
ances, either in the courts or the legislature. Backus had some success in this
role. At one point in 1771 he appealed to the king of England and had the
satisfaction of seeing the king veto a Massachusetts religious tax law as insuf-
ficiently protective of the religious freedom of minorities. As a result, the state
was forced to expand its system of tax exemption for religious minorities.

Yet the tax exemption framework remained cumbersome. It was a system of mere toleration that led to prejudice against the Baptists. They were
considered by many Congregationalists to be tax evaders. The application of
the exemptions was in the hands of local towns and parishes, which at times
abused them. Often local officials denied tax exemptions to Baptists and other
minorities on technicalities or even on mere pretext.

In 1773, the association considered whether it should adopt a denomina-
tion-wide policy of civil disobedience and refuse to seek the exemption or pay
the taxes. In the end, they authorized each church to decide whether to take
this drastic step. At the same time, they voted to publish and distribute copies of Backus's *Appeal to the Public for Religious Liberty*, with its attack on the
"tyranny" of the tax exemption system.

Backus's *Appeal to the Public for Religious Liberty*

In their defenses of religious liberty, William Penn and Elisha Williams had
started at opposite ends of the natural theology spectrum. Penn began with
the nature and rights of God and the heavenly government, Elisha with the
nature and obligations of man and civil government. But Backus started
at a third point not on this continuum—that of biblical revelation and its
teaching regarding the fallen nature of man and the proper roles of civil

and ecclesiastical rulers.[46] Despite these different starting points, the three positions made up a connected triangle of ideas about God, church, society, and the individual. While their arguments began in different places, each of them included all these elements and related them to each other in a similar manner.

Backus explicitly rejected Locke's reasoning about the state of nature. Instead, Backus asserted that because of man's fall, and his subsequent sinful nature, humans possess no real freedom or liberty by nature, but are in bondage to sin. Man does not give up rights and freedom by entering society. Rather, man must "submit to some government in order to enjoy any liberty and security at all."[47] Despite this turn to scripture, Backus drew skillfully on Locke. He quoted the philosopher with approval, especially his *Letter on Toleration*. In other works, including the *Seasonable Plea* (discussed earlier), Backus approvingly cited Locke's views on churches being "voluntary societies," as well as on limiting the civil magistrate's jurisdiction to temporal matters.[48]

Backus also engaged Locke's works on epistemology and human understanding. He agreed with Locke's *Essay on Understanding* that it is not freedom to violate the teachings of reason. He differed with Locke, however, over whether man has the ability to obey reason on his own. Backus insisted that God's grace is needed to live consistently with true reason. Finally, Backus himself saw the parallel between Locke's view of the personal, subjective nature of understanding and the Baptist's view of the role of the Holy Spirit in experiencing spiritual truth. Backus argued that carnal, unconverted men could not be ministers, because ideas were, as Locke stated, the result of a direct sense experience, not just abstract definitions. Men must experience spiritual truths, not just think about them, to be able to preach and teach those truths. As Backus put it, "experimental knowledge" of spiritual things, as mediated by the Holy Spirit, is necessary for ministers to lead others to an experiential knowledge of the truth.[49]

These comments by Backus reveal that he and other dissenting Protestants saw a similarity between Locke's epistemology and views of spiritual knowledge held by Protestant thinkers themselves. Locke's teaching about the need for the individual to exercise his judgment to weigh the probabilities of truth paralleled the dissenting Protestant view that spiritual truths must be internally appropriated and understood to have any worth.

Backus provides an example of the careful and selective manner in which many religious thinkers in colonial America dealt with Locke and his writings. There was neither an unreflective embrace of the whole nor a wholesale rejection of the British philosopher. Rather, there was a careful, critical, reasonably nuanced distinction between those aspects of his philosophy that were seen to be consistent with biblical teachings and those that were seen to conflict with scripture.

As one scholar has put it, "Backus began to use Locke, but at the same time reinterpreted Lock to suit his purposes."[50] In actuality, there was use, reinterpretation, and, in some areas, rejection. But the rejection of certain parts of Locke's views, especially those that seemed to suggest an overly optimistic view of human nature and unaided human effort, did not stop thinkers such as Backus from using other parts that were consistent with scripture and historic Protestant thought. The latter category contained especially ideas of spiritual epistemology and of the differing roles of civil and ecclesiastical government.

Consider Backus's rejection of Locke's views on the original state of nature and the loss of liberty entailed by the creation of a state. Rather than a state of nature, Backus begins with the two kinds of government that God has appointed—civil and ecclesiastical. The civil government, rather than being destructive of rights, is instituted, in Backus's view, to create the possibility of freedom and rights. But because Backus believed that the civil and ecclesiastical governments were very different, he followed Locke's modern enunciation of Luther's two kingdoms model.

Backus's argument for religious freedom was largely based on this model and the differences between the two kingdoms. Locke and Backus agreed in embracing the heritage of dissenting Protestant theology regarding the relationship between civil and church powers. Backus rejected, however, what he viewed as Locke's efforts to place that heritage on different philosophical foundations, such as an enlightened human nature, rather than the biblical foundations that Luther or Roger Williams or the English Baptists had used.

Spiritual Standards of Epistemology, Authority, and Use of Force

In his *Seasonable Plea*, Backus ended up with Elisha Williams and Locke in regard to spiritual epistemology, religious authority, and the use of civil force. On the way there, however, he parted ways with them on two points. He argued, in contrast to Locke and Penn, that the Baptists were not making arguments from natural rights. He insisted that his claims rested on the "Charter privilege," the legal rights of Englishmen to be free of religious discrimination. Even this close to the American Revolution, the Baptists had not yet fully decided which camp, loyalist or revolutionary, would best defend their interests.

In 1773, when Backus published his *Seasonable Plea*, colonists were using the language of rights to propose revolution against England. Yet at this point, the Baptists' best defense against religious discrimination in the colonies came from their appeal to Charter privileges under British law. This protection is illustrated by Backus's earlier invalidation of a colonial law by an appeal to the king. So in 1773, Backus hedged his bets. He rested his case for religious liberty on practical legal protections rather than more grandiose, but less enforceable, philosophical principles, which might actually have undercut the existing legal protections from Britain. Later, after the Baptists largely sided with the revolutionaries, he cited Locke favorably to support the claim that natural rights for mankind included not just life, liberty, and property but also conscience.[51]

Concluding his 1773 tract, Backus directly referred to the principle underlying his arguments—the right of private judgment in religious matters held by each person. Echoing Elisha Williams, he stated that the disability of civil government in spiritual matters rested on the truth that "each one has an equal right to judge for himself, for we must all appear before the judgment seat of Christ" (2 Cor. 5:10). Every man has not only the right but the responsibility to "judge for himself" and to act "according to the *persuasion of his own mind.*" By contrast, the empowerment of civil legislatures to make religious laws meant popery. There was "no more warrant from divine truth" for men to appoint representatives, he wrote, to "impose religious taxes" than they "have to appoint Peter or the Virgin Mary to represent them before the throne above."[52]

To place an earthly power between God and man, he argues, is to usurp the role and place of God. It makes men judges of spiritual matters, a role they have no right to play.[53] The exemption system was based on a notion of inequality. Why do the Baptists need to seek exemptions from the established church, and not vice versa? He then returns to his theme of "no jurisdiction" of civil authority in religious matters.

Backus ultimately rested his defense of full religious liberty on the three points common to Locke, Elisha Williams, and Penn: (1) all spiritual knowledge is personal; (2) there is no ultimate earthly spiritual authority; and (3) therefore, the civil power has no jurisdiction in spiritual matters. In colonial America, these points had become the hallmarks of the principle of the right of private judgment in religious matters for most Protestants. Of course the most direct influence on Backus, as a Baptist, was the writings and work of Roger Williams, which Backus used extensively in writing his history of New England.[54]

Backus's Continuing Public Efforts

A few years later, Backus wrote his famous multivolume *History of New England.* In the first two volumes, he discusses the arguments of Elisha

Williams's *Seasonable Plea for the Rights of Conscience*. He refers to them as undercutting the very system of church/state cooperation that existed in New England. It is not clear from his comments whether he read Williams's work before he wrote his own primary pamphlets on religious liberty in the 1770s.[55]

By the late 1790s, Backus again used language promoting religious freedom that echoed that of both Williams and Locke. A primary example of this was a proposal for a bill of rights in the Massachusetts constitution in 1779. While Backus's proposal did not succeed (the Puritan standing order of church/state cooperation would remain in place for another half century), it did provide a succinct statement of Backus's mature views and those of the Baptists he represented. In the section dealing with rights of conscience he wrote:

> As God is the only worthy object of all religious worship, and nothing can be true religion but a voluntary obedience unto his revealed will, *of which each rational soul has an equal right to judge for itself*; every person has an unalienable right to act in all religious affairs according to the full persuasion of his own mind, where others are not injured thereby. And civil rulers are so far from having any right to empower any person or person, *to judge for others in such affairs*, and to *enforce their judgment* with the sword, that their power ought to be exerted to protect all persons and societies, within their jurisdiction from being injured or interrupted in their free enjoyment of this right, under any pretence whatsoever.[56]

Backus's commitment to religious liberty, though, did not mean a rejection of public or civil morality. William McLoughlin, a leading historian of both Backus and the American Baptists, has documented Backus's commitment to submit to the government in matters related to public peace, order, and morals. Baptists did not abandon Puritan laws restricting profanity, gambling, dancing, theater going, and intemperance, but these were not considered primarily spiritual matters. Rather, they were safeguards of the community's public health and welfare, an important part of which was financial, social, and sexual morality.[57]

This morality, however, was accessible and potentially understandable by all from the teachings of nature: it was not dependent exclusively on revealed religion or scripture. By contrast, Backus felt different about religious duties touching matters revealed only in scripture. For instance, unlike many Protestants of his day, Backus did not support civil Sunday laws. About Sunday laws, Backus wrote: "we believe that attendance upon public worship and keeping the first day of the week holy to God are duties to be inculcated and enforced by his laws instead of the laws of men."[58]

The rising stature of the Baptists in Massachusetts was indicated by the fact that twenty to twenty-five Baptists were part of the four hundred delegates sent to the federal ratifying convention in Boston in 1788. Backus was one of them. He spoke and voted in favor of the new Constitution, noting special approval of the "exclusion of any religious test" for officeholding in the new federal government.[59]

Backus and the Shaping of Baptist Advocacy

Both Backus and Williams were important for the way they melded Lockean ideas with existing Puritan and Baptist thought. This process was, in some ways, less difficult for Backus and the Baptists than for Elisha Williams. Though he was more cosmopolitan and sophisticated in his education, Elisha needed to modify historic Puritan theology to fit with Locke. The Calvinist magisterial tradition had not explored the full consequences of the doctrine of the priesthood of all believers for the role of church and state, and so maintained a quasi-theocratic state order.

Backus, on the other hand, could look back beyond Locke to earlier Baptists who had taken church/state positions very similar to his own. Backus could cite Locke on the incapacity of the civil magistrate in religious matters, but then back it up with a reference to Roger Williams, who wrote forty years prior to Locke.[60] For Backus, Locke was merely a more modern and sophisticated voice articulating concepts basic to Baptist thought for nearly two centuries.

These facts help explain why Elisha Williams's piece was an unusual example of Puritan advocacy for religious liberty. It also explains why Massachusetts continued its established churches for two or three more decades longer than the rest of the colonies. Backus, on the other hand, was by no means the only Baptist to speak as he did. He was merely a leading voice in a Baptist chorus calling for religious liberty. But since he was a prominent spokesperson, Backus's rhetoric was echoed by other Baptists. A dramatic example of his influence is seen in Virginia in the 1780s with the adoption of the Virginia Statute of Religious Freedom.

The story of the passage of the famous Virginia Statute, which disestablished the Anglican church in Virginia, is considered a victory for the

Enlightenment duo of Jefferson, who drafted the statute in 1777, and Madison, who helped pass it in 1786.[61] The Statute represented the culmination of the resistance to a bill submitted by Patrick Henry to lay assessments or taxes for the support of the Christian ministry. The battle over religious assessments was the occasion of Madison drafting his "Memorial and Remonstrance," probably the most detailed defense of religious liberty and disestablishment by an American founder. Madison's *Memorial* has been justly called "a cornerstone in the American tradition of religious liberty."[62]

Less well known are petitions in opposition to Patrick Henry's assessment bill submitted by Baptists. These petitions contained several times as many signatures as Madison's petition, which had about fifteen hundred subscribers on thirteen separate copies.[63] One church petition, known as the Great Baptists petition, garnered nearly five thousand signatures on twenty-nine separate copies.[64] Thousands of others signed Presbyterian petitions that also used religious argument. The Baptist petitions, which invoked the "spirit of the Gospel," presented a Backus-like view of Locke (indeed, some versions of the Baptist petition invoked the "Great Mr. Lock" by name)[65] rather than the more Enlightenment Locke of Madison's petition (although, as we will see, Madison's statement reflects the same elements of Locke, which parallel dissenting Protestant thought).

The Great Baptists petition declared: "We do … earnestly declare against … [the assessment bill] as being contrary to the spirit of the Gospel and the Bill of Rights."[66] It argued that Christianity had been maintained without the aid of the state for its first several centuries. Constantine's support of the church ended persecution of Christianity, but it also opened the church to much "error, superstition, and immorality." The petition also noted the "state of Pennsylvania" as an example of a government that flourished without an established religion.[67]

This overtly evangelical, biblically conservative view of the separation of church and state had a great and even decisive influence on Virginian disestablishment. John Ragosta has just recently documented the influence of religious dissenters in Virginia in bringing about a sea-change in the state's politics and church/state arrangement during the revolutionary period and immediately afterward. He persuasively argues that the Anglican establishment in Virginia had to negotiate and accommodate the dissenters' desire for religious liberty to gain their support and involvement in political matters surrounding the Revolution. Having been drawn into the political fray, though, when the Revolution was over, the dissenters stayed and worked effectively with Enlightenment elements to prevent the establishment from regaining its former control. Thus, it was primarily because of religious dissenters' efforts and views that the sentiments of Madison's *Memorial* and the freedoms of Jefferson's statute won the day in Virginia.[68]

Ten times as many Virginians signed these overtly evangelical petitions, proclaiming the "spirit of the gospel," than signed Madison's more Enlightenment-oriented *Memorial and Remonstrance.* The Baptists in Virginia had been flourishing since the early 1760s. Their separationist views on church and state had begun to influence other religious groups in Virginia that had a more magisterial heritage. A key example is the Presbyterians, led for many years in Virginia by Samuel Davies. In seeking toleration for his church, he had come into contact with Baptists and Quaker liberty advocates during the 1750s and beyond.[69]

Unsurprisingly, the Presbyterian language and rhetoric in seeking toleration began to reflect Baptist rhetoric. In 1776, one Presbyterian averred that the Anglican establishment was in violation of "their natural Rights; and in their consequences a restraint upon *freedom of inquiry and private judgment.*"[70] This petitioner understood the principle of private judgment as essentially Protestant, and believed that any failure to follow it would erect "a Chair of Infallibility which would lead us back to the Church of Rome."[71]

The following year, 1777, the same Presbyterians objected again to a general assessment for teachers of religion. They argued first, in Lockean terms, that "the duty we owe our Creator, and the manner of discharging it, can only be directed by reason and conviction, and is nowhere cognizable but at the tribunal of the universal Judge."[72] But in the next paragraph they invoked the right of judgment in an obviously biblical context: "to *judge for ourselves,* and to engage in the exercise of religion agreeable to the dictates of our own conscience is an unalienable right, which upon the principles that the gospel was first propagated, and the reformation from Popery carried on, can never be transferred to another."[73]

To be sure, the Presbyterians were not entirely united on their approach to the question. Henry's bill had gained momentum in 1784 when certain Presbyterian groups supported his effort.[74] But by the following year, even these Presbyterian groups switched over to join the Baptists in opposing the bill because it made "the Legislature judges of religious truth." The Presbyterians used more language invoking natural religion in their petitions than the Baptists did.[75] But even the Presbyterians combined an appeal to nature with direct biblical references, identifying themselves as "subjections of Jesus Christ, who are wholly opposed to the exercise of spiritual powers by civil authorities."[76] Madison's *Memorial and Remonstrance* has survived most prominently in America's collective memory of Henry's assessment bill. But Madison's work was merely the tip of a much larger iceberg of opposition, with the vast majority of it representing the explicitly biblical, dissenting Protestant thought of Backus, the Baptists, and even the Virginia Presbyterians. Ragosta's observation that "current legal and historic literature and judicial decisions have failed adequately to listen to the voice of Virginia's dissenters" seems absolutely correct.[77]

Moreover, Virginia was not the only place where the Baptists played a central role in disestablishment and where they influenced others to support it. For example, they were also active in Vermont, where over a number of years they petitioned the legislature for a repeal of religious tax laws.[78] The Baptists came fairly late to Vermont; their first church there was founded in 1768, and the second did not form until 1780. But after that their growth was rapid, approaching nearly fifty separate churches by the turn of the century. As their numbers grew, so did their political muscle—and their willingness to flex it through petitions for freedom from the religious tax system.

One petition, delivered in 1794 by several different Baptist churches, said that the enforced church taxes were "subversive of the Rights of conscience ... and of an exceeding dangerous Tendency depriving us of the sacred Rights of free citizens ... for it is our conscientious & avowed Sentiments that civil authority have no Right to intermeddle with ecclesiastical affairs." By the early 1800s, a number of prominent Baptists became members of the Vermont legislature, including Aaron Leland as speaker of the house. Finally, with Baptist efforts from both within and without, the legislature repealed the religious tax statute.[79]

The Baptists came similarly late to New Hampshire, having only one church before 1770. But over the next two decades, the Baptists grew to more than forty churches. They were on the front lines of the battle for religious disestablishment in that state, too. New Hampshire laws were more liberal toward dissenters than those of other New England states. But local towns were still able to assess citizens' property for taxes to support the majority church, and they did not always exempt dissenters. Still, probably in part because of the less onerous burdens on dissenters, it took longer for Baptist efforts to achieve full disestablishment in New Hampshire. By 1817, the struggle was joined by some important Methodist leaders, as well as a Unitarian in the House; in two years they ended establishment in New Hampshire.[80]

The Baptists also played a central role in disestablishment in Connecticut. Following years of guerilla-style politics, including much sniping at the religious establishment in the form of petitions, sermons, and letters, the

Baptists joined forces with the Methodists to mount a concerted effort for full disestablishment at the 1818 state constitutional convention. Both denominations appear to have coordinated internally and with each other. Throughout the state, resolutions by the two groups were passed that shared the identical preamble: "Resolved that no constitution of civil government shall receive our approbation or support unless it contains a provision for securing the full and complete enjoyment of religious liberty."[81]

The declarations themselves urged an offensive against the state-supported religious tax scheme. As one declared,

> *Resolved* as the sense of this meeting that Religion, or the duty men owe their Creator, and the manner of discharging it, ought to be left to the reason, conviction, and conscience of every man—that these rights are inalienable—that all acts of the civil magistrate, either in the form of constitutional provisions or the ordinary acts of the legislature which in any manner restrain the free exercise of religion or compel any man to contribute to the support of religious worship or the public teaching thereof are oppressive.

The efforts of these two denominations, combined with those of the growing community of deists, were enough to achieve victory for the forces of disestablishment when the Connecticut constitution was approved in 1818.[82]

The story of Backus and the Baptists is a signal account of how a group that had originally been minority outsiders in colonial America began to set the church/state agenda on a state-by-state basis in the early republic. Wherever they gained influence, new church/state arrangements soon followed. Remarkable in this story is not the Baptist opposition to the state church in their early years. History is full of outsiders who protest the abuses, perceived and otherwise, of groups in power. Truly unusual with the Baptists was their continued opposition to a state church even when they had the numbers and influence to control the levers of power. This consistency of their church/state views once they gained political power supports the belief that their position was a principled aspect of dissenting Protestant theology. These principles retained their influence and force even when those who held them came to positions of political power.

The same point can be made about the writings of Elisha Williams. Although he wrote from within the majority party in Connecticut, he was willing to extend freedom of religious expression to dissenting minorities. Both he and Backus were influenced by Locke and used his ideas in promoting their own. But they did not do so uncritically. Backus especially was quick to point out where Locke's presuppositions or conclusions conflicted with what Backus viewed as biblical orthodoxy. But on questions of religious freedom, both Elisha Williams and Backus saw Locke as expressing ideas about belief, conscience, and religious freedom that were in fundamental agreement with core Protestant ideas on the right of private judgment and biblical teaching.

Conclusion

We have seen how this principle of dissenting Protestantism influenced thinkers in both the dissenting and magisterial Protestant communities of colonial America. Even the Puritan strongholds of New England began to open up to some of these ideas, through the efforts of moderate members of the establishment like Elisha Williams and the growth of activist Baptists like Isaac Backus. The Middle Colonies were most open to the influence of dissenting Protestantism, in good part due to the influence of Penn on his own colonies and the pressure this influence created in other Middle Colonies, such as New York, to increase religious toleration as a way of competing for immigrants.

The south was not far behind, especially in Locke-influenced North Carolina, which had a practical toleration that matched what was found in the middle colonies. Virginia, though, was resistant to religious equality for many years, given its commitment to class hierarchy and the established Anglican church. But this commitment weakened when a combination of dissenting Protestants, including Baptists and Scotch-Irish Presbyterians, worked with some elite, educated landowners to push back the religious establishment.

How notions of disestablishment made inroads into the educated elite, who were often more influenced by Enlightenment-style thought than the laborer, farmer, or small businessman, is examined in the next chapter. Set in the mid-Atlantic colony of New York, it is the story of the first attempt in America to establish a major educational institution for public, rather than sectarian, purposes. It occurred nearly a half century before Thomas Jefferson founded the University of Virginia on a nonsectarian basis, and it illustrates both the growth of religious freedom in the non-Quaker middle colonies, as well as the strong presence of theology in what is sometimes considered simply secular, Enlightenment thought.

4

Revolutionary and Governor

WILLIAM LIVINGSTON OPPOSES ANGLICAN CONTROL OF KING'S COLLEGE

IN 1752, the founders of King's College, the forerunner of Columbia University, proposed to organize their school as an Anglican institution supported by the public.[1] In so doing, they ran into powerful opposing arguments based on a relatively new and ultimately enduring metaphor—the free marketplace of ideas. The Anglicans' most articulate foe, the New York attorney William Livingston, set out these arguments in a series of articles in a journal called the *Independent Reflector*. He detailed the vital role a college could play in the social and political development of New York, and argued that an Anglican establishment of the college would pose a serious, if not insurmountable, threat to that role.[2]

The contest between the two sides was heated and protracted. Neither side fully prevailed. The heated rhetoric of Livingston and his allies delayed the College's opening for two years. But when it opened, it was under Anglican control. Due to Livingston's influence, however, it did not initially receive certain public funds the founders had anticipated obtaining. Two years later, in a legislative compromise, the College was given a partial allotment of the public funds.[3]

But if the Anglicans won the immediate battle, Livingston and his allies triumphed in the larger war. Until after the Revolutionary War, King's College carried the stigma of illiberality and sectarianism that the *Reflector* had first fixed on it. More important, the separation of religious advocacy and education from public funds that the *Reflector* advocated became the model that the national government, and most state governments, began to follow over the next forty or fifty years.

Indeed, some modern historians point to the free-market-of-ideas construct that undergirded Livingston's arguments as the key principle that drove disestablishment in the early republic. "The Founding Fathers, rather than designing a church-state framework of their own, endorsed the emerging free marketplace of religion." In this view, the growing multiplicity of religious opinions made it necessary, in order to maintain peace, for all views to compete freely and equally in the public arena. The fact of so much diversity made the establishment of any one view impracticable. As James Madison frequently noted, no single group could or would obtain the upper hand for long. Such an establishment was also illogical, since the sheer variety of views meant that the legislature could never be certain which view was correct.[4]

The free-marketplace-of-ideas metaphor is today generally regarded as primarily a secular, Enlightenment construct based on the model of the economic free market.[5] It is thought to rely on the existence of a wide diversity of views and the presumed relativistic nature of those views.[6] Many scholars see its roots as lying largely in the free market thought of the Scottish Enlightenment economist and philosopher Adam Smith.[7] Smith applied his free market economic analysis to the question of the monopoly of religious establishments and advocated a free market for religion.[8] The most vocal American advocates of this religious marketplace view at the time of the founding were Thomas Jefferson and James Madison, also considered primarily Enlightenment rather than religious figures.[9]

Some scholars have concluded that traditional religious views, with their reliance on authority and dogma, were a threat to the freedom of this marketplace. As Gordon Wood put it, "many religious groups resisted the disintegrative effects of the Enlightenment belief in ... separation of church and state."[10] More recently, Philip Hamburger has claimed that the marketplace idea, insofar as it contributed to the actual separation of church and state, was purely a secular, anticlerical idea with no meaningful religious content or basis.[11]

Insofar as evangelical Christian impulses contributed to the free market framework, the story goes, this contribution was primarily due to the multiplication of convictions and groups growing out of the Great Awakening. A nod is usually given to the Great Awakening's focus on the importance of the individual experience and conscience in matters of religion.[12] But the emphasis is on the diversity created by the Awakening rather than religious dissenters' substantive ideological contributions to religious freedom. Bernard Bailyn has described these contributions of religion as "unsystematic, incomplete, pragmatic," and "little grounded in doctrine."[13]

A close examination of the King's College debate calls for a modification of these views. Instead of a thoroughly Enlightenment position replacing a thoroughly traditional one, Livingston's writings suggest a close connection between evangelical, specifically dissenting Protestant thought in relation to the right of private judgment and Enlightenment thought on the free market of ideas. Moreover, the circumstances of Livingston's life reinforce this reading of the religious roots of the idea.

Crucial to the market model, as expressed by Livingston (though the term "arena" serves better to capture the noncommercial conflict between ideas), were the inherent personal rights of private judgment in both scriptural interpretation and other religious questions. The arena model did not assume the denial or relativization of truth, as is often the case today. Rather, it was viewed as a forum in which to sort out truth from error. Indeed, while Livingston often spoke the new language of reason versus blind adherence to authority, he also spoke of the authority of scripture as providing a base for the independence of personal judgment.

Livingston's writings are important for understanding the overlap or mixture of dissenting Protestant and Enlightenment thought in arguments for disestablishment in colonial and early republican America. In particular, he provides a bridge connecting the thought and writing of Elisha Williams, with whom he studied as an undergraduate, and later revolutionary figures like Madison and Jefferson, who were contemporaries and colleagues of Livingston in the War for Independence.

Livingston wrote a great deal on the topic of church and state. He not only published five separate articles on the King's College matter but also penned more than a half dozen other articles in the same year, expressing his views on religion and civil freedom. Thus, his particular arguments in the College debate can be set in the larger context of his religious, political, and philosophical views. They help reveal the close connection between dissenting Protestant thought and what has been termed Enlightenment or republican thought in the quarter century prior to the Revolution. In so doing, they add to the chain of arguments that stretch from Luther and the Anabaptists in the 1520s to the Virginia Baptists in the 1770s. They show that there was more to American disestablishment than just pragmatism, and that even its Enlightenment foundations drew significantly from dissenting Protestant logic and thought.

Livingston played a very public role in the King's College debate and was also a member of the College's founding board of trustees. He went on to have a very influential and active public life. Following a move to New Jersey, he was appointed a delegate to the First and Second Continental Congresses. He later became governor of New Jersey during the Revolutionary War and served as commander-in-chief of the New Jersey militia during that war. He served as governor of New Jersey for nearly fourteen years, essentially the remainder of his life. During this time he was also a delegate to the Constitutional Convention of 1787 and was a signatory to the U.S. Constitution.[14] In short, he was a founder and influential in his day, although somewhat obscure beyond his generation. His relative obscurity today is a special pity, as his *Reflector* articles give probably the most complete and systematic record we have of the thoughts of one of the founders on the topic of disestablishment.[15] His writings on the King's College controversy outlined a mature position on disestablishment in the world of higher education more than fifty years before Thomas Jefferson founded the nonsectarian University of Virginia.

Livingston's writings reveal that the marketplace/arena metaphor was not exclusively or even primarily a secular construct. Rather, religious and theological ideas contributed important and central elements to this model. Enlightenment and evangelical thought are at times viewed as separate and often conflicting modes of analysis and thought. But it has been recognized for some time now that significant strains of Enlightenment thought, most specifically what has been termed the moderate and Scottish Enlightenments, were sympathetic to and even influenced by Protestant thought.[16]

This recognition suggests that moderate Enlightenment views and evangelical thought were more like Siamese twins, conjoined in places, sharing similar, if not identical ideas, while possessing separate identities and vocabularies. Perhaps they were Siamese twins destined to be separated, but they were not separate in the minds of many American religious and political thinkers of the eighteenth century.[17]

This chapter will first look at Livingston's background, educational and religious, in an attempt to place him in the social, intellectual, and religious context of his day. The King's College controversy and Livingston's arguments in the *Independent Reflector* against Anglican control of that institution will then be examined in some detail. Livingston's other articles in the *Reflector* regarding religion and civil liberties, which provide a theological context for his views regarding the College, will then be reviewed. The result will be a more complete grasp of the important role of religious ideas in the American Enlightenment and its contribution to the logic of American disestablishment.

William Livingston: Religious Roots and Whiggish Wiles

In 1723, William Livingston was born in Albany, New York, to a Dutch Reformed family that figured prominently in the political life of the colony.[18] His grandfather had been the speaker of the colonial assembly, and his father, Philip, also served in the assembly and as a member of the council.[19] His great-grandfather had been a pastor in England who had fled to Holland at the Restoration of Charles II, hence the Dutch Reformed connection.[20] His family were the well-to-do owners of a national and international complex of mines, ships, warehouses, and land holdings.[21] Young William was groomed from an early age for a legal career to aid the family business. But he quickly developed other plans.

In 1737, at the age of fourteen, William entered Yale, from which three previous brothers had graduated. Not much is known about his time there, except that he graduated in 1741 at the top of his class.[22] We do know that he overlapped by two years with Elisha Williams, who served as rector of the college until 1739.[23] Williams, as we have seen, had both legal and theological training, and was a forceful intellect on matters of church and state. Livingston was likely familiar with Williams's *Seasonable Plea for the Liberty of Conscience*, given the prominence of Williams's pamphlet and Livingston's breadth of reading in this area. In any event, Livingston was exposed to Williams's views generally during his time at Yale. Livingston's writings in the *Reflector* on religious freedom certainly partook of the same spirit that Williams expressed.

Later in life, Livingston made it known that he did not fully accept or approve of the strong Calvinism found at Yale. But in reflection, he viewed his time there as a happy one.[24] Despite the strong and even rigid theological views of the faculty and administration, they allowed students free access to the wide range of books in the school's library. Livingston appears to have been more influenced, at least in matters of religion, by the progressive authors whose works he found in those libraries, who included John Locke, than by the teachers in its classrooms, with perhaps the exception of Elisha Williams.

Livingston's *Reflector* articles were written more than ten years after he left Yale. But the tolerant and liberal views found in them were well in place very shortly after his graduation. Letters written within two or three years of his graduation already reflect a broad tolerance of religious views. "Every man has a right to think for himself, as he shall answer for himself," he wrote to a former classmate in 1744, "and it is unreasonable for me to be angry with any one for being of different principles, as he has the same pretence to quarrel with me."[25]

But Livingston was no skeptic or deist. After Yale, he traveled to New York City to work as a law clerk and read for the bar. At about this time, he became a Presbyterian, as had many of the Dutch Reformed young men of his generation. The Dutch Reformed Church continued holding its services in the Dutch language, which the younger generation did not speak. This caused many of them to shift to the Presbyterian church.[26] While Livingston was often critical of the clergy, he made clear it was their abuses he was targeting, and not the office itself.

He continued close friendships with several ministers connected with his alma mater, including the older Aaron Burr, who became president of Princeton in 1748. Livingston was no new light enthusiast, but he did appear to hold relatively orthodox biblical views. In various publications throughout his life, including a prayer written in the *Reflector* and in a eulogy written for Burr, he affirmed the authority of scripture, the atoning death of Christ on the cross, and the reality of eternal life.[27]

Livingston worked busily as a law clerk and sought entrance to the bar in the few years after graduation. Admitted to the bar in 1748, he began to take on cases of greater variety and importance than typically handled by new lawyers. But the practice of law alone could not fully occupy such a lively and eclectic mind. In 1752, he published, with a friend, the first digest of the laws of the colony. This heightened his prominence, and his practice continued to grow. But this did stop him from engaging the public in debates on matters of great societal interest. He and two other lawyer friends produced the first issues of the *Independent Reflector* before the end of 1752.[28]

The name of his journal reflected the influence of British Whig views. The title was obviously borrowed from the *Independent Whig*, a journal published in England in 1720 by the two well-known English essayists, Thomas Gordon and John Trenchard.[29] As noted, both Gordon and Trenchard were Whigs, British political reformers with a strong suspicion of centralized power, whether civil or ecclesiastical.[30] In the *Independent Whig*, they advanced the primacy of the individual conscience over church authority. They also wrote *Cato's Letters*, which contained a fuller defense of both religious and civil liberties generally, as well as attacks on particular government abuses and corruptions.[31]

Both sets of essays achieved wide popularity in the American colonies. By 1750, two American editions of the *Whig* papers had been published, and *Cato's Letters* were serialized widely in American newspapers. Colonial Americans likely learned more about Locke's thought through popularizers like Trenchard and Gordon, as well as Livingston and other American

expositors, than they did from reading Locke directly.[32] Bernard Bailyn identified the political Whigs as those who, "more than any other single group of
writers ... shaped the mind of the American Revolutionary generation. To
the colonists the most important of these publicists and intellectual middle-
men were those spokesmen for extreme libertarianism, John Trenchard and
Thomas Gordon."[33]

Late in life, Thomas Jefferson said that the ideas in the Declaration of
Independence expressed the "common sense of the subject" and "an expression of the American mind." That "mind" had been prepared and shaped by
men like Livingston, who articulated Whig and moderate Enlightenment
thought for the American situation. As one Livingston scholar put it, "colonial America had its own spokesmen of the rights of man, and they commu-
nicated the European principles in a distinctively American idiom and to a
distinctively American audience. Livingston was just such a spokesman, and
the *Reflector* was his medium. ... Few publications contain so comprehensive
a statement of the Whig liberalism of the Revolutionary leadership at so early
a date."[34]

That philosophy was set out in the context of specific political issues,
much as Trenchard's and Gordon's had been, and reflected the "style, subject
matter, and attitudes on public questions" found in those writers.[35] The shared
lively style and timely subject matter were what caused *Cato's Letters* and the
Independent Reflector to have such a broad impact in America. Locke's *Second
Treatise* and *Essay Concerning Understanding*, while influential for elites like
Jefferson and educated pastors, seem to have been too theoretical for the average busy colonial. Livingston, by contrast, gained a wide reading by expressing his position on questions of current controversy, such as the creation of
King's College.

King's College and the Independent Reflector

The King's College affair was of special interest to Livingston since it joined
his interests in education and religious freedom. The College was proposed
several years prior to the founding of the *Reflector*, and by 1748 a special public
lottery fund had been created for its founding.[36] Prior to the *Reflector* series,
and prior to Anglican designs on the College, he had written on the importance of a college for New York in a number of letters and a full-length essay.[37]
This earlier support, combined perhaps with a desire to neutralize a potentially formidable enemy, caused Livingston to be appointed to the founding
board of trustees for the College in 1751.[38]

Shortly after this appointment, Anglican plans to operate the College became more widely known.[39] At this time, the *Reflector* was also launched. The timing was likely coincidental, since the *Reflector* had been in the planning stage for three years and the first several articles had nothing to do with the college issue.[40]

The College as Bulwark and Guardian of the Free Marketplace of Ideas

Livingston appears to have undertaken the College dispute on the basis of an honest interest in a free education, rather than antipathy to Anglicans.[41] His concern about Anglican control was driven by what he viewed as the purpose and role of a public college—a training ground for participation in the marketplace of knowledge. It was one of the two main private institutions that allowed the marketplace of ideas to function, the other being a free press—whose functioning Livingston defended in *Reflector* issue 40.[42]

Livingston developed the idea of college as promoting freedom of thought in the first article on the proposed College (issue 17 of the *Reflector* series). It said nothing about the Anglicans but laid the foundation for his theory of education. He elaborated on the purposes of a college and the best means of attaining them. He scorned the notion that a college was merely for the imparting of linguistic, literary, or scientific information. Rather, it existed to "qualify men for the different employments of life," to "infuse a public spirit and love of their country," and generally to "make them more useful and serviceable to the Common-Wealth."[43]

But this "employment" and "service" was not just, or even primarily, about technical skills. Rather, it was about developing people who could continue to attain "greater progress in knowledge" by thinking for themselves. Livingston envisioned these educated minds dropped, like rocks into a pond, into strategic spots in society "on the Bench, at the Bar, in the Pulpit, and in the Senate," and the resulting ripples affecting "civil and religious principles" throughout the whole province. Youth was the perfect time to teach these lessons of critical thought, since the young mind was like wax, which was susceptible to "almost any impression."[44]

The trouble was, argued Livingston, that colleges in reality were "seldom places of candid inquiry." Because students generally received the dogma of their teachers, study was undertaken with an eye to answering objections rather than seeking truth. The system of truth in place at the college was accepted with "implicit faith," and the sole business was to defend it. "Freedom of thought rarely penetrates those contracted Mansions of learning."[45] Here he echoed similar sentiments about sectarian-controlled education found in the *Independent Whig*, which had also accused sectarian institutions of merely seeking to defend their own orthodoxies rather than searching for new truths.[46]

Next, Livingston moved from theory to experience, including his own. He cited the examples of Harvard and Yale, where the "Presbyterian Profession is in some sort established." He noted that at these colleges, the religion of the colleges was taught and principles of other Christian groups combated. The spirit of the college in these matters was diffused, through its graduates, throughout the larger colony. The result was that the Presbyterians maintained a colony-wide ascendancy, preventing the "Episcopalians" from acquiring an "equal strength among them."[47] This inequality would continue, Livingston argued, until the system of education was reformed.

Livingston's assessment of Harvard and Yale may not have been accurate—perhaps those colleges stayed "Presbyterian" because of the character of the colony, rather than the other way around. But it served as an effective reminder to the Anglicans that *they* were disadvantaged elsewhere by the very system they were proposing in New York. He then closed the first essay by noting that in England, both Protestant and Catholic rulers saw that universities influenced the national character and had used colleges as tools to advance their religious agendas.[48] New York, he proposed, should learn from these examples and set up its college free from sectarian control.

Sectarian Control of Education as Threat to the Marketplace of Ideas

Having established that colleges were vital institutions in the free market of ideas, Livingston went on to show how sectarian control or influence would undercut this role. In issue 18, he argued that a college that discriminated among members of the Protestant religion would be "a Nursery of Animosity, Dissention and Disorder." The ascendant sect would tend to disparage and oppress those outside its faith, with the result that outsiders would either be second-class students or forced to attend other schools.[49]

Second, Livingston argued that an establishment within the College would lead to similar results in society at large. If a college promoted the "doctrines of a Party" based on authority, rather than reason, this mentality would seep into society at large. Livingston feared that the ultimate result would be a statewide establishment by the Anglicans, the precise opposite of a free market for religion.[50]

Finally, Livingston noted that initial funding for the college was through the legislature, which could not have intended it to be the engine for one religious party.[51] Livingston observed that New York had a wide range of religious groups, including Anglicans, Anabaptists, Lutherans, Quakers, and Moravians, all of whom would be appalled that their public funds were being used to skew the religious market in favor of one competing sect.

The religious diversity of New York created just the kind of environment where Livingston's free market of ideas model made a great deal of sense. "The variety of sects," as Livingston put it, may be "a Guard against the Tyranny and Usurpation of one over another." Conversely, he argued, any sect given aid by the secular state will "oppress others" who otherwise would defend their cause with the "weapons of reason and argument."[52] Here, Livingston anticipated Madison's arguments in *Federalist* 51 about the balance among sects and factions preventing the tyranny of any.

While Livingston had the negative example of New England as a foil for his proposals, he found in Pennsylvania a positive model of tolerance and freedom. Perhaps Pennsylvania went too far, Livingston reflected, in allowing "Papists" the "common and equal benefits of society."[53] Yet the "rising Prosperity of Pennsylvania," he believed, was connected with "their vast importation of religious Refugees," which contributed to "Their Strength and their Riches."[54] This free market of religion was the model to emulate.[55] But a sectarian college would be a serious obstacle to this emulation.

Livingston ended the series on the role of the college by appealing to the civic values and patriotism of his readers to oppose "the rule of the College" being "the *Monopoly* of any single Denomination."[56] Livingston's use of the word "monopoly" to describe a religious establishment appeared about twenty-five years before Adam Smith in 1776 applied ideas of commercial monopoly to establishments in the religious world. Livingston's use of the monopoly language here underscores the propriety of attaching the term "free market" to Livingston's views.

Livingston addressed, in turn, the Anglicans, the Dutch Reformed, the Presbyterians, the Quakers, and then the Moravians, Lutherans, and Anabaptists, reminding them of how they had fared under religious monopolies. He argued that once the "Fountain of Learning" was directed and all public offices "engrossed by one sect," they would once again lose their hard-won freedoms. He closed with a peroration on the rights of Christians and Englishmen and the need to assert those rights with vigor to prevent the College from being run by the Anglicans.[57]

Although he wrote further on the topic elsewhere in letters and articles, the important elements of the argument were outlined in the *Reflector* pieces.[58]

More important, the *Reflector* contained companion pieces on religion and freedom that give context to the King's College arguments. These other articles are especially helpful for illuminating the religious ideas, including the Protestant right of private judgment, that underlay Livingston's market-place-of-ideas model.

Other Reflector Articles Relating to Religion and Civil Liberties

Critics of Livingston accused him of merely being anticlerical and even antireligious.[59] They claimed that he was perhaps a closet deist or even an atheist who did not merely oppose the Anglican establishment generally, but denied revealed religion altogether. In this view, his marketplace model was a rejection of all claims to authority based on revealed truth and a promotion of the importance of diversity because of the inherent uncertainty of truth. It was, in other words, a simple product of the skeptical Enlightenment.

But Livingston's articles on religion and religious freedom rebut this charge. They reveal that his commitment to the marketplace of ideas was, in good part, based on religious and theological ideas, not least the Protestant principle of the right of private judgment. In these articles, Livingston explored the beliefs of some minority religious groups and also revealed some of his own beliefs, including his view of the clergy. A careful reading shows him not to be antireligious, or even broadly anticlerical. Rather, he opposed the abuse and misuse of religion and scripture.

Livingston's Attitude toward Other Religious Groups

Livingston instinctively defended marginal groups because he often saw in these groups a greater sincerity and spirituality than in the established churches. The latter were, in his opinion, too often corrupted by power and wealth. This analysis appeared in his first *Reflector* article on religion, a defense of the Moravians. This German Pietist sect aroused hostility due to its members' pacifisms, opposition to slavery, and refusal to take oaths in court. Livingston contrasted the "honest simplicity and spirituality" of the Moravians with the "antic mimickry, and idolatrous Trumpery" of their enemies.[60]

He continued by sarcastically arguing that the real trouble with the Moravians was that they acknowledged "no other rule than the scriptures ... wickedly preferring the Word of God, to the establish'd Orthodoxy." He described the enemies of the Moravians as the "High Church" and left no doubt as to who was being criticized. In a footnote that appeared calculated to offend all the mainstream religious groups equally, he said: "By High Church in this Place, I do not mean any church in particular; but the Popes and Persecutors of all Churches, whether they be Popes of Rome, England, Holland or Geneva."[61]

This footnote helped kindle the vigorous opposition that characterized the short life of the *Reflector*. But it also nicely clarifies Livingston's real target in much of his religious polemics: not practical, biblical Christianity, which he found in the behavior and teachings of the Moravians. Rather, his target was the human additions and accretions to the gospel of Christ represented by the creeds and religious systems that he viewed as extrabiblical.[62] Livingston consciously used a critique that dissenting Protestants had often brought against the magisterial and national Protestant churches.

Livingston's Religious Beliefs and Attitude toward the Clergy

In his writings on religion, Livingston emphasized the rational and moral elements of Christianity. But what separated him from a pure Jeffersonian rationalism was his high regard for scripture. While much criticism of religion can be found in his writings, there is no criticism of scripture, but only of its misuse or abuse. Livingston would have had no sympathy with Jefferson's cutting the New Testament apart to separate its moral teachings from its miraculous stories.

In outlining his view of scripture, Livingston contrasted "primitive Christianity" with "modern Christianity."[63] According to him, early Christianity taught a few simple doctrines and rituals, including the atonement of Christ, the restoration of human nature, and the remembrance of his sacrifice in the simple ceremony of communion. "All the Faith it requires," Livingston declared, "is that Christ was the promised Messiah, and its moral directions may be contained in a sheet of paper."[64] Just as important, this record was given in a style "so artless and perspicuous" as to be easily understood by any sincere believer. He then catalogued some of the many systems of Christianity that had grown up, and needlessly complicated this simple affair. This diversity showed, Livingston argued, that all should seek for truth "where alone it may be found, in the pure and genuine Oracles of Truth and Inspiration."[65]

This commitment to scripture as a basis for truth stayed with him throughout his life. Many years later in 1784, when governor of New Jersey, Livingston wrote an essay on the liberty of the press in which he raised the issue of contradictions in scripture. He quoted two passages from Proverbs, and then wrote "Is not this a contradiction?—Profane and deistical men may indeed give it that turn. . . . But all the contradiction is merely verbal." That is, there was no real contradiction. He explained: "The scripture, which contains an inexhaustible magazine of human, as well as of divine knowledge, never *really* contradicts itself, though in many instances it may, to superficial readers or corrupt wranglers, appear self-contradictory."[66]

Livingston's assumptions regarding the unity and coherence of scripture separated him, as he himself acknowledged, from the deists of his day. Although he did not fit easily into any neat religious category, he strongly denied accusations of either atheism or deism. His insistence on scriptural authority seems to have been deeper and more sincere than merely a cover for an underlying skepticism. His position appears to be similar to Ezra Stiles, renowned president of Yale. During a period in his life when he came close to semideism, Stiles emphasized the rationality and morality of Christianity, while downplaying the miraculous. Yet he never abandoned his high view of scriptural inspiration, and this conviction appeared to be instrumental in causing him to return to a more fully "orthodox" Christianity.

Interestingly, Livingston hosted Stiles at his home in New York for dinner and discussion of politics during Stiles's period of semideism in the 1750s.[67] Livingston was perhaps Stiles's alter ego, the man Stiles would have been had he opted for law rather than the ministry. But whatever their journeys, neither man ultimately deviated from a foundational commitment to scriptural inspiration and authority.

Livingston did not clarify things overly much when he set out his personal "creed" in *Reflector* 46 in 1753.[68] This issue delivered a sarcastic argument that purported to defend penitential confession and systems of creeds, but really attacked them.[69] We need creeds, he said, as "surely every man has not sufficient abilities to understand the Scriptures."[70] He then parodied the thirtynine articles of the Anglican creed with his own series of beliefs.

While Livingston's articles were not overly theological, the place where he began was most significant. At the very start of his discussion, he stressed the importance of individual scriptural interpretation. For this purpose he used sarcasm, though he clearly counted on his readers to sense his real views. In attacking creeds, by apparently defending them, he wrote, "besides, for us to determine what Creeds are agreeable or repugnant to Scripture, is in Reality claiming a Right of private judgment; when by the very Supposition, to *judge for us*, is the Prerogative of our ghostly Directors."[71] His first "article of faith" started seriously by stating that "I believe the Scriptures of the Old and New Testament, without any foreign Comments, or human Explications but my own." But he could not hold his serious pose for long, and immediately followed this with "for which I should doubtless be honoured with Martyrdom, did I not live in a Government which restrains that fiery Zeal which would reduce a Man's body to Ashes for the Illumination of his Understanding."

The rest of the "Articles" were largely a series of criticisms of the pretensions of the clergy. He criticized transubstantiation, extravagant clergy apparel, and misguided attempts to explain "incomprehensible mysteries." He focused again on the practical fruits of Christianity, arguing that "he who feareth God and worketh righteousness will be accepted of him, even tho' he refuse to worship any man," and that "a man may be a good Christian, tho' he be of no sect in Christendom."[72]

Some might consider Livingston's criticism of the clergy to reveal his true, antireligious agenda, as when he claimed that for every honest pastor there were "fifty who assume the gown by the instigation of mammon." He held that there was "more iniquity committed under the Robe, than is repented of under the Gallows."[73] This was strong stuff that certainly reflected the tone of persistent anticlericalism found in the *Independent Whig.*[74]

Yet Livingston distinguished, elsewhere, more generally between good and bad clergy. In 1753, he dedicated an entire article to the "veneration and contempt of the clergy" in which he contrasted the good and bad. Here he wrote that "to contemn the Priesthood itself, for the wickedness of those who dishonour it, was as unreasonable as to insult a good Man, because his Grand Mother was a strumpet. The Order is a valuable Institution while it is kept within due Bounds, and confined to instructing instead of riding the laity. An indiscriminate contempt of ecclesiastics, is, therefore, absurd and immoral." In the same article, he wrote: "there is not a more lovely character in nature, that that of a good clergyman. He is the glory and ornament of society; forever rever'd be his name, who goes into orders for the reformation of mankind."[75]

Livingston seems to have been honest in his assertions that he was attacking only the corrupt and abusive clergy. A few years after the *Spectator* controversy, he wrote a glowing eulogy on the death of his correspondent and friend the Reverend Aaron Burr.[76] Burr, who was serving as president of New Jersey College, was also an active, orthodox clergyman. Livingston celebrated Burr's pastoral role: "What he preached in the pulpit, he lived out of it. His life and example were a comment on his sermons: and by his engaging deportment, he rendered the amiable character of a Christian still more attractive and lovely. ... The pastoral function he discharged with equal fidelity and success."[77] These are not the words of a man who is "ag'in" all clergy.

An even clearer instance of his support for the clergy appears in an article published just after his death in 1790 entitled "Observations in the Support of the Clergy." Here, Livingston argued for a fair and even generous support of the clergy. He wrote: "I said that 'the labourer is worthy of his hire': and by this I mean that the clergy is entitled to a generous support." But he argued that this support should be private. Indeed, the "hirelings" criticized by scripture were those who were "politically introduced through the door of human establishments" and "bribed by the prince."[78]

This evidence supports the view that Livingston's criticisms of the clergy and religion were of their abuses and were not criticisms of revealed religion or clergy generally. One of his last articles in the *Reflector* was a defense of the immortality of the soul. This belief, Livingston asserted, "imparts an unutterable Dignity to human nature," and can only be known by "Revelation alone."[79]

But again, it is not important for our purposes to figure out exactly where Livingston fit on the spectrum between orthodoxy and heterodoxy. Rather, it is enough to show that his critique was made in terms that reflected the long tradition of dissenting Protestant thought. His acknowledgement of the Moravians and their beliefs, as well as other minority religious groups, shows his awareness of this stream. When he couched his arguments in religious terms, with an emphasis on biblical authority, he showed he was writing to be appreciated by these groups. Whether Enlightenment thinker with religious sensitivities or educated evangelical, he framed his advocacy in terms drawn from dissenting religious roots of freedom of thought and belief. His articles on religious freedom illustrated this point most clearly.

Livingston's Views of Religious and Civil Freedom

In the latter part of the *Reflector*, in issues 36 and 37, Livingston laid down the principles that underlay his earlier arguments for church/state separation.[80] Entitled "The Absurdity of the Civil Magistrate's Interfering in Matters of Religion," these articles detailed two main bases for freedom. The first was the natural limits on the jurisdiction of the magistrate, which confined his judgments to civil, and not religious, matters. The second was the rights of conscience held by every individual, based on that individual's responsibility to obtain truth from God through nature and revelation.

In the first of the two-part series, Livingston described in Lockean terms the limits of the civil magistrate's authority—defending "his subjects in the peaceable possession of their rights." "Nothing," he insisted, "but what is injurious to society, or some particular member of it, can be the proper object of civil punishment." But "Matters of religion relate to another world, and have nothing to do with the interests of the state."[81]

It followed from this principle that "every subject has a right to be protected in the exercise of the liberty of thinking about religion, as he judges proper, as well as of acting in conformity thereto." Both religious thoughts and acts were protected, at least until the acts threatened others. Should the magistrate attempt to adjudicate in the area of religion, "all his decisions … are to be regarded as unauthoritative adjudications."[82]

Livingston not only sounded Lockean, he quoted directly from Locke in a number of places. But, curiously, he did not mention Locke by name. Rather, he referred to him as "one of the greatest Patrons of English Liberty and Learning," or "a great Philosopher" or as "a Man of great Learning." This is somewhat unusual, as he did refer to some other authorities by name, but most of them were directly religious. These included references to St. Luke and St. Paul; he also cited a religious poem about King William.[83] Possibly he did not mention Locke by name because he wanted to make clear the religious, scriptural basis of his argument; he did not want to detract from that basis by introducing a name associated by some with more secular traditions.

In underscoring his religious argument, he developed the principle of the right of private judgment by reference to scripture. He asserted that "surely it could never enter into the Heart of Man to submit *his Judgment in Matters of Religion* to his Ruler, not only because it is impossible for all his Subjects to concur with him in Opinion, but also because no Man, of any Religion at all, would reduce himself to the Necessity of worshipping God in a Manner he thought disagreeable to him."[84] From this, he argued, it follows that "the civil Power hath no Jurisdiction over the Sentiments or Opinions of the Subject, till such Opinions break out in Actions prejudicial to the community, and then it is not the opinion, but the Action that is the Object of Punishment."

While this sounds like Locke, Livingston did not cite Locke in support. Rather, he told a biblical story from Acts, where St. Paul is brought to trial by the Jews for preaching about Christ. The civil magistrate, an official named Gallio, "accurately distinguishes," Livingston argued, "between political Offences and religious Opinions." It was the difference between civil breach versus theological speculations. Livingston quoted a large portion directly from Acts 13, verses 12 and following. He concluded with these worlds of Gallio: "if it were a Matter of Wrong, or wicked Lewdness, O ye Jews, Reason would that I should bear with you; But if it be a Question of Words and Names, and of your Law, look ye to it; FOR I WILL BE NO JUDGE OF SUCH MATTERS. And he drove them from the Judgment Seat."[85]

For Livingston, religion consists of "a choice or obligation to do certain Acts in conformity to the will of our Creator, which the laws of reason, or any other method of discovering his will, dictate to us." These religious duties, discoverable by either reason or revelation, "must infer a right in him to chuse his own religion." To take that choice away is to do one of two things: either to destroy the two means, reason or revelation, of discovering God's will; or to usurp the role of God and allow that man can supersede divine obligations.[86]

Livingston ties the free exchange of ideas and the advancement of learning with the private right of judgment he defended with scripture. "The restraint of civil authority, in different countries and ages, upon the free exercise of human reason, has ever been attended with a decay of all valuable knowledge and literature.... The advancement of learning depends up on the free exercise of thought." Where the "right of private judgment" has been surrendered, "the state has generally sunk into barbarism, and every appearance of real substantial masculine piety has vanished from the nation."[87]

The right of private scriptural interpretation and the broader notion of the private right of religious judgment are the foundations for Livingston's arguments about the importance of a free marketplace of ideas. In his identification of the right of private judgment with religious and biblical thought, Livingston follows in the tradition of Elisha Williams, with whom he studied, as well as a long line of dissenting Protestant thinkers, including Locke, John Milton, and the English Baptists.

Indeed, Milton, nearly a hundred years before Livingston or Smith, wrote vividly about the importance of the free play of ideas: "And though all the winds of doctrine were let loose to play upon the earth, so truth be in the field, we do injuriously by licensing and prohibiting to misdoubt her strength. Let her and falsehood grapple; who ever knew truth put to the worse, in a free and open encounter?"[88] Milton's market of ideas was not based on the relativism of all ideas or the impossibility of knowing truth amid great diversity. Rather, his arena was founded on Puritan views of the individual's obligation to pursue truth that existed and was attainable, at least in meaningful part, in both nature and revelation.[89]

Milton's view was a Protestant vision of the progressive nature of truth finding or recovery. A less-quoted passage from Milton's *Areopagitica*, his famed defense of press freedoms, graphically reveals this vision:

> Truth indeed came once into the world with her divine master, and was a perfect shape most glorious to look on: but when he ascended, and his apostles after him were laid asleep, then straight arose a wicked

race of deceivers, who … took the virgin Truth, hewed her lovely form into a thousand pieces, and scattered them to the four winds. From that time ever since, the sad friends of Truth … went up and down gathering up limb by limb still as they could find them. We have not yet found them all, Lords and Commons, nor ever shall do, till her Master's second coming; he shall bring together every joint and member, and shall mold them into an immortal feature of loveliness and perfection.[90]

For true Protestants, according to Milton, the Reformation is a continuing process. Any sort of licensing regulation or censorship could interfere with this all-important task of reconstructing the sacred body of truth, at least as best as possible, prior to the second coming of Christ.

Milton's arena of truth differs from modern views of the commercial marketplace in that the latter is driven by preferences, the former by convictions. A main conviction of dissenting Protestants, which was held also by Livingston, was that the nature of truth is progressive, and its seekers have a duty to walk in its unfolding light without interference from the state.

Conclusion

Livingston's writings reveal that the consilience in colonial America between dissenting Protestant thought and Enlightenment thought on religious disestablishment was not mere chance. Rather, those articulating philosophical, Enlightenment-type arguments for the public policy of disestablishment explicitly made use of existing concepts of dissenting Protestantism. This cooperative relationship made for a powerful combination of popular and elite thought that was influential and lasting.

Indeed, in 1831, James Madison, in the waning years of his life, reflected in a letter to a biographer of Livingston on the use to which he and other students had put Livingston's *Reflector* essays. Madison wrote that the essays were admired for their "energy and eloquence" and were frequently read and cited in student debates at Princeton.[91] One modern scholar, echoing Madison's views of Livingston's writings, declared the King's College dispute was the "major" church/state controversy that shocked Americans into a "true awareness of the necessity and validity" of ideas of religious disestablishment.[92] This may be overstating it, as many colonists realized earlier the importance of these ideas. They had, however, lacked a common, nonsectarian vocabulary to share these ideas with a wider audience.

Livingston played this role inside America, as Locke had done outside America. Livingston's efforts helped create a common American nonsectarian language of disestablishment based on dissenting Protestant principles. The stage was now set for the right of private judgment to move from being a regional phenomenon—focused in the Middle Colonies, with pockets of support in the South and New England—to becoming a truly national principle. To this next, and final, stage we now turn.

5

Theologian and Politician

JOHN WITHERSPOON AND JAMES MADISON MAKE
A NATIONAL PRINCIPLE

Prologue—Mission in Philadelphia

He would certainly have endured the hot and humid summer more comfortably in the shade at his rural estate. The Pennsylvania summer of 1787 was one of the most stifling in living memory. European visitors to Philadelphia wrote home that they could hardly breathe. "At each inhaling of air," one complained, "one worries about the next one. The slightest movement is painful."[1] But national business beckoned him once again. He knew that duty lay, at least one more time, in the stifling rooms and halls of urban Philadelphia. Principles of liberty and freedom he had long fought for needed one more—hopefully final—push to become part of the fabric of the new nation.

He had walked the bustling streets of Philadelphia more than ten years earlier—also in the summer—when the Continental Congress had birthed the idea of independence for the colonies. He had signed the Declaration of Independence and had also helped rally the cause that summer for a unified nationhood in an impassioned speech to the delegates on the importance of a union of states after independence.

And he had been there again in 1778—November, this time—when the Articles of Confederation were drafted. He had desired—prophetically it turned out—stronger taxing and commercial oversight powers for the new central government than the Articles provided. But believing a confederated union was better than none at all, he had approved and signed the Articles.

Now he was embarked on his most important project to date. Many had come to the conclusion that stronger national ties were needed. State and local authorities were no substitute for the order and organization of a disciplined national unit. Changing times were calling for an adjustment in principles of governance, including those relating to the roles of church and state. The call had gone out for delegates to come to Philadelphia in May 1787 to create a new, national constitution. And that was why he walked those muggy, gritty Philadelphia streets once again.

He was destined to play the role of a primary author and shaper of this new government. It may not be too strong, given his role in visioning its three-part structure, to call him the "father of the Constitution." But it would probably just be better to call him "a father of the church"—because that is what John Witherspoon was in his role as pastor, theologian, and university president. In addition, the former title has already been given to another visitor to Philadelphia that summer—a former pupil of his—attending another constitutional convention taking place at the very same time just down the street.[2]

Of course, everyone remembers that summer for the *other* convention, the one where Washington silently presided, Franklin sagaciously philosophized, and Madison's penmanship won for him the honorific of *pater* of our national constitution. It is Madison's records of that convention, as well as his other writings, especially those relating to the First Amendment, that scholars comb through to try to understand what the founders had in mind for the role of church and state in the new republic.

If it had not been for his church commitments, Witherspoon himself would have likely been a delegate at that other convention. But ironically, John Witherspoon's work in Philadelphia in drafting the new national Presbyterian constitution may actually provide greater insight into the role of church and state in the early republic than the records of the far more famous federal constitutional convention. This is hardly to say that Madison was not important on this topic. On the contrary, he was arguably the most thoughtful and influential founder on church and state issues. Rather, it is only to recognize that the federal Constitution concerned national and federal principles. As a legal document, the Constitution was agnostic as to the relationship of church and state at the state and local level.

On the other hand, the Presbyterian constitution was not concerned with issues of political federalism. It spoke about the role of the magistrate and the church as a general matter. Its principles of church and state were applicable at every level—federal, state, and local—where the church itself operated. And those principles were truly revolutionary. The Presbyterian deliberations provide an insight into the way many biblically conservative people viewed the proper roles of church and state in the early republic in ways that the federal Constitution cannot. But to understand and appreciate the story of Witherspoon and Madison in 1787 in relation to church and state, we must return a few years to the events of another revolutionary year, 1776.

Witherspoon and Madison: Backgrounds

It was 1776 when both John Witherspoon and James Madison made their entrances as significant American public figures. Witherspoon had already been an important figure in his church and as president of the College of New Jersey, predecessor to Princeton University. But events in that year vaulted both Witherspoon and Madison onto a wider public stage than either had previously walked. It was here that the church/state principles began to emerge that eventually came to fruition as national documents in the late 1780s.

Due to their public influence, the lives and thought of Witherspoon and Madison shed much light on the American story of church and state. One was a pastor, professor, college administrator, and practicing theologian who was also involved in national politics. The other was a legislator and statesman, but with early theological training under Witherspoon that appears to have directly affected his public thinking. Of all theological thinkers in eighteenth-century America, they were probably most responsible, with perhaps the exception of William Penn, for applying to actual governance the implications of the private right of judgment in religion. Both in their influence and in their thought, they qualify as founding theologians par excellence.

I will examine the course of their lives between 1776 to 1787 in relation to the right of private judgment and religious freedom. I will first look at contributions Witherspoon and then Madison made in 1776 to the public development of that principle. I will then move to the events of Virginia in 1786, where Madison made probably the most forceful ideological exposition of that principle in his opposition to Patrick Henry's bill for religious assessments. Finally, I will return to that muggy Philadelphia summer of 1787 and examine Witherspoon's role in making this principle part of the constitution of a great national church, and thus part of the fabric of the new nation.

Witherspoon: Foreign Bishops and Basic Freedoms

Witherspoon was the senior of the two, the teacher and tutor of Madison, so it is only right to begin with him. Pastor, college president, founding politician—Witherspoon's life spanned three careers, and he found success in all of them. He was a Scot by birth and education, a Scottish Presbyterian who was conversant with the ideas of the Scottish Enlightenment. His natural Scottish independence and love for freedom was no doubt deepened by a misadventure he suffered during his first year of ministry. When he tried to observe a battle between the royalist troops and the rebelling Highlanders of Bonnie Prince Charles, he was captured by the Highlanders and held for a month in a decaying Scottish castle. Forgoing a night escape with some friends, he was eventually released as a noncombatant. The experience was profound, and was said to have given him a serious and sober turn of mind, and one that had a deep and practical appreciation for liberty.[3]

Before coming to America, Witherspoon had already enjoyed a successful career as a prominent Scottish clergyman. He had led the conservative forces of the popular wing of the Scottish National Church against the Enlightenment-influenced Moderates.[4] Indeed, it was his reputation for orthodoxy and learning that had caused the leadership of the College of New Jersey at Princeton to seek his services as president in 1766.[5]

But despite his national and international reputation within Presbyterian circles, Witherspoon would today be a figure unknown outside the arcana of ecclesiastical history had his career merely ended successfully at Princeton. Even having educated a future president, a vice-president, more than seventy-five congressmen and senators, and three Supreme Court justices would not have guaranteed him a place in posterity.[6] Leaders at William and Mary and Yale colleges could make similar claims, but they do not have the prominence of Witherspoon.[7] It is the fact that Witherspoon was also directly involved in the passage and/or ratification of the three major organic documents of the nation—the Declaration, the Articles, and the Constitution—that gives him his place in the pantheon of the founders.

None of this might have happened, but for a bold sermon Witherspoon preached on May 17, 1776. This occurred a little over a month prior to his being named a delegate to the Second Continental Congress, scheduled to meet in Philadelphia that summer.[8] While Witherspoon had already been active in New Jersey politics in the cause of independence, he had kept his political views out of the pulpit. The Continental Congress had, however, appointed a "general fast" day throughout the colonies for May 17.[9] Given the special day, and the background of hostilities already commenced, the time had come, Witherspoon decided, to address the political situation from the pulpit.

A Revolutionary Sermon

Entitled "The Dominion of Providence over the Affairs of Men," the sermon has long been recognized as an important revolutionary address. Its key significance in relating religious freedom to the Revolution, however, has often been overlooked. Psalm 76:10 ("Surely the Wrath of Man shall praise thee") provided the scriptural basis to preach about the actions of those "men of wrath"—the British.[10] How could God be praised by the unjust and oppressive actions of the overbearing British? In various ways, according to Witherspoon: by showing the sinfulness of human nature; by chastising sinners; and by glorifying God when the evil plans of men self-destruct.[11]

How should the colonials react to this evil? First, by seeking more deeply and fervently for their souls' salvation. Next, they should acknowledge the providences of God and resist relying on the arm of flesh.[12] Here Witherspoon was on relatively safe pastoral ground, as he exhorted his listeners to purely spiritual activities. But when he touched on his third point of response—the active role of church members in the struggle for independence—he knew he was stepping into less familiar, riskier waters.

He acknowledged this risk by stating "you are all my witnesses that this is the first time of my introducing any political subject into the pulpit." But, he believed, he was now justified in declaring from the pulpit that the armed uprising was the "cause of justice, of liberty, and of human nature." And what was this justification? Because the revolt was not based on "pride, resentment, or sedition." Rather, it rested on a "deep and general conviction that our civil and religious liberties ... depended on the issue."[13]

Developing this theme of the importance of civil and religious liberties, he noted that "there is not a single instance in history in which civil liberty was lost, and religious liberty preserved entire." Thus, at stake in the American resistance was religious freedom and conscience itself. "If therefore we yield up our temporal property, we at the same time deliver the conscience into bondage."[14] No mere justification of political expediency or policy could suffice for a man who had in Scotland maintained that ministers should avoid meddling in civil affairs, that they should resist the temptation to "claim the direction of such matters as fall within the province of civil magistrates."[15]

But what was this threat to "religious liberties" and "conscience" that justified the public intervention of a clergyman in political affairs? Oddly, in his fast-day sermon, Witherspoon did not directly say. But there can be no real doubt as to what he was referencing, and his listeners would have been well aware of it. Most well knew that Witherspoon had been active in a group of religious organizations opposing the appointment of an Anglican bishop in American.[16]

The American Bishop Question

From today's vantage, the issue of an American-Anglican episcopacy appears to be nothing more than sectarian squabbling. But at the time it was viewed as part of an English attempt to subjugate the colonies, civilly and ecclesiastically. Anglican bishops had certain common law rights and powers that made them civil as well as religious forces. This authority included the power to tax, impose coercive tithes, and operate "spiritual" courts.[17] The imposition of an Anglican bishop on America was seen as a first step to achieving a full-blown, British-controlled, Anglican establishment throughout the colonies—a direct threat to the colonists' civil and religious liberties.[18]

The ecclesiastical conflict had percolated along at varying levels of strength since the late seventeenth century. One expert on the conflict adjudged that, in the "American colonies," the conflict over religious control was "the most enduring and absorbing public question from 1689 to 1776."[19] By the middle of the eighteenth century, that conflict had taken the form of a standoff between the official Anglican church and the many dissenting groups in the colonies. One notable skirmish had been William Livingston's conflict in the 1750s in New York over the Anglican religious identity of King's College.[20]

Livingston, through his pamphleteering, was also involved in the opposition to the appointment of an American Anglican bishop.[21] But even before Livingston's involvement, Ezra Stiles, the Congregational preacher and president of Yale, preached on the topic in Rhode Island in 1760.[22] Stiles's sermon was a stirring call for American religious unity against outside interference. "Churches can then alone be said to be *perfectly free*," Stiles asserted, "when each congregation has an *unlimited, absolute*, and *self-determining* power in the choice of their officers." Only when churches are guaranteed the power to regulate their own affairs will "this fundamental principle of *universal liberty*" be secured.[23]

According to Stiles, this right of religious autonomy was closely connected with the right of individual biblical interpretation. He viewed the idea of freedom from imposed creed as an element or expression of the foundational rights of liberty of conscience and the right of private judgment. "The *right of conscience and private judgment* is unalienable; and it is truly the interest of all mankind to unite themselves into one body, for the liberty, free exercise, and unmolested enjoyment of this right, especially in religion. ... God be thanked we are not embarrassed with subscriptions and oaths to uninspired rules for defining truth, in this land of liberty, where the SCRIPTURES are professedly our only RULE."[24] To defend these rights, Stiles and other prominent non-Anglican religious leaders formed an active coalition of about seven hundred churches to work with dissenting groups in London to oppose the appointment of an American bishop.[25]

Witherspoon had been in Scotland during much of the activity of this antiepiscopal group. But even in Scotland, he had been dealing with very similar issues. One of the concerns of the Popular party in the Scottish church was the imposition of pastors on congregations by elite patrons.[26] In the very year that Stiles was asserting the right of private judgment and biblical understanding against external religious authorities and creeds, Witherspoon was doing the very same thing—with remarkably similar language—in Scotland.[27]

An occasion of Witherspoon's defense of this principle was the imposition of the patron's choice of a certain pastor on the unwilling congregation of Kilconquhar in 1760, the same year that Stiles preached in Rhode Island. The General Assembly upheld the prerogative of the patron, and Witherspoon entered a dissent. In his speech, Witherspoon protested, "has not every man a natural right, well secured in this happy island, to *judge for himself in matters of religion*, and in fact to adhere to any minister he pleases?"[28] Witherspoon's connection of the right of private judgment with the natural right of religious liberty shows that the connection was broadly known. Not only was it "well secured in this happy island" but also it was one of the "few principles, in which, I should think, hardly a man in this assembly would disagree."[29]

But while the connection between the private right of judgment and religious liberty was apparently well known, a dispute existed about the contours and implications of that right. Both Witherspoon and Stiles, however, viewed the right as opposing external interference in ecclesiastical matters, either by a church hierarchy in local matters, or a state-established church. It is not surprising, then, that shortly after coming to America in 1768, Witherspoon should join up with the antiepiscopacy forces. In fact, he arrived just in time to witness a renewed barrage of antiepiscopacy writing by William Livingston, who held forth almost weekly on the topic between the spring of 1768 and the summer of 1769 in the *American Whig*.

Witherspoon himself became an active member of the antiepiscopacy group, writing letters and making recruiting visits to clergy on its behalf.[30] The organization had been active right up to the time of Witherspoon's fast-day sermon, holding its annual meeting in 1775, with one planned for 1776 that was mooted by the events of the Revolution.[31] Given the liveliness and currency of the episcopacy debate, its identification as a core matter of religious liberty in relation to the British, and Witherspoon's ongoing involvement on the issue, it seems apparent that this was the main religious liberty issue referenced by his fast-day sermon.

But for our present understanding, the historic issue of the American bishop controversy is less important than the principle in which both Stiles and Witherspoon explicitly wrapped it—the right of private judgment. This principle appears scores, even hundreds of times throughout the American eighteenth-century literature of religious pamphlets and sermons. While a version of the concept had branched in a more liberal, deistic direction, religiously conservative thinkers also continued to use it.

Indeed, Witherspoon's and Stiles's own use of the term, tying it to the right to study and believe the Bible for oneself, reveals its religious roots. Witherspoon, in his *Lectures on Moral Philosophy*, which he delivered regularly to all seniors as the capstone of the Princeton educational experience, talked generally of rights in a state of natural liberty, and included among those the "right of private judgment in matters of opinion." Phrased in this manner, the concept does have an Enlightenment ring to it. But in the same lectures he also spoke of the distinction between alienable and unalienable, including among the unalienable "a right to judge for himself in all matters of religion." This has a decidedly more religious tone to it.[32]

Witherspoon and Stiles were generally theologically conservative, but they also engaged with Enlightenment thinkers, usually John Locke and those from the Scottish Enlightenment.[33] But even though Witherspoon and Stiles opposed those thinkers from the skeptical Enlightenment, it is at times thought that their high view of reason was a sort of "contagion" that filtered into their religious systems.[34] Some might argue that their references to the private right of judgment could be viewed as an invasion of Enlightenment categories into their religious thought.

But both men were widely respected for their theological and biblical orthodoxy in church circles. As we have seen, Stiles flirted with a form of Christian deism early on. But according to his most prominent biographer, by 1758 Stiles had come to an orthodox and evangelical appreciation of scripture and traditional Christian doctrines.[35] As for Witherspoon, during his time in Scotland, he had consistently opposed the Moderates in his church who absorbed the latest Enlightenment ideas into their theology. He wrote a widely circulated satire essentially ridiculing what he viewed as the Enlightenment faddishness of the Moderates.[36] It was generally acknowledged that his theological views steered clear from the "laxity of the Moderates."[37]

Witherspoon and Stiles had raised the principle of private judgment in a directly religious context, the appointment of ecclesiastical leadership. But more people were seeing the civil and societal implications of the ideal. As Trenchard and Gordon noted, the idea was being used increasingly to justify an assortment of civil and religious liberties as matters of right rather than merely convenience or even toleration. James Madison, former student of Witherspoon, was in the forefront of those who applied the concept directly in the political environment. He did so prominently for the first time in the same year of Witherspoon's fast-day sermon, 1776.

Madison and Virginia: Toleration to True Religious Freedom

Ironically, it may have been the threat of an American Episcopal bishop that first brought Madison and Witherspoon together. Madison's failure to attend William and Mary, the Virginia college favored by the elite of the colony, has puzzled biographers. Madison's family was Anglican, yet he passed up his home state's Anglican college for the Presbyterian College of New Jersey.[38]

Later in life, Madison claimed the "unhealthy" climate of William and Mary persuaded him to go north. While Madison was something of sickly lad, health offers an incomplete explanation.[39] Madison's major biographers also point to certain divisions existing at the Virginia college as causing the young Madison to look elsewhere. One primary controversy was that the college's president supported the established church in the "excitement which then prevailed on the disturbing question of the American Episcopate" and was "suspected of too eager aspirations to the mitre."[40] The College of William and Mary became a focal point for episcopacy advocates in Virginia and was the location of meetings of proepiscopacy clergy.[41]

Despite being Anglican, the Madison family was known to be opposed to an American episcopate as strengthening the royal power and as a threat to colonists' civil and religious freedom.[42] Health may have played a role in Madison's choice. But the historical evidence suggests that questions of religious establishment in general, and the episcopacy issue in particular, may have also helped guide the young Madison to Princeton.

Once at Princeton, Madison was no doubt aware of the campaign against a state church by Witherspoon and others.[43] Given Witherspoon's own involvement in the antiepiscopacy campaign, cooperative efforts by Madison would be unsurprising. But the point is that Witherspoon was fostering, rather than originating or creating, antiestablishment concerns in the young Madison. The connection between the younger and older man was no doubt strengthened by Madison's decision to stay on for six months after graduation to study Hebrew, divinity, and moral philosophy under Witherspoon's tutelage.[44]

If Madison had some antiestablishment sentiment in coming to Princeton, he possessed it more so by the time he returned home. In 1774, Madison wrote to a friend in Philadelphia of the unhealthy influence of the established clergy in Virginia who had "great influence" because of their "connection with and dependence on the Bishops and Crown." He wrote approvingly of his Pennsylvania friend's good fortune to be "happy in dwelling in a land" where the "public has long felt the good effects of this religious as well as civil liberty."[45]

Furthermore, Madison contrasted the bustling arts and commerce of Philadelphia with what he felt was the stifling influence of religious establishment in Virginia. He argued: "If the church of England had been the established and general religion in all the northern colonies as it has been among us here … it is clear to me that slavery and subjection might and would have been insinuated among us. … [E]cclesiastical establishments tend to great ignorance and corruption."[46] One can see in the young Madison, years before either the First Amendment or even the Virginia Statute, already a deep opposition to religious establishment.

These early comments are crucial, since some argue that Madison's antiestablishment concerns, like Jefferson's, were driven by a committed deism and rejection of orthodox and organized Christianity.[47] Indeed, it has been claimed that the intent behind Madison's "free market in religion" was not to vitalize religion, but may have been to "sap its potency."[48] But even accepting the enigmatic status of his religious beliefs later in life—with his apparent drift toward a kind of deism—the above statements regarding religious establishment came early in his life at a time when he was passing through a period of pious—even fervent—Christian orthodoxy.

At the same time he criticized religious establishments, he also encouraged his friend to consider the ministry. Madison wrote that they both should aim toward "becoming fervent Advocates in the cause of Christ."[49] Certainly, he would have received no encouragement to heterodoxy from Witherspoon, who had written scathingly of the Scottish church Moderates and their drift toward Enlightenment-influenced, liberal religious views.

Thus, one cannot ascribe Madison's early commitment to antiestablishment principles to antireligious sentiments, as some have proposed.[50] Rather, he connected antiestablishment ideals with the positive virtue of religious freedom and freedom of conscience. In the same letter in which he criticized the established church for its tendencies to slavery, he wrote—in reference to the

jailing of some Baptist preachers—that the "diabolical, hell-conceived principle of persecution rages among some" in Virginia.[51] Madison had engaged
in some local activism on the issue and "squabbled and scolded, abused and
ridiculed … about it," but to little effect. He begged his friend to pray for
"liberty of conscience to all."[52]

Madison and the Virginia Constitution

Standing outside a jail and hearing Baptist dissenters—imprisoned by the
Virginia church/state establishment—preaching from behind bars could
only have strengthened in Madison's mind the connection between disestablishment and religious liberty. It also powerfully joined antiestablishment
principles and concerns for liberty of conscience with the right of individuals
to read and preach the Bible as they understood it. But Madison's depth of
commitment to religious freedom as a fundamental right, and the connection
of that right to disestablishment, was not widely apparent until the Virginia
constitutional convention of 1776. At that meeting, Madison, as a delegate,
played a significant role in moving religious freedom from the realm of toleration to that of fundamental rights.

George Mason's original draft of an article on religion for the proposed
Virginia constitution acknowledged the right of judgment and reason in
worshiping God. It read that "as religion or the duty which we owe to our
divine and omnipotent Creator, and the manner of discharging it, can be
governed only by reason and conviction, not by force or violence; and therefore all men should enjoy the fullest *toleration* in the exercise of religion."[53]
Madison concurred on the importance of reason and conviction as the basis
of the duty of worship. He was concerned, however, that the reference to "toleration" weakened what in his mind was a right into a policy extended by the
will of those in power.

The legislature accepted Madison's proposal to change "toleration" to
equal right, or "equally entitled" as he put it. This change of wording is justly
celebrated as an example of the shift in the view of religious freedom from
being a concession made by those in power to being perceived as a pre-exist-
ing, God-given, natural right.[54] What is less noted is Madison's connection
of free exercise of religion and the dictates of conscience with his support
for disestablishment. Madison had originally proposed a more far-reaching
change to Mason's original draft than was eventually accepted, a change that
would have resulted in the practical disestablishment of the Anglican church.
After the relevant statements on "reason and conviction" and the "exercise of

religion" and "dictates of conscience," Madison had inserted the statement "and therefore that no man ... ought, on account of religion to be invested with peculiar emoluments or privileges."[55]

Madison's wording—"and therefore"—shows his belief that disestablishment was an imperative that followed logically from the principles of religious freedom and conscience articulated in the first portion of the clause. Rather than two separate ideas, liberty of religion and conscience versus the disestablishment or the voluntary support of religion, Madison saw one main idea: the right and duty of persons to learn for themselves, before God, what their religious convictions and duties were. From this principle flowed the rights against the state in religious belief and conduct, as well as the duty of the state to refrain from supporting or promoting religion itself. For Madison, it was one main idea, with two distinct consequences: the safeguarding of individual religious freedom and conscience, both by protecting private religious conduct from interference, consistent with the peace and safety of society, and by restraining the state from the implementation or promotion or support of religion.

Most Virginians were not ready for this momentous second step. Thus, this part of Madison's change was dropped. But the proposal provides a clear insight into Madison's early thinking on the topic, at a time when he displayed considerable theological piety. Madison eventually resurrected his disestablishment proposal in 1786, when he helped defeat Patrick Henry's bill for religious assessments, and pushed through Thomas Jefferson's statute for religious freedom. The wording he used on that occasion was very similar to his efforts in 1776. Indeed, the basic theology seems identical. Whatever his changed personal views and convictions on matters of religion at that later time, he still operated on the same public theology concerning God, the duty of reason, the importance of personal conviction, and the foundation of private conscience, as he had in 1776.

The importance of the 1786 effort is that it produced arguably the most important statement on the reasons for disestablishment in American history. The statement is far more extensive and complete than any other that Madison—or any other constitutional founder for that matter—gave on the topic. Yet it has received somewhat modest attention in both First Amendment jurisprudence and historical scholarship. It is a key document in understanding the theological roots of the First Amendment.

Madison Opposes Religious Assessments

The Virginia conflict over religious assessments was a battle of founding heavyweights. Patrick Henry's bill was supported by no less than George

Washington; opposing it was James Madison, supported from afar by the sentiments and pen of Thomas Jefferson. The dispute lasted over a year, with Patrick Henry introducing his bill in late 1784.[56] Madison had thought it not likely to pass, but a switch of position by the Presbyterians, who had originally opposed a religious assessment, gave the bill real momentum.[57] Madison and his allies were unable to defeat the bill and were only able to delay a vote until the following session. In the meantime, they hoped to build support for the opposition. It was in this context that Madison wrote his famed *Memorial and Remonstrance against Religious Assessments*.

But the *Memorial* was only his second full-blown attack on Henry's bill. The first public opposition came in a major speech to the legislature in late 1784 as part of seeking to delay a vote on the bill. While no full transcript survives of this speech, we have Madison's fairly elaborate notes, which provide a sense of his argument.[58] The speech reveals, in ways the *Memorial* only intimates, the core theological and biblical issues that lay at the heart of Madison's belief in the right of personal liberty.

Beginning with the axiom "Rel. not within the purview of civil authority," a statement itself with theological provenance, he moves through a series of philosophical, historical, and pragmatic arguments against establishment. The last third of the speech, however, under the heading "probable defects of Bill," is focused almost entirely on issues of biblical study, interpretation, and the inability of courts to decide issues of religious orthodoxy. "What is Xnty? Courts of law to Judge." "What edition: Hebrew, Septuagint, or Vulgate? What copy? What translation?" He pointed out the split among Christians on the question of the canon and the role of the apocryphal books. He also raised questions on views of inspiration. Should the courts treat them as "dictated every letter" or the "essential parts only" or the "matter in general?" How should the court choose between "Trinitarianism, Arianism, Socinianism," between "salvation by faith or works" and "free grace or will?" Henry's bill would result, he concludes, in the civil authorities saying "what is orthodoxy, what heresy," and this ultimately "dishonors Christianity."[59]

Madison's argument draws distinctly on the idea of the right of private judgment, both in its religious and Enlightenment forms. On the religious front, the speech points out the religious and theological pitfalls of civil judges interpreting and applying the Bible. This warning served as part of the foundation for the reasoning in the more famous *Memorial*, written a few months later. The lack of a clear consensus on scriptural form, content, or interpretation was part of the reason that the duty of religion could be "directed only by reason and conviction" of "every man," and it was the "right of every man to exercise it as these may dictate."[60]

A few months later in the *Memorial and Remonstrance*, Madison explored further the reasoning behind the right of religious freedom. "This right," Madison declared, is "an unalienable right." He then articulated this right in terms of both Enlightenment and religious principles. This right is unalienable, he proposed, for two reasons: the first, "because the opinions of men, depending only on the evidence contemplated by their own minds, cannot follow the dictates of other men."[61] Here is the Enlightenment's priority of reason in the mind of man. The second reason was that "because what is here a right towards men, is a duty towards the Creator." In this statement, Madison shifted his emphasis from the Enlightenment's focus on reason to more of a religious view of man's duty toward God. He expanded on the religious reason in words remarkable for any state or government leader, acknowledging a power superior to that of the state. They are worth quoting in full:

> It is the duty of every man to render to the Creator such homage, and such only, as he believes to be acceptable to him. This duty is precedent both in order of time and degree of obligation, to the claims of Civil Society. Before any man can be considered as a member of Civil Society, he must be considered as a subject of the Governor of the Universe: And if a member of Civil Society, who enters into any subordinate Association, must always do it with a reservation of his duty to the general authority; much more must every man who becomes a member of any particular Civil Society, do it with the a saving of his allegiance to the Universal Sovereign. We maintain therefore that in matters of Religion, no man's right is abridged by the institution of Civil Society, and that Religion is wholly exempt from its cognizance.[62]

Madison was not unique in recognizing that man had duties to God, and that these were properly known as religious duties. The entire religious world of the day would have concurred. Where his formulation of this duty was unique—at least from that held by the magisterial Protestant churches—was his insistence that the individual had an obligation to learn this duty for himself; that no state or government could transmit that duty to him. Thus, the duty was "precedent" both in "time and degree of obligation" to the claims of the state. Thus, in matters of religious belief, conviction, and worship, the civil magistrate, indeed, the entire legislature, was inferior to the individual conscience.

Madison spent less time in the *Memorial* than he had in his speech on the question of the difficulty of magistrates interpreting scripture. But his fifth argument in the *Memorial* made an explicit reference to questions of biblical interpretation. "Because the bill implies either that the Civil Magistrate is a competent Judge of Religious Truth; or that he may employ Religion as an engine of Civil policy. The first is an arrogant pretension falsified by the contradictory opinions of Rulers in all ages, and throughout the world: the second an unhallowed perversion of the means of salvation."[63]

Finally, Madison's other primary theological point in the *Memorial* as it relates to the importance of private judgment is the fourth argument, where he insists on the "equal rights" humans enjoy to choose their own religion. "We cannot deny," he writes, "an equal freedom to those whose minds have not yet yielded to the evidence which has convinced us." Once again, he expresses this principle as a theological concern. "If this freedom is abused, it is an offence against God, not against man."[64]

Henry's bill was not a bill many people would consider to have real implications for the free exercise of religion. It seemed to impose no religious duties on the unwilling or disbelieving. Rather, it merely sought to provide a tax mechanism to raise money for religious education, with those being taxed having the opportunity to send the money to the church or religious school of their choice. There was even an exemption for "Quakers and Menonists," who were opposed in religious principle to such a scheme, and a general fund that non–church members could contribute to. It was, in modern terms, as neutral and nonpreferential a system of government benefits as could be envisioned in the eighteenth century.

It is thus all the more remarkable that Madison makes use of such an extended argument based on soul freedom before God and the right and duty of personal conviction in worship, an argument today typically associated with free exercise rather than establishment concerns. It goes to show how we have lost most of the sense of the theological arguments and impetus behind the moves to disestablishment in the early republic.

It is also remarkable that Madison's *Memorial* has not, in the modern era, been given more attention by those studying the constitution and question of establishment in the early republic. The lion's share of attention goes to Jefferson and his "wall of separation" letter to the Danbury Baptists. But Jefferson's letter is far briefer, almost cryptic in its content compared with Madison's *Memorial*. The *Memorial* is far richer and broader in argumentation, and certainly has far more theological content to it. But modern scholarship tends to focus on the Danbury letter, with several recent books being devoted entirely to it or its picturesque metaphor. I could not locate one book given over to the *Memorial*.

By contrast, the federal courts have given a similar quantity of attention to the two documents, citing Jefferson's wall about 125 times and Madison's *Memorial* about 105 times.[65] But, given the richness, audience, and impact of the *Memorial*, one would have thought that *it* would be the primary historical document reviewed for the meaning of disestablishment in the early republic. The Danbury letter was signed by one man, Jefferson, who, though hugely important in many ways, did not represent the religious mainstream, or really even the acceptable religious Protestant periphery of his day.

The *Memorial*, on the other hand, was written to appeal to a highly religious public and to provoke as much support as possible. It was signed by over one thousand citizens of Virginia, with another ten thousand signing similar petitions. Many have puzzled over Madison's true religious beliefs, but these become largely irrelevant in the context of a public petition.[66] Such a document uses language and ideas that the author knows will be accepted and supported by the signers—in Madison's case, a strongly biblically based, religiously conservative community with many Baptist and evangelical dissenters.[67]

Whether or not Madison meant to put these ideas into the federal Constitution—as has often been the point of contention and argument—is also not of great import.[68] This is because the *Memorial*, and Jefferson's statute, became the face of what disestablishment meant to what we might call colonial middle America. Or rather—as the middle American colonies had had this sort of disestablishment for multiple decades already—it became the face of the new wave of state-level disestablishments that swept all but a handful of New England states between 1776 and 1798.[69] If we take Madison seriously—and we must because Virginians did, and eventually many other Americans—we must take seriously the *Memorial*'s theological principles regarding the right of private judgment in relation to Bible study and interpretation.

This observation is supported by what happened the following year in Philadelphia, not so much at the federal constitutional convention but with John Witherspoon and the national Presbyterian convention. In fact, John Witherspoon's experiences in Philadelphia in 1787—rather than Madison's—show the real "nationalizing" of the principles of the Virginia bill.

The Right of Private Judgment Goes National

The exact role of John Witherspoon in drafting the new national Presbyterian constitution is not fully known. Some claim that he was a "veritable bishop of the churches," the leading figure in the reorganization, and the primary author of the new plan of government, his draft proposal being "adopted with scarcely any alteration."[70] Others claim he was a mere figurehead, lending the dignity of his prestige to the event—a sort of Washington figure—with others taking the laboring oars.[71]

We do know, however, that whatever his role in its formation, Witherspoon must not have disapproved of the final version of the new church documents. He preached the opening sermon and presided as the initial president-moderator at the ratifying convention for the new organizing documents in 1789.[72] In neither role did he make any recorded objections to the constitution and statements of belief. Further, "all scholars [agree] that Witherspoon was the sole author of the Introduction" to the constitution and that it was "adopted by the Synod without any substantive changes to its original draft."[73] Thus, Witherspoon actively and intentionally applied the principle of the right of private judgment to help make a dramatic alteration in the way the Presbyterian church expressed its view on the role of the civil magistrate in religious affairs.

That such a dramatic change took place is a matter of historic record. In setting out their confession of faith, the Synod reasserted the Westminster Confession of Faith of 1647 virtually verbatim. The only meaningful changes dealt with church and state. The key article that was changed was article 3 of chapter 23, "Of the Civil Magistrate." The original article had read as follows:

> The civil magistrate may not assume to himself the administration of the Word and Sacrament, or the power of the keys of the kingdom of heaven: yet he hath authority, and it is his duty to take order that unity and peace be preserved in the Church, that the truth of God be kept pure and entire, that all blasphemies and heresies be suppressed, all corruptions and abuses in worship and discipline prevented or reformed, and all the ordinances of God duly settled, administered, and observed. For the better effecting whereof he hath power to call synods, to be present at them, and to provide that whatsoever is transacted in them be according to the mind of God.[74]

This formulation had given the civil magistrate a role in overseeing the discipline of the church, as well as in suppressing blasphemy and heresy. The changed American version took the magistrate entirely out of these matters. It reads as follows (the changes and additions are in italics):

> The civil magistrate may not assume to himself the administration of the Word and Sacrament, or the power of the keys of the kingdom of heaven, or, in the least, interfere in matters of faith. *Yet, as nursing fathers, it is the duty of civil magistrates to protect the church of our common Lord, without giving preference to any denomination of Christians above the rest, in such a manner that all ecclesiastical persons whatever shall enjoy the full, free, and unquestioned liberty of discharging every part of their sacred function without violence or danger. And as Jesus Christ has appointed a regular government and discipline in His church, no law of any commonwealth should interfere with, let, or hinder the due exercise thereof among the voluntary members of any denomination of Christians, according to their own profession or belief. It is the duty of the civil magistrate to protect the person and good name of all their people, in such an effectual manner as that no person be suffered, either upon pretense of religion or infidelity to offer any indignity, violence, abuse or injury to any other person whatsoever; and to take order that all religious and ecclesiastical assemblies be held without molestation or disturbance.*[75]

The American version dramatically cuts back on the role of the magistrate in religious affairs. It does refer to civil leaders as "nursing fathers" of the church. But that role is limited to protecting the free exercise of religion, both for individuals and assemblies, on an impartial and equal basis to all churches. There is no claim for financial support for or promotion of religion by the state. Rather, it is a call for the protection of the free exercise of religion for all. Like Madison's *Memorial*, the revised article recognizes the priority of religious commitments over "laws of the commonwealth" that might interfere with not merely the belief but with the "due exercise" of Christians.

And what was the principle driving this new vision of church and state? We are not left to guess, because we have it in Witherspoon's own words. In the introduction, which he authored, he wrote this: the Presbyterians "consider *the rights of private judgment*, in all matters that respect religion, as universal and alienable [*sic*]: they do not even wish to see any religious constitution aided by the civil power, further than may be necessary for protection and security, and, at the same time, equal and common to all others."[76]

Essentially, this is a succinct summary of the changes found in chapter 23. It is perhaps even clearer that no aid or support from the civil power is sought, except an equal "protection and security." Witherspoon's final article of the introduction insists that church discipline "be purely moral or spiritual in its object, and not attended with any civil affects."[77] This also is an explicit rejection of the original Westminster Confession, which had allowed that those in violation of church rules could be proceeded against by church leaders "and by the power of the Civil Magistrate."[78]

Thus, again the "right of private judgment" is associated with not only religious freedom and freedom of conscience, but also freedom from state interference with or support of the church. It is used in as purely a religious context as can be found outside a sacred writing—a preamble to a doctrinal statement of belief by a church synod. It is identified as the foundation principle on which the major changes in relation to church and state are made. At last, the right of private judgment in matters of religion had been expressed as a truly national principle, at least within certain influential religious circles. The legal and political framework would soon follow, at least at the state level.

Despite championing this right of private judgment on a national level, Witherspoon should not be confused with a modern-day church/state separationist. In his *Lectures on Moral Philosophy,* he had argued for a limited role of the magistrate in enforcing laws against "profanity and impiety."[79] In the same place, he said "many are of the opinion" that the magistrate ought also to make public provision for the worship of God, although none should be constrained to do so. Despite putting this opinion onto others, he said that he himself thought there might be a "good deal of reason for it," as the "great bulk of common people" may never have the inclination or resources to provide for their own religious education.[80]

These sentiments seem to run contrary, in spirit if not in letter, to the provisions and language of the new Presbyterian constitution, which said that no aid should be provided by the state to religion. Perhaps Witherspoon had reconsidered his already somewhat halfheartedly held views, written about twenty years earlier. Or it may be that the give-and-take and compromise of the convention had not allowed for the full expression of his personal views on the topic. Whatever the case, the full separation of the magistrate from matters of religion, except in its evenhanded protection of religious freedom, became the public expression of the national Presbyterian church.

Conclusion

Recently, scholars and some judges have argued that the First Amendment did not represent a national consensus about how the church and the state should relate to each other at the state or local level.[81] At best, some argue, it was meant merely to prevent a single, national established church. Indeed, some say that far from disestablishing religion, it was meant to *protect* existing state establishments.[82] Our modern-style disestablishment and church/state separation, some propose, is a product of the anti-Catholic bigotry of the mid-nineteenth century and the growing secularism of the late nineteenth and twentieth centuries.[83]

There can be no doubt that our understanding of disestablishment has evolved and grown over our more than two-hundred-year history. Such is the nature of constitutional principles and growing societies. But to contend that meaningful church/state separation is a post-1940s, secular/liberal interpretation of the most radical of the founders should be reconsidered in light of the story told here. National church organizations were, in the late eighteenth century, on their own initiative changing their statements of belief to dramatically alter the role of the magistrate in spiritual affairs. This change cannot be explained by anti-Catholic bigotry or modern secularist influence.

The Presbyterians were not the only ones to make these changes. In 1801 their example of removing the civil magistrate from religious affairs was "followed by the Protestant Episcopal Church in the revision of the political sections of the Thirty-Nine Articles of Religion."[84] The fact that both the formerly pro-establishment Presbyterians and Anglicans shifted their positions in America on establishment by 1800 shows that something had indeed dramatically changed the manner in which most people viewed the roles of church and state.

Of course, dissenting groups had had this separationist language in their articles of beliefs decades earlier, whether Baptists, Quakers, Anabaptists, or Mennonites. What the Presbyterian document shows is that this principle of dissenting Protestantism had now become an accepted part of American Protestantism generally. As church historian Phillip Schaff put it in the mid-19th century, expressions of religious liberty and equality of all denominations before the law was not just a principle of major denominations, but "has become the common law of the land."[85]

These churches were not constrained by federalism. They did not speak to the issue of religion only on the national level. Rather, they addressed the issue as that of how government in principle—all governments, whether federal, state, or local—should relate to religion. They argued for the kind of freedom of belief, freedom from magisterial involvement, and even independence from state aid that Madison had helped implement in Virginia.

There would still be discussions and arguments over the lines between civil and spiritual. Some churches would continue to receive state support in New England states, such as Connecticut and Massachusetts, for decades after 1787 and after the First Amendment was enacted. There was also the question about where moral issues might rise to the level of impacting the peace and safety of society. Examples of these issues were blasphemy laws, Sunday laws, and slavery.

Some have argued that the continued existence of blasphemy and Sunday laws, and Bible reading in the public schools, meant that nothing fundamentally had changed, and that the notion of American religious freedom is a popular myth.[86] But this claim overlooks the undeniable historical reality that the terms and contours of the law, religion, and morality debate had now fundamentally changed. It is certainly true that many Protestant notions of morality continued to hold sway during the 19th century in both society and law. For the greatest part, though, this morality was considered to be part of the teaching of the natural law, and did not involve the intentional enforcement of faith-based or sectarian religious views.

Those defending the states' role in suppressing blasphemy or promoting Sunday observance almost never spoke in terms of the magistrate's responsibility to promote religious or spiritual truths. Rather, they argued that church attendance had direct, positive civil impacts on society, or that laws against blasphemy and Sabbath-breaking were aimed at preventing breaches of the peace. Thus, the magistrate could regulate these for the peace and order of society. But even these arguments lost traction over time, as the purely religious bases of blasphemy and Sabbath keeping became clearer to people as society became more diverse.[87]

Education and schools was something of a special case. Most education at the time of the founding was private, and run by churches or religious orders, and thus early disestablishments did not impact education much. The transition to public run schools throughout the 19th century forced a debate over the relation of education to religion, and to morals and values generally, that remains with us to the present day.[88] But the case of religion and schools is a peculiar and perplexing one. Americans had to adjust to the notion of public institutions now occupying the spaces held formerly by private groups that were responsible for transmitting fundamental community values and morals. The wrestling over this difficult issue should not obscure the fact that, in almost all of 19ᵗʰ century America, clearly and historically public entities, such as courts, legislatures, and political leaders were now under an obligation to operate and justify their actions on the basis of a practical, civic public good, and not in terms of promoting religious rituals, beliefs or practices.

Under magisterial Protestantism, no defense of public acts or decisions in terms of a practical public good was needed, since the role of the magistrate in both protecting and promoting religion, as well as punishing heresy, was largely unquestioned. But now, the new ideal of American Protestantism meant that the terms of the discussion were changed. Only those acts that were directly linked to public concerns could engage the magistrate's attention and action. The discussion about the lines between the civil and the spiritual would continue for the next century, and even to the present, but the ground rules of those discussions were fundamentally altered.

The coincident timing of the U.S. Constitutional Convention with the Presbyterian national convention is one of those serendipities of history that can open the mind to larger insights. At the same time that America was becoming truly an American nation, American Protestantism was becoming, well, truly Protestant—in the sense that dissenters had used the term to mean religious liberty and the rights of conscience. It might be more historically accurate to say that American Protestantism was becoming more radically Protestant—a trend that would only intensify under the effects of the Second Great Awakening. In its church/state views, the Protestant church in America would look fundamentally different from the magisterial churches of Europe—and much more like the minority, dissenting members of the radical wing of the Reformation.

The confluence of political and religious events in the summer of 1787 was an important foundation for the Protestant America that emerged over the next 150 years. This is because the revisionist legal historians are right on this point—the First Amendment on its own did not disestablish state churches. Whatever principles of disestablishment Madison and others intended to place there, the fact remains that for almost 150 years, states could have whatever church/state arrangements they chose. The example of the First Amendment no doubt influenced some states to follow a similar church/state course. But that they all eventually chose full disestablishment had more to do with the influence of the Presbyterian constitution, and the similar positions of other church groups, than it did with the effect of the federal Constitution.

It took both a Madison *and* a Witherspoon—a politically acute theologian and a theologically astute politician—to turn the right of private judgment into a truly national principle of church and state. The current religious vitality of America, often ascribed to the religious energy unleashed by avoiding state-supported religious monopolies, may be owed in good part to the fact that neither Witherspoon or Madison chose to spend that muggy Philadelphia summer at home in the shade.

Back to the Future of Church and State

IT HAS BEEN more than 220 years since Witherspoon and Madison helped nationalize the dissenting Protestant contribution to America's system of church and state. Much has changed in the American handling of church and state since that time. It would be another entire project to trace the final decline of state establishments, with the last one expiring in Massachusetts in 1833, the continued struggle over remaining elements of civil religion, including school Bible-reading, blasphemy laws, and Sunday blue laws. Many blame the loss of these elements on the eventual incorporation of the First Amendment and its Establishment Clause against state governments. But the fact is that most of these elements were either gone from state law, or were unenforced, before the process of incorporation began, as the logic of disestablishment played itself out during the nineteenth century.[1]

This logic was aided by the rise of a secular stream of thought that, while present earlier in the thought of Thomas Paine, Thomas Jefferson, and others, gained new force in the late nineteenth century. During this period a lingering, informal, nonsectarian, Protestant establishment—evidenced by generic Bible readings and prayer in public schools—gave way to a more thoroughgoing secular establishment that pushed almost all vestiges of religion to the fringes, or off the edges, of the public square.

Indeed, from the early twentieth century to the present, rather than a contest between dissenting and more magisterial strains of Protestantism, the competition has been between religion and nonreligion, belief and skepticism. In this battle, the differences between religiously based views of church and state have become overshadowed by the apparent gulf between skeptics and believers. The implication of my research is to suggest, however, that the modern contest is not two-sided, but three-sided. There is a moderating position between the so-called religious right and secular left, one based on the dissenting Protestant heritage that came to be forcefully expressed at the constitutional founding. This position can be understood by examining differing approaches of each to the relationships between the individual, church, state, and God.

The best place to see these models outlined is the historical period when legal thinkers thought theologically and theologians thought about the legal consequences of their ideas. To understand our possible futures, it will be helpful to revisit the past: specifically, the end of the seventeenth century, when the revocation of the Edict of Nantes sent legal thinkers to their libraries to prepare defenses of religious toleration. At that time, these positions were ably expressed by three of the most brilliant legal and theological minds of that time.

The three were Samuel Pufendorf, a Lutheran natural rights lawyer and counselor to the king of Sweden; John Locke; and Pierre Bayle, an influential French Huguenot theologian and philosopher. In their writings can be found the basic outlines of the Puritan, semitheocratic model; the separationist model based on the right of private judgment; and the secular, liberal separationist model.[2]

Pufendorf and Medieval Privileges

Born in 1632 in Saxony, Pufendorf was best known for his works on international law, especially *The Law of Nature and Nations*.[3] Published in 1672, this work was widely influential on the continent, in Scotland, and in the newly formed American colonies.[4] When the Edict of Nantes was revoked, Pufendorf took the opportunity to write what has been described as an "appendix" to this work, which applied his natural law theory to issues of church and state.[5] Entitled *Of the Nature and Qualification of Religion in Reference to Civil Society*, it was published in 1687. It set out a principled basis for what was ultimately a pragmatic, anemic toleration. It represented the magisterial Protestant continuation of the medieval view of church and state.

Pufendorf dedicated the book to the elector of Brandenburg-Prussia and used it to recommend himself for a post in the elector's Berlin court, which he indeed received.[6] The intended audience perhaps helped shape the work. He sets out a high view of the state and its power, and a rather limited and weak basis for religious toleration. The work begins with apparently strong principles of separation between ecclesiastical and civil spheres, as well as a commitment to individual rights. But the last third of the book returns spiritual powers and oversight to the "Christian" ruler that are denied to secular rulers in the first portions of the book. To simplify his thinking in a useful way, we

can diagram it. The diagram contains
four basic elements: Truth/God, the
church, the state, and the individual.
Pufendorf's arrangement of these elements would look like the arrangement
shown in figure E.1.

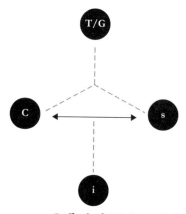

Here, God and the accessibility
of truth are recognized. A distinction between church and state is also
accepted, but that distinction allows
for a great deal of cooperation, especially when the ruler is a Christian. The
importance of the individual is mini-

FIGURE E.1 Puffendorf's Medieval Model

mized, because of one's need to go through the organs of church and state to
obtain truth, whether spiritual or civil. It represents the world of the divine
right of kings and popes, where no individual rights exist, but only privileges
extended by the rulers. It is one where church and state are distinct entities,
but play a role in cooperating to civilly enforce the majority religious beliefs
and practices of society. Under this system, the church in theory has a superior position in society, as kings and rulers are subject to the superior spiritual
authority of church. Bishops and popes at times provided legitimacy to the
claims of leaders to civil authority, at times crowning them, as Pope Leo III
did for Charlemagne. This relationship is shown in figure E.1 by the capital *C*
and lowercase *s*.

Pufendorf criticized the revocation of the Edict of Nantes, but not because
the Huguenots had some sort of natural right claim to religious liberty. Rather,
he believed that the Crown, once having extended the toleration, should keep
its word and not withdraw it. It was a question of honoring agreements and
contracts, and the social stability protected by that practice. Pufendorf had no
principled or moral argument for why the Edict should have been entered into
in the first place. That was a policy calculation that brought political peace in the
face of an aggressive and armed minority. In Pufendorf's model, religious liberty
became a question of policy, a privilege to be extended or denied at the inclination of the ruler. His philosophical fruit fell not far from the medieval tree.

Locke and Protestant Rights

I have already examined John Locke's church/state principles in his *Letter on
Toleration*. His views show the shape of the new world that Luther helped

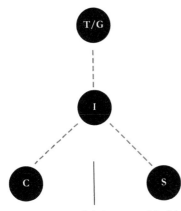

FIGURE E.2 Locke's Protestant Model

create in proposing that each person should access God through prayer and Bible study. The priesthood of all believers inverted the bottom half of Pufendorf's diagram. The belief vaulted the individual to a position above the church and the state, with direct access to God and truth. Locke's model of these four elements would look like figure E.2.

This model accepted, like the medieval model, that God exists and that certain truths could be ascertained about both the world and spiritual things. But the new, Protestant view placed the individual above church and state. Each person now had the duty and right to seek this truth from God, through both the Bible (especially about spiritual things) and nature (especially political matters and civil morality). The church and the state existed to support and protect the rights of the individual, one as a member of the spiritual world, the other as a citizen of the temporal world. There was a separation between these two powers, since their jurisdiction was limited to their separate spheres of concern, whether spiritual or civil. It was a separation of equality and mutual respect, with each entity respecting the sovereignty of the other in its own sphere. Hence, both are represented in figure E.2 by the capital letters *C* and *S*.

One's rights against the state as an individual, in turn, derived from the duties one owed to God. This is essentially the political expression of the Protestant model of the priesthood of all believers. It serves as a robust foundation for individual rights, hence the individual is shown by a capital *I*. This is the model we have traced through the early modern West and seen to be an important part of the impulse to disestablishment in colonial America.

Bayle and Skeptical Rights

Pierre Bayle, while ostensibly a Calvinist theologian, was actually a strongly skeptical thinker who based his view of toleration on broad epistemological skepticism. Bayle was accused by fellow Calvinist theologians of supporting atheism, and he was deprived of his professorship at his Protestant university as a result.[7] Rather than an heir of Calvin and ancestor of the New England Puritans, Bayle was more an heir of Pyrrhonius and ancestor to Hume, Voltaire, Rousseau, and eventually Franklin and Jefferson.[8]

Bayle largely shared Pufendorf's view on the supremacy of the state over the individual. He rejected Locke's notion of a reciprocal contract between ruler and people, denied the right of rebellion, and upheld a strong duty of obedience to the ruler.[9] But unlike Pufendorf, Bayle held a skeptical view of the world. Especially in the area of speculative truths, including religion, he affirmed a strong difference from mathematical or empirical truths. For speculative truths, he believed one could only attain a "reputed" truth rather than actual truth.[10]

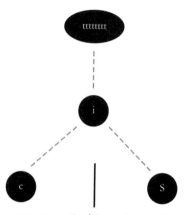

FIGURE E.3 Bayle's Secular Model

This uncertainty led Bayle to defend the notion of individual conscience.

Other thinkers of the day often spoke of the rights of conscience, but it was generally understood that they were not talking about erroneous conscience or acts against one's conscience. Bayle was one of the first to propose that rights of conscience should extend to consciences that were believed to be in error—the so-called erroneous conscience.[11] Even if one could know that someone else was in error, Bayle argued, how could one know that the other person was convinced of that error?[12] This question was a central point of contention in the debate between Roger Williams and John Cotton over the issue of toleration and persecution.

Bayle's strong defense of conscience, then, was based on a weak view of truth, or at least human ability to know truth. This led him to view individual judgment and conscience as important. Thus, he held a strong view of the duty of the state to tolerate religious differences. To put Bayle's view into our diagram looks like figure E.3.

The lowercase *t*s represent the individualistic conception of truth, where no universal view of truth exists, but everyone conceives his or her own truth. Church and state are still separate, but it is not a separation of mutual equality and sovereign spheres. Rather, it is a separation based on a suspicion of the truth claims made by religious people. The tolerance in this scheme is dependent on a commitment to skepticism—from the logic that if truth cannot be known, then no one can or should enforce it. The real threats to this system are those who claim knowledge of absolute truths.

Churches and people who believe in special revelation were such a threat. Therefore, religious people and their beliefs are to be kept far away from politics and the public square generally. Separation of church and state, rather than being based on a view of separate sovereignties, comes to be founded on hostility to the truth claims of religious people and their views of special revelation. Religious people and their ideas are kept not only out of government, but on the fringes of the public square generally. The attitude under this view of the state toward the church was symbolically expressed by Napoleon when, in contrast to Charlemagne, he crowned himself emperor in the presence of the pope. Even more substantively, Napoleon's new legal code became the secular replacement of many of the Christian-favoring legal systems of Europe that had evolved under the influence of the Code of Justinian. The marginalization of the church and religion in this system is represented in figure E.3 by the lowercase *c*.

Rights in this system are not quite as secure as under the Lockean view. Individual autonomy is a somewhat fragile thing when it is based merely on skepticism rather than on individual duties to, and rights before, God. The solitary autonomy of the individual becomes fairly quickly outweighed by the interest of the group once accommodation of the individual becomes anything more than a slight inconvenience. This is seen very clearly in the skeptical/atheistic communist systems, where respect for the individual is very quickly submerged to the common good. A similar thing happens in a democracy, we have seen, when terrorism threatens national security. Liberal thinkers known for their defense of human rights begin writing apologias for "enhanced interrogations" and even torture.[13] Hence the *i* for individual is lowercase.

Under this model, there is no real reason why religious claims to truth should obtain greater protection than claims to convictions in other areas. Why should religious claims have special protection beyond that received by a wide range of special interest claimants, such as environmentalists, animal rights supporters, or advocates of unions and labor? People feel strongly about all these issues. If it is the individual conviction only that provides the basis for rights, as this model suggests, then all these convictions should be treated equally. But ultimately, if all convictions are equally protected, none can be meaningfully protected, or democracy will ultimately become gridlocked amid a cacophony of clashing rights claims.

Three Views in American History

My discussion of the third view has moved beyond what Bayle himself would have suggested into how at least parts of modern liberalism has developed this view. All three of these views, the Pufendorfian, the Lockean, and the

Baylean models, have had varying influences throughout American history. (A good case has been made by political scientist Phillip Munoz that all three views were present at the constitutional founding period in the persons of George Washington, James Madison, and Thomas Jefferson.[14]) A side-by-side comparison of these models, a representative advocate, the historical periods they represent, and their time of greatest influence in America is represented in figure E.4.

The American Puritans developed a Pufendorfian-like church/state arrangement in early New England, with a civil magistrate involved in enforcing ecclesiastical rules and discipline. Thus, the earliest American colonies were founded on the theory of the medieval model on the left in figure E.4, with the exception of Rhode Island. Some later ones, especially New Jersey, Pennsylvania, Delaware and North Carolina, were founded basically on the Protestant theory in the center box, which also guided the formation of the national Constitution. Despite Pufendorf's enormous influence in both Scotland and the American colonies, the founders of the American republic explicitly rejected his form of church/state arrangement.[15] At the time of the Revolution and the formation of the Constitution, Pufendorf's model of toleration was limited to two or three New England states, and within a few years vanished from even there.

It was Locke's formulation, mediated by Madison, Witherspoon, and other key American thinkers, of dissenting Protestantism that carried the day in the founding of the American republic. Their views of the separate roles of the two powers were the ideological victors on the topic of tolerance and religious freedom in the early republic. It is this shift from a medieval, paternalistic,

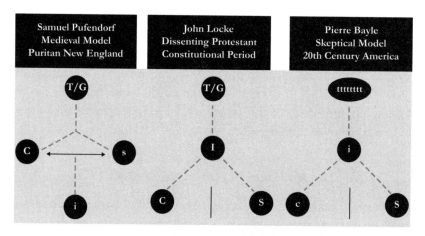

FIGURE E.4 A Comparison of the Three Models

hierarchical model to an individualistic, egalitarian, rights-based outlook that Gordon Wood so ably documents in his justly famed work *The Radicalism of the American Revolution*.[16] Wood broadly and convincingly documents the change from hierarchy, patriarchy, aristocracy, and patronage to democracy, equality, republicanism, and the rule of law in colonial America. Figure E.4 can perhaps shed light on one of the puzzles in Wood's book. In his subtitle, he asserts that the book shows "How a Revolution Transformed a Monarchical Society into a Democratic One Unlike Any Other That Had Ever Existed." While he is right about the uniqueness of American society, it seems apparent from the story in his book that the Revolution did not cause the shift from a monarchical to a republican ethos. Rather, the Revolution was a symptom of a shift that had already occurred in American culture and society.

Wood does an excellent job of describing that shift from monarchical to republican outlook, but offers, in my view, less than convincing arguments for the reasons or causes of the shift. He focuses on the Enlightenment, arguing that "for the revolutionary generation America became the Enlightenment fulfilled."[17] This raises the problem, earlier discussed, of trying to explain a movement with tremendous popular involvement and appeal by appeal to an elite affinity and state of mind. Wood is unwilling to give religious thought any real credit for the paradigm shift to a republican outlook, instead crediting Enlightenment and rationalistic sources. Indeed, he views religion as a conservative force that largely resisted that shift.[18]

But it seems that Wood is looking at only one version of religion in telling this story, that of magisterial Protestantism. This is most obviously displayed when he describes the belief in "liberty of conscience and separation of church and state" as an "Enlightenment belief" that was resisted by "many religious groups."[19] Indeed, there were religious groups that opposed religious liberty and the separation of church and state. But the dominant religious groups in early republican America had taken on a dissenting Protestant perspective, which Wood seems to miss almost completely. Wood's larger story becomes much more explicable when religion, and religious belief, are given their due weight in shifting popular views forward from a medieval to a Protestant outlook on church, society, and the individual.

The religious support for American independence as well as religious liberty was well understood by those closer to the Revolution, such as Edmund Burke, the British parliamentarian. Burke explained the independent character of the American colonists by the fact that "the people are Protestants, and of that kind which is the most adverse to all implicit submission of mind and opinions. … All Protestantism, even the most cold and passive, is a sort of dissent. But the religion most prevalent in our northern colonies is a refinement on the principle of resistance: it is the *dissidence of dissent, and the Protestantism of the Protestant religion.*"[20] Burke, a strong critic of the Enlightenment-driven ideology of the French Revolution, saw very different, and much more religious and Protestant, principles at work in America.

But by the late nineteenth century, the rise of uncertainty in theology and philosophy undermined the American Protestant outlook and laid the groundwork for a toleration based on skepticism. John Stuart Mill's view of skeptical individualism increasingly became the prism through which Locke was understood. As a consequence, the twentieth century saw a wholesale move, at least in the elite centers of thought, to toleration based on epistemological uncertainty and moral relativism.

After the Civil War, the rise of Darwinism and the growth of philosophical uncertainty caused many American elite institutions, including colleges and universities, the professions, and the media, to move toward the much more skeptical view represented by Bayle. This shift did not happen overnight, and much has been written on the involved process of secularization in American history.[21] The Protestant umbrella broadened to include an even more generic and diffuse sense of American spiritual identity.

The influence of German higher idealism, with its attendant historicism and philosophy of relativism, in the mid-to-late nineteenth and the early twentieth centuries called into question the natural law foundations of the country. This philosophy also undercut the Protestant model of church and society that was based on these views of natural law and natural rights. New approaches to the law based on social and pragmatic concerns accompanied the gradual acceptance of legal positivism. These ideas gained ground in the early twentieth century and especially influenced legal thought in the second half of the twentieth century.[22]

These new ideas made progress to different degrees in differing parts of society. They made greater inroads earlier in many leading colleges and universities, and thus into other elite social institutions such as the media and Hollywood.[23] Old paradigms continued to hold sway at more popular levels. The Civil Rights Movement of the 1950s and 1960s could be described as the last gasp of Protestant-style natural rights/public morality arguments at the popular level, which combined with a more modern, liberal rights perspective among its leadership, the media, and the courts.[24]

But the cycle of ideas has continued to roll, and now a vocal segment of the American public, especially after the events of 9/11, is vigorously rejecting the skepticism and relativism that has come to be associated with our current system of rights. Rather than returning to a Lockean, Protestant founding view, however, there are many who appear ready to embrace a model more like that of Pufendorf.[25] In this post-9/11 world, significant segments of American society are simultaneously rejecting moral relativism as well as seeking the security provided by a stronger, centralized government.

This rejection of the modern paradigm moves society from the right side of the tolerance diagram generally leftward. It does not require a conscious repudiation of the importance of the individual to move from the Locke column over into the Pufendorf column. The difference between Locke and Pufendorf was not over their ostensible commitment to the individual and freedom to worship. Rather, it was that a strong view of the supremacy of the state generally negated Pufendorf's theoretically positive view of the individual.

In the last few years trends within American politics have undercut its traditional system of separation of powers and checks and balances—a system that lies at the heart of an accountable, limited government, and the rule of law. The unitary executive, the growth of the power of unelected administrative agencies, the greater use of executive orders, the willingness of Congress to delegate the declaration of war to the executive—all these trends tend to diminish the role of the people in overseeing their government.[26]

Rather than the citizens monitoring a government accountable to them, as Locke envisioned, American citizens are becoming increasingly content to let the government monitor itself and them. Unwittingly, they have adopted an attitude towards government that is more consonant with Pufendorf's view—that of the paternal state which can be trusted to look out for our best interests. In Pufendorf's model, a paternalistic view of government power also accepts a role for government in religious matters. It comes as no surprise, then, that the recent moves toward a diminishment of the separation of powers and an increase in centralized authority has been accompanied by an increase in the state's involvement with religion.

The Sovereign and Religion

Much of this shift to a greater role for the presidency happened under the conservative, Republican administration of President George W. Bush, but it began earlier, under not only the Democratic presidency of Bill Clinton, but also those of George H. W. Bush and Ronald Reagan. The shift continues at some level under the oversight of Barack Obama's administration, as we have seen, as of this writing, in President Obama's skirting of the War Powers Act and his failure to seek the approval of Congress in his commitment of

American forces to the hostilities in Libya. It is thus a bipartisan, or nonpartisan, development.

In his treatise on church and state, Pufendorf made a list of appropriate involvements of the "Christian prince" with the church. It is interesting to compare his list with actual events from the last few years:

1. *The sovereign funds Christian organizations:* Presidents Clinton, Bush, and Obama have sponsored legislation or policies to send tax monies to religious groups and churches to carry out social welfare programs. In practice, the vast majority of this money goes to Christian groups.[27] The Bush administration also supported school voucher programs aimed at supporting private religious schools.[28]

2. *The sovereign provides oversight and surveillance of religious groups:* The Department of Justice has implemented rules that allow it to monitor and infiltrate religious groups based on suspicions of illegal activity, suspicions that do not need to meet the traditional law enforcement standard of probable cause.[29]

3. *The sovereign sets standards for teachers in religious schools:* Once schools accept state voucher funds, they generally are required to admit students and even employ teachers regardless of religious affiliation or practices. This can also be true for employees of religious organizations whose salaries are paid out of government money given for faith-based social programs.

4. *The sovereign uses religion for civil unity:* While most presidents have employed religious language in their speeches, President George W. Bush's administration took this practice to new levels of pervasiveness, invoking faith and belief in God on a wide range of personal, domestic, and foreign policy matters. While ostensibly acknowledging America's religious diversity, he treated explicitly Christian language and symbols as a kind of unifying theme in his public communications. Leaders of both parties have participated in this trend, as neither wants to be left out in the race to gain the support of religious America. The 2012 presidential race has taken this use of religious language to new heights, as one Republican candidate after another finds it important to cast himself or herself as the true evangelical candidate who will oppose the media's "war on religion." The Mormon candidates in the field have had to go to extra lengths to assert that their religious views are acceptably Christian and American. Indeed, in his 2008 candidacy, Mitt Romney felt it necessary to publicly declare that he believed "that Jesus Christ is the son of God and the Savior of Mankind."[30]

5. *The sovereign creates church standards and oversees discipline:* Just prior to the 2004 American presidential campaign, the media reported efforts by the Bush campaign to influence the Catholic hierarchy in Rome to encourage American bishops to enforce conservative Catholic social teachings on topics such as gay marriage and abortion. These topics were an important point of contention between President Bush and his challenger, John Kerry, a Catholic, in that presidential race.[31]

6. *The sovereign promotes "consensus" religious beliefs and opposes atheists:* Attempts by secularists to remove "under God" from the Pledge of Allegiance or the Ten Commandments from public spaces has resulted in a backlash against the beliefs of atheists and unbelievers. A sitting Supreme Court justice not long ago wrote that because the "vast majority" of believers, Christian, Jewish and Islamic, believed in God and the validity of the Ten Commandments, there was nothing "unconstitutional in a State's favoring religion generally, honoring God through public prayer and acknowledgment, or, in a non-proselytizing manner, venerating the Ten Commandments."[32]

Some of the above items, especially the careful use of some religious language by civil leaders, are perhaps an appropriate corrective to the last half century of increasing secularization of the public sphere. We have recently passed through a period where a kind of secular orthodoxy reigned in the public sphere, and many religious people felt marginalized. The Lockean/Protestant model does not view all public mentions of God as violative of a healthy separation of church and state. Both Madison and Jefferson, who were both very sensitive to issues of church/state separation, still used language referencing a creator God in their works of public advocacy and policy. The most obvious example of this is Jefferson's reference in the Declaration of Independence to all men being "endowed by their Creator" with rights. Madison's *Memorial and Remonstrance* likewise invokes the notion of a creator God to whom humanity owed certain duties.

But their God was the God of natural theology and philosophy. He was the God accessible by all, according to Lock's philosophy, through the application of reason to the natural world. For them, religion was not the same thing as an acknowledgment of God's existence, his role as creator, or even that humans should relate to him. These truths, they believed, could be arrived at by a natural philosophy. Religion, on the other hand, in a definition used by both James Madison and George Mason in framing the Virginia constitution, was "the duty which we owe to our Creator and the manner of discharging it."[33] In this view, religion was not just the mere conception of a Supreme Being. Rather, it was those specially revealed ideas, either through holy books, prophets, or even an inner light, about how people should worship and behave toward Him.

Indeed, the founders, including Madison and Jefferson, viewed the notion of God and a sacred realm as important, perhaps even indispensable, to a view of limited government and preservation of individual rights. In their view, if there was no authority outside the state, there would be no theoretical limit on the powers or prerogatives of the state. Thus, it was a conception of God that placed limits on government, rather than creating new prerogatives for the state.

This issue of limits perhaps provides the essential test for whether theistic language in public ceremonies or objects (money, pledges, oaths, etc.) is improper establishment of religion, or proper political philosophy. Does the reference to the Deity serve to remind the body politic, both the rulers and the citizens, of its limits? Does it point to a sphere of inviolable human rights beyond the authority of the state, especially the freedom of conscience, and put the state on notice that it must restrain and limit its conduct accordingly? Or is the theistic language used to enlarge the state's power into the realm of the sacred and to justify the state's promotion or otherwise favoring of some religious view or group within society? The former would be consistent with the founders' political philosophy/theology. The latter would be to pervert their use of theistic language. It turns what was meant to limit the power of the state into an excuse for the state to exercise illegitimate and inappropriate powers.[34]

Certain items on Pufendorf's list move well beyond the language of theistic limits on the state. Proposing that somehow the state can promote the biblical Ten Commandments overlooks the fact that the first four describe our duties of worship to God. In addition, for political leaders to encourage religious leaders to enforce their internal discipline to gain an advantage in political contests is to politically meddle in questions of worship and duty to God. As far as funding religious entities and churches, the dissenting Protestant tradition is quite clear that such support steps over the proper bounds of church and state. This was true in any of Penn's mid-Atlantic colonies, Roger William's Rhode Island, and Madison's and the Baptists' Virginia.

Conclusion: America Caught between Extremes

Often the rhetoric of one extreme helps "validate" the criticisms and claims of the other extreme. Certain left-wing advocacy groups attempt to "de-Christianize" America by challenging the use of God language on coins, public buildings, or in pledges. This emboldens right-wing Christian groups to respond with intemperate claims about American being founded in some legal sense as a "Christian nation" or that "the separation of church and state" is a Soviet invention that has no role in our constitutional republic.

The basic problem is that both left and right draw on models of church and state that are foreign to the prevailing philosophy of our state and national founders. One side promotes a quasi-medieval system that our national founders rejected, the other a secular model that had a home in the French, but not the American, Revolution. Both extremes jockey for supremacy in a world made tense by an apparently interminable war on terror and a bleak economic environment.

But moments of crisis are also times of opportunity. The Revocation of Nantes provided a moment for European thinkers to set a public idea of religious toleration and religious freedom on principled grounds. The challenges of our Revolutionary War and constitutional founding created a time and place for these ideas to come to practical fruition in government. It has been creditably proposed that it was the crisis of the Civil War that moved America away from a Protestant framework of rights and duties and toward its encounter with and embrace of the uncertainty of secularity.[35]

American's latest crisis—the encounter with a radicalized militant extremist element of Islam—has caused the middle of the country to strongly question and doubt the elite's embrace of a relativistic secularity. Average contemporary Americans believe in right and wrong, truth and error. They believe that suicide attacks on innocent civilians are a virulent type of evil that needs to be responded to by severe justice, if not outright vengeance. A commitment to uncertainties is no longer seen as a sufficient basis for societal or state restraint or inaction in the name of "rights."

Thus, middle America has stayed astonishingly mute in the face of the well-documented reports of "enhanced" interrogations, secret renditions, secret evidence, secret courts, long-term detentions of suspects without trial, even assassinations of U.S. citizens, all carried out by American government officials and agents in our war on terror.[36] These deeds have occurred under the oversight of both Republican and Democratic presidents, and appear to have popular support.[37] There was little public outcry when Congress passed, and President Obama signed, the National Defense Authorization Act of 2011, which allows the president to indefinitely detain terror suspects, including U.S. citizens arrested in the United States, without charge.[38]

These were actions that until a decade ago most Americans would, and our government often did, classify as torture, kidnapping, murder and the violation of fundamental civil and human rights. We routinely condemned conduct such as waterboarding, use of stress positions and sleep deprivation, monitored beatings, detentions without timely charges and trial, and executions without meaningful trial, as the acts of rogue or totalitarian states. The federal courts would have certainly condemned many of these acts as violative of fundamental guarantees in the US. Constitution. It shows how far our national mental mode has slipped into the medieval model when we view these rights as dispensable once the state, in its wisdom, chooses to withdraw them in the face of some real, and many hyped, threats.

This phenomenon also shows how the church/state model of a country affects its larger system and conception of rights. A loss of an understanding of the religious roots and Protestant heritage of the antimajoritarian, anti-establishment aspects of the religion clauses is accompanied, unsurprisingly, by a loss of the sense of the antimajoritarian and sacrosanct nature of rights generally. A reacquaintance with the dissenting Protestant model of religious freedom, including a principled commitment to a balanced separation of church and state, might also help revitalize a broader sense of the sanctity of other basic human rights and freedoms.

The right could learn that it need not sacrifice meaningful freedom for people of all faiths and no faith to protect either security or morality. The left could learn that a shared civil morality and overarching sense of transcendence and stewardship are important and even necessary conditions of the freedoms we all cherish. Even secularists and agnostics might recognize that a respect for the possibility of the transcendent and the sacred, and the individual's connection to it, can make for a richer, more humane outlook on the importance and rights of people.

If this moment of crisis brings about such a moment of historical insight and national self-reflection, then the result might be to the benefit of the nation and the world. If we continue, however, on our present course of polarization, we will increasingly divide into the two extreme camps—a medieval-like absolutism and an ironic, skeptical secularism. Eventually, what remains of the center cannot, and will not, hold. It is high time to reevaluate how we got here, and where we came from.[39]

Sometimes the future lies somewhere back in the past; one just has to be sure to find the right past. That is why the founders themselves were such students of history, especially the history of Protestantism, in its various streams. We would do well to reacquaint ourselves with that history—its hopes, ambitions, and limitations, and most important, its concern, at least in its dissenting branches, for the commitment to both freedom and truth.

The founders believed that the individual needs freedom to undertake the search for truth, and that truth is a necessary goal that shapes both the contours and purposes of that freedom. They believed that one could not truly have one without the other, and that society constantly has to seek a proper balance between the two. This is the stuff of our heritage; but we are only its heirs if we know it, and understand it, and constantly judge the balance between truth and freedom for ourselves.

One scholar of John Locke has described Locke's conception of freedom this way: "genuine freedom cannot be inherited through custom or tradition, not can it be imposed by some all-knowing legislator. The freedom that defines us as human beings must be enacted by each individual through the arduous process of self-government."[40] Or to put it more simply, only those retain the right of private judgment who are willing to constantly, actively, and thoughtfully exercise it for themselves in the active pursuit of practical and transcendental truths for themselves and for society.

Significant Works on Religious Freedom and Early America

Church and state in early America must be understood in the larger context of the rise of ideas of religious toleration in Europe and England. Two multi-volume works that provide a framework for such studies are Joseph Lecler's *Toleration and the Reformation* and W.K. Jordan's *The Development of Religious Toleration in England*.[1] While somewhat dated, these books are still valuable and provided a helpful orientation for my project. The particular arguments of my book also explore European territory more recently covered in Peter Zagorin's *Rise of Religious Tolerance in the West*, Benjamin Kaplan's *Divided by Faith: Religious Conflict and the Practice of Toleration in Early Modern Europe*, and John Coffey's *Persecution and Toleration in Protestant England: 1558–1689*.[2]

Kaplan and Coffey provide helpful summaries of a series of thinkers dealing with issues related to toleration in England and western Europe, but they do not seek to connect these thinkers to each other theologically. Nor do they bring the story across the Atlantic to the American colonies. Of these three, Zagorin is the only one to deal with the connections between European and American views of religious freedom, and then only briefly. His main argument is that the growth of religious pluralism and the development of pragmatic concerns were the main engines of growth in toleration. While he treats a number of theological thinkers, he does not suggest a continuous or consistent line of Protestant argument.

Two other relevant works dealing with toleration in Europe are John Marshall's important books on John Locke and toleration.[3] While both works focus on Locke personally, the more recent study, *John Locke, Toleration and Early Enlightenment Culture*, attempts a serious overview of the rise of tolerance and religious freedom in western Europe. Marshall uses Locke as a focus to argue for the central role of the early secular Enlightenment in the rise of religious liberty. My work draws on many of Marshall's historical observations, but contests his claims that the main impetus to toleration was secular Enlightenment thought and that Protestantism played little role in the rise of liberty.

The modern telling of the story of disestablishment and the rise of religious freedom in America essentially began in 1950 with the issuing of Leo Pfeffer's and Anson Phelps Stokes' monumental three-volume *Church and State in the United States*.[4] The work is encyclopedic in its scope and has major sections on: colonial and revolutionary historical backgrounds; the constitution and Supreme Court decisions; and the role and contribution of various denominations and religious groups to the American church/state arrangement. It also discusses the major contemporary church/state issues, such as religion in public education, private religious schools, and social legislation. The work's comprehensiveness, though, is attained at the expense of some detail and analysis. It necessarily relies heavily, especially in its historical sections, on secondary and tertiary materials. It provides, however, an essential matrix for any significant work on church and state in America.

About three years later, Pfeffer contributed *Church, State and Freedom*, which covered similar ground, but had an even greater analysis of court decision.[5] Pfeffer, a constitutional lawyer who wrote in the 1950s, traced the history of toleration and disestablishment from the Middle Ages through American history down to the 1940s. His legal history focuses on the Supreme Court's twentieth-century religion decisions. Again, in covering so much ground, Pfeffer's work relies for its history almost entirely on secondary and tertiary sources. He also does not grapple with the questions of religious influences on legal ideas. But again, its role in providing a sense of the larger framework is invaluable.

A more recent work that provides an overview of religion and American politics from the founding to the present is the multi-authored *Religion and American Politics*.[6] While spanning the period from the early colonial settlements to the presidency of George Bush, it has five or six very useful chapters on the colonial period and the early republic. The authors are a virtual who's who of American religious and political history, including Harry Stout, John Wilson, Mark Noll, Nathan Hatch, Daniel Walker Howe, and George Marsden.

Another foundational work for those wanting to focus on church and state in colonial America is Thomas J. Curry's *The First Freedoms: Church and State in America to the Passage of the First Amendment*.[7] Before Curry, American church/state scholarship focused on the events surrounding the passage of the Constitution and the First Amendment, with some attention to what happened in Virginia in the preceding years. Curry took several important steps backward and provided the first comprehensive and meaningfully detailed overview of the church/state arrangements and developments in all the original American colonies from their founding to the time of the federal constitution. His attention to variation among the colonies, as well his ability to spot similarities, contributed to the geographical framework I used in my book, with the grouping of New England, Middle, and Southern colonies. Curry does not deal much with European background and influences, but his work is indispensable for understanding what was happening on the ground throughout the colonies in early America.

In the same year (1986) that Curry published his work, his former professor, Leonard Levy wrote probably the most comprehensive study to that point on the meaning of *The Establishment Clause*.[8] Writing during the Reagan years, Levy countered the argument then growing in popularity that early American disestablishment was meant only to prevent the creation of a single national church. He showed that a number of colonies had multiple establishments—even types of nonpreferential aid programs that supported all churches evenly—and that these programs were all equally targets of those seeking to disestablish religion. Levy also recognized the existence of religious influences on disestablishment, acknowledging Roger Williams, rather than Thomas Jefferson, as the true originator of the "Wall of Separation" metaphor. Still, Levy's work is primarily concerned with legal developments and not religious thought. He concentrated on analyzing the drafting of the First Amendment, with much less concern to understand the background and substance of the religious influences that shaped the thinking behind the Amendment.

More recently, two of the better efforts to deal with church and state in early America are Frank Lambert's *The Founding Fathers and the Place of Religion in America* and John Witte's *Religion and the American Constitutional Experiment*.[9] Both deal with the topic of religion and American constitutionalism, examining the question of disestablishment in some detail. Lambert's work is a nuanced history of the middle to late colonial period, although he gives priority, in my view, to Enlightenment ideas at the expense of theology. He proposes that the dominant church/state view at the time of the founding was captured by the metaphor of the free marketplace of ideas, which he considers to be a largely Enlightenment concept. As I argue, this concept owes as much, if not more at its foundations, to dissenting Protestant theology as to humanist conceptions.

In contrast, Witte gives more credit to theology, but combines all theological influences of the day, whether New England Puritan, mainstream Anglican, or dissenting Baptist, into one large religious influence on the First Amendment. He tends to blur the distinctions between the doctrinal commitments and emphases of the various Protestant groups. Nor does he explore which sects or denominations might have been more important in promoting disestablishment. Indeed, Witte argues that "Puritan Calvinism" and its "ideas of conscience, confession, community, and commonwealth" were the foundation for "American religious ... and political liberty."[10]

Witte's remarkable assertion overlooks and obscures, in my view, the diversity of Protestant thought in Europe, as well as the ongoing clashes in colonial New England between the Reformed establishment and Baptist, Quaker, and other dissenting thinkers. There is ample historical evidence to support the view that Puritan commitments to rule of law, to covenant, and to a republican polity influenced American constitutionalism. But defense of "erroneous" conscience or religious pluralism or disestablishment was just not part of the Reformed Puritanism agenda. To claim that it was is to attribute to Puritans views of freedom and disestablishment that most Puritans were actually actively opposing during the colonial period. It is certainly a claim that would have astounded Roger Williams, Isaac Backus, and even Elisha Williams, who wrote from within the Puritan establishment, but recognized that his was a minority position within his larger community.

Witte's historic Calvinistic Puritan imperialism aside, the emphasis on the role of religion in most modern works on American disestablishment is that of a pragmatic response to American pluralism, rather than the principled outgrowth of religious ideology. The common view is that the two main religious impulses represent either a pragmatic desire by religious minorities to avoid persecution, or a practical recognition by mainstream religious groups that living peacefully in a diverse religious community required some kind of widespread tolerance and eventually disestablishment. In this picture, theology was an afterthought to justify what was otherwise a social, cultural, or political necessity.

All these works on the American founding are much more sensitive to religion than some earlier historical works that barely mentioned religion. Written in what might be termed a modern liberal tradition, they focus almost entirely on secular Enlightenment and republican influences. Both Bernard Bailyn's *Ideological Origins of the American Revolution* and Gordon S. Wood's *Radicalism of the American Revolution* represent this de minimis approach to religion. These books are not about disestablishment, but when the issue is discussed, it is framed as an Enlightenment development that religious people opposed.[11]

Written in this same vein of marginalizing, or even demonizing, the role of religion in the development of American freedom are two more recent works, whose theses are aptly described by their titles. The first is *The Impossibility of Religious Freedom*, by Winnifred F. Sullivan, and the other *The Myth of American Religious Freedom* by David Sehat.[12] Sullivan uses a case out of Florida involving a claim to put religious symbols on gravesites to argue that religion cannot be sufficiently well defined in a pluralistic society to protect it. While it is not a book on American history per se, it does discuss the history of religion and religious freedom in America in the context of legal discussions of the case.

In his work, David Sehat argues that the early American republic was not characterized by religious freedom, but that the First Amendment was really an umbrella for religious coercion. This coercion continued, Sehat argues, throughout the 19th century and into the mid-20th. He believes that both liberals and conservatives have it wrong, the former by believing that American freedom actually existed before the mid-20th century, and the latter that religion had, or has, anything positive to do with religious freedom.[13] These two books, while well written and containing much useful material, are, in their larger arguments, almost caricatures of the popular view that secular liberal elites devalue, dismiss, or oppose religion.

Fortunately, not all those that might be identified as academic liberals believe that religious freedom is either entirely impractical, impossible, mythical, or, even worse, a cover or ruse of religious people to actually further religious oppression. Indeed,

a number of such writers refute these claims, and give religious influences on disestablishment and religious freedom a much more sympathetic reading. Martha Nussbaum's
Liberty of Conscience: In Defense of America's Tradition of Religious Equality includes
a provocative, if somewhat unorthodox, analysis of Roger Williams' religious objections to religious establishment. She provides some helpful insights into the differences
between the thought of John Locke and Roger Williams. She certainly refutes the
notions that either religious freedom did not exist, or that all religious people opposed
it. Her argument, though, that Locke was a religious writer who wrote from religious
"Protestant premises" whereas Williams developed "an independent ethical argument
for his political principles," seems just basically backwards.[14]

Nussbaum portrays William's central principle as being that of a philosophically-
based equality of respect for conscience. This characterization appears an uphill battle
to make a 17th century theologian into a 21st century pluralist. But still, it is heartening to
see modern legal and philosophical thinkers grappling seriously with the contributions
of early religious thinkers. Nussbaum does make a number of points worth considering,
such as Williams openness, in contrast to Locke, to religious exemptions from neutral
laws, as well as the sophistication of William's exploration of the psychology and causes
of persecution.[15]

Jon Meacham's *American Gospel: God, the Founding Fathers, and the Making of a
Nation*, while also generally written from a conventional, secular view, gives a reasonably
fair and balanced accounting of the combination of religious and enlightenment influences on the founding. Meacham tends to want to boil the religious thread in American
politics down to a watered down and somewhat vacuous civil religion, but he is open
to acknowledging the importance of religion not just at the founding, but throughout
American political history. His book is written at a popular level, is very readable, and
would be appropriate for high-school and even collegiate classes on American history
and religion.[16]

Another historiographical stream that my book encounters, and opposes at least in
part, is that of what might be called the neo-Puritans. This group of scholars argues that
America's true church/state foundations lay in the Christian republicanism espoused
largely by the Puritans and their heirs in New England. They contend that the separation of church and state was at most meant to be a barrier against the establishment
of a single national church. Notable recent scholarship in this genre includes Philip
Hamburger's *Separation of Church and State,* Daniel Dreisbach's *Thomas Jefferson and
the Wall of Separation between Church and State,* and James Hutson's *Church and State
in America: The First Two Centuries.*[17] Hamburger's is the more ideologically ambitious
work, Dreisbach's the bolder in its historical claims, and Hutson's the more historically
grounded, even if his history tends to be somewhat selective.

Hamburger, a professor of law, takes on the whole of the United States' history of
church/state relations. He argues that at the time of the founding, the "wall" was the
view of a small minority of anticlerical deists. He alleges that it came to prominence
only many decades later through a combination of anti-Catholic bigotry and religiously

hostile secularism. He attempts to paint almost all orthodox Christian thought as very much in the mold of New England Christian republicanism. In some ways, this work is a response to Hamburger's account, since it shows that Hamburger's reading of the founders' religious thought is, in my view, somewhat selective and not representative of early American society as a whole. He especially overlooks, in my view, the contribution of the Middle Colonies and dissenting protestant sects.

Dreisbach, a professor of history, focuses intensively on Thomas Jefferson's "wall of separation" letter from 1802. His book is essentially a microhistory of this single document, but he exploits it to draw some very broad conclusions. Using textual criticism, including X-ray examinations of original manuscripts to expose earlier drafts of the letter, Dreisbach proposes that Jefferson's "wall" was not between church and state, but between the federal government and state governments.[18] In Dreisbach's view, the First Amendment was intended to *protect* state establishments of religion from interference by the federal government—a conclusion exactly opposite the Supreme Court's twentieth-century interpretation. Once again, his argument is that all seriously religious people of the time, even those on the margins, viewed disestablishment as a purely federal limitation that was not meant to prevent church and state mixing in the states. While this is accurate insofar as it is a description of the legal effect of the First Amendment when drafted, it is misleading, my book argues, in terms of the societal and cultural expectations of how most Americans viewed the proper roles of church and state by the end of the 18th century.

Hutson undertakes a similar argument about religious federalism in his book, although he covers a broader period than Dreisbach and goes back earlier than Hamburger. His *Church and State in America* is only one of his more recent efforts in an ongoing project to promote a kind of Puritan Christian republicanism as the founding church/state philosophy.[19] He documents his claims for puritan priority with extensive quotations from primary material as he sets out his case that the New England establishment provided the primary founding philosophy for the nation. While citing more broadly than Hamburger, and reading in a less strained way than Dreisbach, Hutson also, in my view, basically overlooks the middle-colony, dissenting Protestant impulse.

What Hutson, Hamburger and others in their camp, including Donald Drakeman, in his *Church, State, and Original Intent,*[20] do successfully show is that there was another side to the disestablishment argument during the founding period. Disestablishment, at either the state or federal level, did not take place without vigorous arguments on both sides. It is good to be reminded of the existence and vigor of the opposing argument, as it can help provide context and even insights into the content of the winning side of the debate. One such insight is that both sides of the debate accepted and embraced the importance of a natural law, civic morality for society. But it just confuses the matter, and history, to suggest that some version of a Puritan Christian Republican view on church and state carried the day in the early Republic.

As I believe this book shows, New England Christian Republicanism, at least in its church/state order, was specifically rejected, on both religious, theological and natural law grounds, by the rest of the country, and then ultimately by New England itself, well before the rise in popularity of American secular liberalism. By the time of the Constitutional Convention, and probably a good deal earlier, it was the dissenting Protestant church/state impulse that prevailed in most parts of the country. And that dissenting view, I argue, was the primary popular ideological impulse behind disestablishment in America.

While a great number of the above books have provide helpful backgrounds and materials for my work, those books closest in argument to my work include *Beyond Toleration: The Religious Origins of American Pluralism,* by Chris Beneke, and *Revolution within the Revolution: The First Amendment in Historical Context, 1612–1789,* by William Estep. Beneke notes the central role that the "right of private judgment" played in turning the culture of eighteenth-century America into one open to pluralism and disestablishment.[21] Beneke even identifies this principle with Protestants, but suggests that a policy of pragmatism was first given ideological, principled form by Enlightenment thinkers and the "radical political ideology known as liberalism."[22]

Estep's book does the historical work of tracing toleration within Protestantism from its earliest days, focusing almost entirely on the Baptist contribution.[23] He deals with theology, but the focus is on telling the stories of the men involved in the transmission of the idea, not the theological makeup of the idea itself. He thus does not deal with the connections the idea itself exhibits between apparently disparate groups and people like the Anglican Locke, the Quaker Penn, and the Puritan Elisha Williams. None of these men were Baptists, yet they were impacted by the same stream of thought, I argue, of which the Baptists were the most visible example.

My book makes observations about a three-way discussion over church and state in early America similar to those made by Vincent Phillip Muñoz in *God and the Founders: Madison, Washington, and Jefferson.* During the period of the founding of the constitution, he holds up Madison, Washington, and Jefferson as holding three competing views of church and state. While Munoz's categories are not quite the same as mine, I think there is meaningful overlap in our analysis. His Washington's Anglican establishment would correspond meaningfully with my Puffendorf/medieval category, Madison with my Locke/dissenting protestant category, and Jefferson with my Baylean/liberal category. We differ somewhat in how we characterize the Madison/dissenting Protestant view, but our observations largely support each other in the importance of understanding the early American church/state debate as basically a three-way affair.

Finally, one of the best books showing the interplay between dissenting Protestant and establishment thought in colonial America is John Ragosta's *Wellspring of Liberty: How Virginia's Religious Dissenters Helped Win the American Revolution and Secured Religious Liberty.*[24] Ragosta shows how the impulse to disestablishment in Virginia was led primarily by biblically conservative, dissenting Baptists and Scotch-Irish Presbyterians. These minority groups gained influence during the revolutionary period, where the establishment needed their support. The dissenters then used their newfound influence after the war to change the church-state landscape of Virginia.

Ragosta's story of a rag-tag band of dissenters who, from the margins, and empowered by a core religious ideal, finds a publicly accessible version of that ideal to promote to a larger audience is a micro-version of the macro-story advanced in my book. It is not the story of a religious doctrine that itself gains ascendancy in the American political framework, as that would have the ironic effect of defeating the very principle of disestablishment itself. Rather, it is the story of a religious doctrine that provides insight and impetus for conservative religious groups of various persuasions to embrace and promote a publicly accessible, reason-based principle of conscience, duty, and choice. This latter principle, then, led quite directly to ideas of disestablishment and religious freedom that have become synonymous with the American model of church and state.

Notes

PROLOGUE

1. Given the cultural biases of the early eighteenth century, a solo visitor taking a trip to all of the major regions of colonial America would in all likelihood be a man rather than a woman. Thus, our hypothetical visitor is male. The description of Boston, New England, and Puritan views in the following paragraphs is taken, in good part, from Edwin Gaustad and Leigh Schmidt, *The Religious History of America: The Heart of the American Story from Colonial Times to Today* (San Francisco: HarperSanFrancisco, 2002), 49–65, and Thomas Curry, *The First Freedoms: Church and State in America to the Passage of the First Amendment* (Oxford: Oxford University Press, 1986), 1–28, 83–88.
2. Ralph Barton Perry, *Puritanism and Democracy* (New York: Harper Torchbooks, 1944); Edmund S. Morgan, *Puritan Political Ideas* (Indianapolis: Bobbs-Merrill, 1965), xx–xxv.
3. George Lee Haskins, *Law and Authority in Early Massachusetts* (Lanham, Md.: University Press of America, 1960), 43–45.
4. The descriptions of Williamsburg and the Virginia church/state arrangements in the following paragraphs are taken, in good part, from Gaustad and Schmidt, *Religious History of America,* 36–48, and Rhys Isaac, *The Transformation of Virginia 1740–1790* (Chapel Hill: University of North Carolina Press, 1982), 58–68.
5. The following paragraphs on Philadelphia and its church/state arrangements draw on the descriptions found in Joseph E. Illick, *Colonial Pennsylvania: A History* (New York: Scribner's, 1976); J. William Frost, *A Perfect Freedom: Religious Liberty in Pennsylvania* (Cambridge: Cambridge University Press, 1993); Gary B. Nash, *First City: Philadelphia and the Forging of Historical Memory* (Philadelphia: University of Pennsylvania Press,, 2002).

INTRODUCTION

1. The phrase "dissenting Protestantism" is admittedly somewhat ambiguous. The view that there should be no official state church and that toleration should be given to all, or nearly all, religious groups was definitely a minority, dissenting

position within Protestantism in early modern Europe. Still, the word "dissenting" is often used to describe many Protestant groups that dissented from the Protestant majority in any country on any number of positions, and not just on the question of church/state arrangements. Most of the English Puritans, for instance, complained about issues of liturgy, vestments, and worship styles within the state church, and were thus viewed as "dissenters" for much of their history. They, however, generally had no problem with a state-established church. They just thought that the "wrong" kind of church was established in England. When they got to New England, they established the "right" church. In light of this, some might consider "Radical Protestants" a better phrase to use for those early modern Protestants who opposed religious establishments, since it is generally accepted that the radical wing of Protestantism, the Anabaptists, etc., usually believed in religious disestablishment. Except, of course, when they did not, like Thomas Müntzer during the Peasants' War of 1525, and the Anabaptist uprising in the city of Münster in 1535. While neither of these events represents the core of the mainstream of Anabaptism, they are considered to fall generally under the umbrella description of the Radical Reformation. See George Williams, *The Radical Reformation* (Kirksville, Mo.: Truman State University Press, 2000), 148–171, 553–588; Brad Gregory, *Salvation at Stake* (Cambridge, Mass.: Harvard University Press, 1999), 200–201. Another problem with using "radical" is that most of the people in this project would not be considered part of the "Radical Reformation" as generally understood, whether early Luther, Castellio, Milton, Locke, Williams, or Witherspoon. But all these men were, at certain times and in various ways, dissenters against magisterial Protestantism. While elements of the Radical Reformation, including various Anabaptists and Mennonites, helped keep this part of the Protestant heritage alive, that does not make the belief in religious freedom and disestablishment a heritage of only the Radicals. Thus, I have stayed with "dissenting," with the understanding that in this work the word is used to describe those who dissented from magisterial Protestantism on issues of the appropriate roles of church and state.

2. Benjamin J. Kaplan, *Divided by Faith: Religious Conflict and the Practice of Toleration in Early Modern Europe* (Cambridge, Mass.: Harvard University Press, 2007), 356. Kaplan identifies this story of secularization as being the explanation for tolerance as a modern "myth" that forecloses the possibility of religious countries or peoples nurturing tolerance. As he notes, the "secularization story suggests that religious fervor and commitment are fundamentally incompatible with toleration, and that the latter will flourish only as the former fades." This view, Kaplan maintains, blinds us to the "varieties of bona fide religion" and "encourages us to associate religion in general with certain intolerant forms of religion. Equating religion with a destructive fanaticism, it tempts us to fear and condemn religion in general"; 357–358.

3. Authors that develop these themes include Kaplan, *Divided by Faith*; John Witte, Jr., *The Reformation of Rights: Law, Religion, and Human Rights in Early Modern Calvinism* (New York: Cambridge University Press, 2007); Andrew R. Murphy,

Conscience and Community: Revisiting Toleration and Religious Dissent in Early Modern America (University Park: Pennsylvania State University Press, 2001); John Coffey, *Persecution and Toleration in Protestant England* (Harlow, England: Longman, 2000); John C. Laursen, *Religious Toleration: "The Variety of Rites" from Cyrus to Defoe* (New York: St. Martin's Press, 1999); John C. Laursen and Cary J. Nederman, eds., *Beyond the Persecuting Society* (Philadelphia: University of Pennsylvania Press, 1998); B. W. Young, *Religion and Enlightenment in Eighteenth-Century England: Theological Debate from Locke to Burke* (Oxford: Clarendon Press, 1998); William R. Estep, *The Revolution within the Revolution: The First Amendment in Historical Context, 1612–1789* (Grand Rapids, Mich.: Eerdmans, 1990; Marci A. Hamilton "The Religious Origins of Disestablishment Principles." *Notre Dame Law Review* Vol. 81, no. 5, (2006): 1755–1791, 2006.

4. Alister McGrath, *Christianity's Dangerous Idea: The Protestant Revolution—A History from the Sixteenth Century to the Twenty-First* (New York: HarperCollins, 2007), 2.

5. Ibid., 52–53.

6. Ibid., 199–200.

7. Anson Phelps Stokes, in his encyclopedic *Church and State in the United States,* in three volumes, acknowledges Luther's role in laying the theoretical foundations of the "Protestant doctrine of the 'right of private judgment' … [which] is closely related to the freedom of conscience"; vol. 1 (New York: Harper, 1950), 103. But Stokes does not trace the route by which this theory became practice in colonial America more than two hundred years later.

8. Chris Beneke, *Beyond Toleration: The Religious Origins of American Pluralism* (Oxford: Oxford University Press, 2006).

9. Ibid., 32–33.

10. A number of authors and books that document this are discussed in the appendix, which discusses some significant works on toleration and religious freedom in America.

11. Carl H. Esbeck, "Dissent and Disestablishment: The Church-State Settlement in the Early American Republic," *Brigham Young University Law Review* 4 (2005), 1590.

12. The fact that disestablishment was primarily a local, state-by-state phenomenon, both before and after the passage of the First Amendment, also undercuts the neo-Puritan claim that movement for disestablishment was solely or primarily concerned with preventing the formation of an official national church. Indeed, the popular efforts for disestablishment at the state level were not just aimed at preventing the formation of a single, official state church, but also sought to prevent the state from giving aid and funds to any single church or a combination of churches. Patrick Henry's assessment bill in Virginia, which Madison and the Baptists defeated, would have given funds for education to all Christian churches, which were basically the only religious groups in existence in Virginia at the time.

The best discussion and refutation of the nonpreferentialist arguments have been made by Leonard Levy, *The Establishment Clause* (New York: McMillan, 1986).

13. Esbeck, "Dissent and Disestablishment," 1590.

14. Fox's martyrology "came to exert a greater influence on the consciousness of early modern England than any other book aside from the English Bible and the Book of Common Prayer." John King, *Foxe's "Book of Martyers" and Early Modern Print Culture* (Cambridge: Cambridge University Press, 2006), 2. Being mainly dissenters from the Anglican church, the American colonists had less regard for the *Book of Common Prayer* than their English brethren, but they were no less devoted to Foxe's work than them. After the Bible, it was one of the most frequent books found in colonial wills passing along collections of books. See David D. Hall, *Worlds of Wonder, Days of Judgment* (Cambridge, Mass.: Harvard University Press, 1989), 51, 75.

15. Some have called into question the conventional, "orthodox" nature of much seventeenth- and early eighteenth-century religion. But even these scholars acknowledge that it was a popular, superstitious, supernaturalist view that competed with conventional religion, not some kind of Enlightenment influence or ideology. As David Hall puts it, "the people of seventeenth-century New England lived in an enchanted universe. Theirs was a world of wonders. Ghosts came to people in the night, and trumpets blared, though no one saw the trumpeters. ... Voices spoke from heaven and children in the cradles." *Worlds of Wonder*, 71–72.

16. Thomas J. Curry, *The First Freedoms: Church and State in America to the Passage of the First Amendment* (Oxford: Oxford University Press, 1986).

17. Ibid., 78–104. A good summary of Curry's views about religious thought on church and state throughout colonial America is his comment that "by about 1700 ... a consensus had emerged within Protestantism that captivated and held most writers and thinkers on the subject of Church and State until the American Revolution. Toleration of dissenters from the dominant religion of a region or country, which in the seventeenth century some groups resisted or only grudgingly accepted, came in the eighteenth century to be commonly embraced as a matter of principle." Ibid., 78. Of course, Curry agrees that views of the nature of that principle, and its implementation, differed from place to place, and he does not explain how this view came to predominate.

18. Anthony Gill, *The Political Origins of Religious Liberty* (Cambridge: Cambridge University Press, 2008); Frank Lambert, *The Founding Fathers and the Place of Religion in America* (Princeton, N.J.: Princeton University Press, 2003).

19. Lambert, *Founding Fathers*, 15–18, 72–77.

20. Richard W. Pointer, *Protestant Pluralism and the New York Experience* (Bloomington: Indiana University Press, 1988), 1–3.

21. Curry, *First Freedoms*, 55–56.

22. See John Coffey & Alistair Chapman, "Introduction: Intellectual History and the Return of Religion," in Alister Chapman, John Coffy, and Brad Gregory, eds., *Seeing Things Their Way: Intellectual History and the Return of Religion* (South Bend, Ind.: University of Notre Dame Press, 2009), 1–2.

23. John Coffey, *Persecution and Toleration in Protestant England, 1558–1689* (New York: Longman, 2000), 14–16.

24. Ibid., 15.

25. For a discussion of modern theorists and their limits and shortcomings in understanding the religious beliefs and motivations of early modern Christians, see Gregory, *Salvation at Stake*, 8–15.

26. For a good discussion of this renewed role for religion in the writing of history, see John Coffey and Alister Chapman, "Introduction: Intellectual History and the Return of Religion," in Chapman et al., *Seeing Things Their Way*, 1–19. Mack P. Holt, "Putting Religion Back into the Wars of Religion," *French Historical Studies* 18 (fall 1993), 352–353.

27. Mack Holt recognizes that this resurgence in religious interest revolves around religion as a cultural and social force, where issues of ritual, and broad categories, such as sacred versus profane, eclipse questions of religious belief and theology. Holt, "Putting Religion Back," 352–353. Also see Mack P. Holt, "Religion, Historical Method, and Historical Forces: A Rejoinder," *French Historical Studies* 19 (spring 1996), 864–865, arguing that "religion has been redefined ... as something social" and that "religion as culture (something social) rather than religion as ideas (something intellectual)" characterizes the new approach.

28. Jonathan Scott, *England's Troubles: Seventeenth-Century English Political Instability in European Context* (Cambridge: Cambridge University Press, 2000), 44.

29. Ibid., 45, 51.

30. Brad S. Gregory, "Can We 'See Things Their Way'? Should We Try?," in Chapman et al., *Seeing Things Their Way*, 34–35.

31. Anthony Gill, *The Political Origins of Religious Liberty* (Cambridge: Cambridge University Press, 2008).

32. Ibid., 75.

33. Ibid. He accepts also that there might be a fourth main cause, the desire to cultivate French Catholic assistance during the Revolutionary War, which pragmatically led them to treat Catholics with greater favor.

34. Ibid., 165.

35. Ibid., 165.

36. Ibid., 57.

37. Ibid., 59.

38. As well stated by John Coffey and Alister Chapman, "religious thought [should] be afforded the same respect, and be studied in the same manner, as scientific or political thought. ... Religious ideas should be on the radar of all historians, not merely dedicated specialists. If historians of political thought, for example, can explore the biblical and theological dimensions of political argument, they will produce more rounded expositions of their key texts. Only when religion is reinserted into our accounts will we be able to deliver a richer and more complete intellectual history." "Introduction: Intellectual History and the Return of Religion," 4–5.

CHAPTER I

1. Diarmaid MacCulloch, *The Reformation: A History* (New York: Viking, 2003), xviii, 166.

2. Ibid., 160–161.

3. J. H. Merle D'Aubigne, *History of the Reformation of the Sixteenth Century* (Edinburgh: Oliver and Boyd, 1846), 517.

4. Ibid., 518.

5. http://en.wikipedia.org/wiki/Speyer_Cathedral.

6. D'Aubigne, *History of the Reformation,* 519, 520.

7. Ibid., 521.

8. MacCulloch, *Reformation,* xviii.

9. D'Aubigne, 519.

10. George Waddington, *A History of the Reformation on the Continent* (London: Duncan and Malcom, 1841), 263.

11. Mark Greengrass, *The Longman Companion to the European Reformation, c. 1500–1618* (London: Longman, 1998), 104.

12. Brad Gregory, *Salvation at Stake: Christian Martyrdom in Early Modern Europe* (Cambridge, Mass.: Harvard University Press, 1999), 6, 201.

13. MacCulloch, *Reformation,* 166–168.

14. R. W. Southern, *Western Society and the Church in the Middle Ages* (New York: Penguin, 1990), 16.

15. Ibid., 18.

16. Ibid., 19, 20–21.

17. Greengrass, *Longman Companion,* 103–104.

18. Heiko A. Oberman, *Luther: Man between God and the Devil* (New York: Image Books, 1992). There is some uncertainty whether Luther actually uttered the "here I stand" portion of this phrase, or whether it was inserted by a later editor as a sort of summary statement.

19. Ibid., 204.

20. Charles V finessed the question of the pope's authority in his initial papal condemnation by insisting that the hearing at Worms was not to revisit or reopen the question of heresy, but rather to merely establish whether Luther was the author of all the books attributed to him, and to determine if he was truly recalcitrant.

21. Oberman, *Luther,* 227–229.

22. Greengrass, *Longman Companion,* 57.

23. Martin Luther, "An Appeal to the Ruling Class," in *Martin Luther: Selections from His Writings,* ed. John Dillenberger (New York: Anchor Books, 1961), 406–417.

24. Ibid., 407–408.

25. Ibid., 409.

26. Ibid., 411.

27. Ibid.
28. It has been argued that Luther's Two Kingdom theology flowed from epistemological insights associated with Italian Renaissance humanism, especially the work of Lorenzo Valla. See William J. Wright, *Martin Luther's Understanding of God's Two Kingdoms: A Response to the Challenge of the Skeptics* (Grand Rapids, Mich.: Baker Academic, 2010), 11–16. There does seem to be good historical support for the argument that Luther was influenced by both the humanists' general call to return to the original sources, as well as by Valla's distinction between the certainties of faith and the uncertainties of reason; 79–112. But Wright acknowledges that, while aided by these humanist methods, "Luther developed a renewed Pauline view of God's two kingdoms directly from the Scriptures"; 112.
29. Martin Luther, "An Appeal to the Ruling Class," 383.
30. Ibid., 389.
31. Ibid., 414.
32. Hans J. Hillerbrand, ed., *The Protestant Reformation* (New York: Harper and Row, 1968), 35–36.
33. Reformation historians are well aware that Luther's early views on church, state, and religious freedom differed from his later views. As one prominent author on toleration and the Reformation puts it: "during the first years of his career as a reformer, Luther showed optimism and confidence in his cause. He had the Word of God on his side. This, he thought, was bound to triumph over his enemies without help of carnal weapons. … Like the Apostle [Paul] he considered himself the herald of religious freedom, of Christian liberty—the title of one of his first manifestoes. … He spontaneously contemplated at first only the recourse to the Word of God and as his only weapon the sword of the Spirit, preaching. Boldly he meant to repudiate the methods of the Inquisition, all forms of compulsion, and even the support of the state." Joseph Lecler, *Toleration and the Reformation,* vol. 1 (New York: Longmans Green, 1960), 153–154; one of Luther's modern biographers acknowledges that in his *Secular Authority* of 1522 Luther made "an outright repudiation of the medieval laws against heresy." These early views, he argues "made an important contribution to the history of freedom of conscience," though how this happened is not detailed. Brecht, *Martin Luther 1521–1532: Shaping and Defining the Reformation* (Minneapolis: Augsburg Fortress, 1990), 118–119. Brecht also does not discuss meaningfully Luther's shift in thought, though his narrative of events acknowledges the shift; 152, 344; *John Coffey, Persecution and Toleration in Protestant England, 1558–1689* (New York: Longman, 2000), 51. For a general overview of Luther's theological thought in relation to his political views, see Quentin Skinner, *The Foundations of Modern Political Thought,* vol. 2, *The Age of the Reformation* (Cambridge: Cambridge University Press, 1978), 3–19. Skinner's analysis, though, tends to focus on Luther's later thought, and overlooks the independence his earlier thought gave to believers in spiritual matters from civil oversight. See especially 15.

34. Martin Luther, "The First Sermon, March 9, 1522, Invocavit Sunday," in *Selected Writings of Martin Luther 1520–1523,* vol. 2, ed. Theodore G. Tappert (Minneapolis: Fortress Press, 2007), 234.

35. Martin Luther, "The Second Sermon, March 10, 1522, Monday after Invocavit," in ibid., 239–241 (emphasis added).

36. MacCulloch, *Reformation,* 136–138. Some will argue that Luther had ulterior political motivations in making these arguments for freedom, so that when the political circumstances changed, he abandoned these views. But his restraint in Wittenberg, where the forces of reform were in charge, suggests more was involved. This debate need not detain us, however, since it is secondary to the question of whether Luther's early-stated views on freedom provided a coherent, biblical basis for religious liberty, which others then picked up on. This study provides evidence to support that this was the way at least some in the sixteenth century read and understood early Luther. Luther's original sincerity, or lack of it, in pressing these arguments is not vital to showing whether others were indeed influenced by these teachings.

37. Ibid., 155; for an extended discussion of Luther and his responses to the Peasants' Revolt, see Lloyd B. Volkmar, *Luther's Response to Violence* (New York: Vantage Press, 1974), 140–166.

38. Martin Luther, "Friendly Admonition to Peace Concerning the Twelve Articles of the Swabian Peasants" (1525), in Hillerbrand, *Protestant Reformation,* 67–87.

39. Ibid., 71; as Brecht noted about this early writing, "here the crucial limits of Luther's political theology were not violated." His writing to the princes is an "enduring statement that one must suffer divergent religious views." It is where "they lead to violent acts, however, [that] the princes must step in ... ." Brecht, Martin Luther 1521–1532, 152. One must believe that Brecht uses the word "enduring" as a statement that the general principle endures rather than that it endured in Luther's thought, as Brecht later acknowledges Luther's subsequent defense of force in civil matters; 344.

40. MacCulloch, *Reformation,* 157.

41. Ibid., 156.

42. John S. Oyer, *Lutheran Reformers against Anabaptists* (The Hague: Baptist Standard Bearer, 2000), 116.

43. H. S. Bender, "Luther, Martin," in *The Mennonite Encyclopedia* (Scottdale, Pa.: Mennonite House, 1957), 419.

44. Ibid., 128.

45. MacCulloch, *Reformation,* 161.

46. Francis Oakley, "Christian Obedience and Authority, 1520–1550," in *The Cambridge History of Political Thought 1450–1700* (Cambridge: Cambridge University Press, 1991), 174–175.

47. Ibid., 173–175.

48. The "evangelical" label identifies the group of Anabaptists committed to scriptural authority and pacifism. This distinguishes them from those groups that also

advocated infant baptism, but also promoted the use of violence and prioritized the Spirit over and above the authority of the Word.

49. Walter Klaassen, ed., *Anabaptism in Outline: Selected Primary Sources, Classics of the Radical Reformation* (Scottdale, Pa.: Herald Press, 1981), 244.

50. George Williams, *Radical Reformation* (Kirksville, Mo.: Truman State University Press, 2000), 189, 248, 290, 379.

51. Ibid., 292–293.

52. Torsten Bergsten, *Balthasar Hubmaier: Anabaptist Theologian and Martyr* (Valley Forge, Pa.: Judson Press, 1978), 72–73, 130–132.

53. Henry C. Vedder, *Balthasar Hubmaier: The Leader of the Anabaptists* (New York: AMS Press, 1971), 84–88.

54. William R. Estep, *Revolution with the Revolution: The First Amendment in Historical Context, 1612–1789* (Grand Rapids, Mich.: Eerdmans, 1990), 30–31.

55. Williams, *Radical Reformation*, 288–289, 293–294; Guy F. Hershberger, ed., *The Recovery of the Anabaptist Vision: A Sixtieth Anniversary Tribute to Harold Bender* (Scottdale, Pa.: Herald Press, 1957), 65, 192.

56. Hershberger, *Recovery of the Anabaptist Vision*, 290.

57. Alastair Duke, *The Reformation and Revolt in the Low Countries* (London: Hambledon and London, 2003), 16, 19, 31, 57–59.

58. Williams, *Radical Reformation*, 589–596.

59. Ibid., 590–591.

60. A recent and extended discussion of Castellio and his dispute with Calvin can be found in Perez Zagorin, *How the Idea of Religious Toleration Came to the West* (Princeton, N.J.: Princeton University Press, 2005), 93–144.

61. Hans R. Guggisberg, *Sebastian Castellio, 1515–1563: Humanist and Defender of Religious Toleration* (Surrey, England: Ashgate, 2003), 127–128.

62. Ibid., 128.

63. Sebastian Castellio, *Concerning Heretics; Whether They Are to be Persecuted and How They Are to be Treated. A Collection of the Opinion of Learned Men Both Ancient and Modern,* ed. Roland Bainton (New York: Columbia University Press, 1935), 203.

64. Ibid., 125–126, 141–142.

65. Guggisberg, *Sebastian Castellio, 1515–1563,* 127.

66. Zagorin, *How the Idea of Religious Toleration Came to the West,* 100.

67. Ibid., 101.

68. Castellio, *Concerning Heretics,* 213–214.

69. Ibid., 214, 253.

70. Ibid., 251–253.

71. Ibid., 253.

72. Ibid., 107–114.

73. Ibid., 115–116; Zagorin, *How the Idea of Religious Toleration Came to the West,* 152–153.

74. Castellio, *Concerning Heretics,* 117–118.

75. A good description of British dissenter interaction with Mennonites in the Netherlands can be found in Jeremy D. Bangs, "Dutch Contributions to Religious Toleration," *Church History* 79, no. 3 (September 2010), 595–600, as well as in Estep, *Revolution with the Revolution,* 34–48.

76. Champlin Burrage, *The Early English Dissenters in the Light of Recent Research (1550–1641),* vol. 1 (Cambridge: Cambridge University Press, 1912; reprint, Paris, AR: Baptist Standard Bearer, 2001), 41–42, 65–67.

77. Coffey, *Persecution and Toleration in Protestant England,* 97.

78. Ibid., 118–131.

79. Ibid., 156, 222–223.

80. Ibid., 224.

81. William R. Estep, *The Revolution within the Revolution: The First Amendment in Historical Context, 1612–1789* (Grand Rapids, Mich.: Eerdmans, 1990), 37.

82. Ibid., 252–253.

83. This group thus served as the beginnings of the "general Baptists," as opposed to a later formed group of English "particular Baptists," who held on to Calvin's idea of a limited atonement.

84. H. Leon McBeth, *A Sourcebook for Baptist Heritage* (Nashville: Broadman Press, 1990), 70.

85. Ibid.

86. Bangs, "Dutch Contributions," 596–597.

87. Ibid.

88. McBeth, *A Sourcebook for Baptist Heritage,* 72.

89. Estep, *Revolution within the Revolution,* 53–54.

90. E. B. Underhill, *Tracts on Liberty of Conscience and Persecution* (London: J. Haddon, Finsbury, 1846; reprint, Paris, Ark: Baptist Standard Bearer, 2006), 6 (emphasis in original).

91. Ibid., 18.

92. Ibid., 23.

93. Ibid., 77.

94. Ibid., 185–186.

95. Estep, *Revolution within the Revolution,* 58–59.

96. Bangs, "Dutch Contributions," 603.

97. John Murton, "An Humble Supplication to the King's Majesty," (1620), in E. B. Underhill, *Tracts on Liberty of Conscience and Persecution* (London: J. Haddon, Finsbury, 1846; reprint, Paris, Ark: Baptist Standard Bearer, 2006), 190 (emphasis in original).

98. Ibid., 196.

99. Ibid., 197.

100. Ibid., 199.

101. Ibid., 200.

102. Ibid., 220–222.

103. James P. Byrd, Jr., *The Challenges of Roger Williams* (Macon, Ga.: Mercer University Press, 2002), 159–160.

104. For an overview of the type of religious arguments used, see ibid., 58–68.

105. Coffey, *Persecution and Toleration in Protestant England, 1558–1689*, 59.

106. Frank Allen Patterson, editor's introduction to John Milton, *The Student's Milton: Being the Complete Poems of John Milton, With the Greater Part of His Prose Works* (New York: Appleton-Century-Crofts, 1957), ix–xii.

107. George Newton Conklin, *Biblical Criticism and Heresy in Milton* (New York: King's Crown Press, 1949), 24–26.

108. Ibid., 24–25.

109. See Warren Chernaik, "William Chillingsworth," in *Oxford Dictionary of National Biography*, vol. 11 (Oxford: Oxford University Press, 2004), 456.

110. Ibid., 459.

111. William Riley Parker, *Milton: A Biography* (Oxford: Oxford University Press, 1996), 491–492.

112. Ibid.

113. Conklin, *Biblical Criticism and Heresy in Milton*, 24–26.

114. Thomas N. Corns, "John Milton, Roger Williams, and Limits of Toleration," in Sharon Achinstein and Elizabeth Sauer, eds., *Milton and Toleration* (Oxford University Press, 2007),

115. Edwin S. Gaustad, *Liberty of Conscience—Roger Williams in America* (Grand Rapids, Mich.: Eerdmans, 1991), 61–66.

116. Ibid., 72–73.

117. Parker, *Milton: A Biography*, 410, 1008; Corns, "John Milton, Roger Williams, and Limits of Toleration,"Achinstein & and Sauer, *Milton and Toleration,* 75–76; Theo Hobson, *Milton's Vision: The Birth of Christian Liberty* (New York, NY: Continuum Intern. Pub. Group, 2008), 61.

118. Milton, *Student's Milton,* 864.

119. Ibid., 863–864.

120. Ibid., 865 (emphasis added).

121. Ibid., 865.

122. Ibid., 865.

123. Ibid., 866.

124. Ibid., 866.

125. Ibid., 870.

126. Ibid.

127. Parker, *Milton,* 497.

128. Milton elsewhere expressed this basic concept in equally clear and theological terms, but it was in *The Christian Doctrine*, which was not published in his lifetime. Thus, the clearest public expression of these comments is in the *Treatise on Civil Power*. The relevant section in *Christian Doctrine* reads: "Every believer has

a right to interpret the Scriptures for himself, inasmuch as he has the Spirit for his guide, and the mind of Christ is in him .... It is not therefore within the province of any visible church, much less of the civil magistrate, to impose their own interpretation on us as laws, or as binding on the conscience .... The rule and canon of faith, therefore, is Scripture alone. Scripture is the sole judge of controversies; or rather, every man is to decide for himself through its aid, under the guidance of the Holy Spirit." Milton, *Student's Milton*, 1040.

129. Parker, *Milton*, 524.
130. John Milton, *Of True Religion, Heresy, Schism, Toleration: And What Best Means May Be Used Against the Growth of Popery*, in *Student's Milton*, 916–917.
131. Corns, "John Milton, Roger Williams, and Limits of Toleration," 85.
132. John Milton, *Of True Religion, Heresy, Schism, Toleration: And What Best Means May Be Used Against the Growth of Popery*, in *Student's Milton*, 917.
133. A. G. Dickens, John Tonkin, and Kenneth Powell, *The Reformation in Historical Thought* (Cambridge, Mass.: Harvard University Press, 1985), 101.
134. *John Milton: Complete Poems and Major Prose*, ed. Merritt Hughes (Indianapolis: Hackett, 2003), 856.
135. John Milton, *The Present Means and Brief Delineation of a Free Commonwealth*, in *Student's Milton*, 899. In this work, Milton repeats his argument for the basis of religious freedom being that "the whole protestant church allows no supreme judge or rule in matters of religion, but the Scriptures; and these to be interpreted by the Scriptures themselves, which necessarily infers liberty of conscience"; 911.
136. Ibid., 551–552, 557–558.
137. Ibid., 571–576.
138. John Witte, Jr., *The Reformation of Rights: Law, Religion, and Human Rights in Early Modern Calvinism* (New York: Cambridge University Press, 2007), 247.

CHAPTER 2

1. John Marshall, *John Locke: Resistance, Religion and Responsibility* (Cambridge: Cambridge University Press, 1994), 357.
2. H. R. Fox Bourne, *The Life of John Locke*, vol. 2 (New York: Harper & Brothers, 1876), 46–47.
3. Nigel Smith, "Milton and the European Contexts of Toleration," in Sharon Achinstein & Elizabeth Sauer, eds., *Milton and Toleration*, (Oxford: Oxford University Press, 2007), 40. >
4. Bourne, *Life of John Locke*, vol. 2, 2–3.
5. Ibid., 19–20.
6. Ibid., 20–21.
7. Ibid., 23.
8. Catherine Owens Peare, *William Penn: A Biography* (Ann Arbor, MI: University of Michigan Press, 1966), 9–11, 25–26.

9. Ibid., 209–210.

10. Indeed, Penn was sufficiently principled in his advocacy of freedom for Quakers and other dissenters that he explicitly argued before parliament that Catholics should be extended toleration. This unpopular position placed him in a position of jeopardy, even at times to his personal safety. Ibid., 199–201.

11. John Marshall, *John Locke, Toleration and Early Enlightenment Culture* (Cambridge: Cambridge University Press, 2006), 152–153.

12. John R. Harrison and Peter Laslett, *The Library of John Locke* (Oxford: Oxford University Press, 1965), 206.

13. Marshall, *John Locke, Toleration and Early Enlightenment Culture,* 493.

14. Roger Woolhouse, *Locke: A Biography* (Cambridge: Cambridge University Press, 2007), 239, 249; Marshall, *John Locke, Toleration and Early Enlightenment Culture,* 489.

15. See especially Locke's *A Discourse on Miracles* and *The Reasonableness of Christianity*, in *John Locke: Writings on Religion*, ed. Victor Nuovo (Oxford: Oxford University Press, 2002), 35–50, 91–226.

16. John Locke, *An Essay Concerning Human Understanding*, ed. P. H. Nidditch (Oxford: Oxford University Press, 1975), 694–695, 704.

17. In his essay on human understanding, Locke devoted an entire chapter in book 4, "Of Enthusiasm," to the dangers and perils of being led in religious matters by impulse and impression. Locke, *Essay Concerning Human Understanding,* 696–706.

18. The details found in this summary of Penn's early life were taken from Mary K. Geiter, *Profiles in Power: William Penn* (Singapore: Pearson Education Asia, 2000), 13–21; Mary Maples Dunn, *William Penn: Politics and Conscience* (Princeton, N.J.: Princeton University Press, 1967), 3–6; and William Penn, *The Political Writings of William Penn,* ed. Andrew R. Murphy (Indianapolis: Liberty Fund, 2002).

19. Bourne, *Life of John Locke*, vol. 2, 86–87.

20. Roger Nicole, *Moyse Amyraut: A Bibliography* (New York: Garland, 1981), 4–11.

21. Brian Armstrong, *Calvinism and the Amyraut Heresy: Protestant Scholasticism and Humanism in Seventeenth-Century France* (Eugene, Ore.: Wipf and Stock, 2004), 88–95.

22. Ibid.

23. William Penn, *The Great Case of Liberty of Conscience* (1670), in *Political Writings of William Penn,* 79–119.

24. Ibid., 84.

25. Ibid., 86–88.

26. Locke, *The Two Treatises of Government*, chap. 2, para. 6.

27. Penn, *Great Case of Liberty of Conscience* (1670), in *Political Writings of William Penn,* 90–91.

28. Ibid., 90.

29. Ibid., 92.

30. Ibid., 92.

31. Ibid., 93.

32. Ibid., 95–100.

33. Ibid., 98–99.

34. Steven M. Dworetz, *The Unvarnished Doctrine: Locke, Liberalism, and the American Revolution* (Durham, N.C.: Duke University Press, 1994), 138.

35. That I have placed Roger Williams on the margins as an influence in the 17th and early 18th centuries in America does not mean that the study of his life and thought cannot be tremendously useful for both understanding the thought of Baptists and other dissenters in the 17th century, as well as for providing examples and models of good, reflective, religiously sympathetic thinking about religious persecution and the individual conscience. A number of fine books have been written about him and his thought on church and state, including Timothy L. Hall, *Separating Church and State: Roger Williams and Religious Liberty* (Urbana and Chicago, IL: University of Illinois Press, 1998); Edwin S. Gausted, *Liberty of Conscience: Roger Williams in America* (Grand Rapids, Mich.: Eerdmans, 1991); Martha Nussbaum, *Liberty of Conscience: In Defense of America's Tradition of Religious Equality* (New York, NY: Basic Books, 2008); and most recently, John M. Barry, Roger Williams and the Creation of the American Soul (New York, NY: Viking Adult, 2012).

36. Hamburger, *The Separation of Church and State,* 38–53; James H. Hutson, *Church and State in America: The First Two Centuries* (Cambridge: Cambridge University Press, 2007), 22–25.

37. Patricia U. Bonomi, *Under the Cope of Heaven: Religion, Society, and Politics in Colonial America* (Oxford: Oxford University Press: 1986), 34.

38. Perry Miller, *Roger Williams: His Contribution to the American Tradition* (New York: Atheneum, 1953), 225–227.

39. As the Baptist historian William G. McLoughlin puts it, "Roger William's experiment was a failure because of the inability of Rhode Islanders to shape, by example or evangelism, the destiny of either New England or any of the other colonies. Despite the valiant efforts of Williams, almost no one in colonial New England ever praised his experiment, sought his advice, quoted his books, or tried to imitate his practices. Even in Rhode Island he was often assailed as unsound—and to the other New England colonies, Rhode Island was always the prime example not of virtues, but of the horrors of religious liberty. Those who fought hardest for religious freedom in Massachusetts, Connecticut, Vermont, and New Hampshire considered Rhode Island an embarrassment rather than an asset to their cause." *Soul Liberty: The Baptists' Struggle in New England, 1630–1833* (Hanover, N.H.: University Press of New England, 1991), 19–20.

40. Nathaniel Morton, *New-Englands Memoriall: Or, a Brief Relation of the Most Memorable and Remarkable Passages of the Providence of God, Manifested to the Planters of New-England in America* (Cambridge, Mass.: S.G. and M.J. for John Usher of Boston, 1669), 78.

41. William Douglass, *A Summary, Historical and Political, of the First Planting, Progressive Improvements, and Present State of the British Settlements in North America* (Boston: Rogers and Fowle, 1749–52), 76–77.

42. Isaac Backus, *A History of New-England, With Particular Reference to the Denomination of Christians Called Baptists* (Boston: Edward Draper, 1777).

43. Miller, *Roger Williams,* 254.

44. Ibid., 255.

45. According to a Westlaw search in the Supreme Court database for "Roger Williams," May 13, 2009.

46. According to a Westlaw search in the Supreme Court database for "William Penn," May 13, 2009.

47. *Church of the Holy Trinity v. U.S.,* 143 U. S. 457, 471 (1892).

48. Ibid., 467.

49. James Madison to William Bradford, April 1, 1774, in *The Writings of James Madison, 1769–1783,* ed. Gaillard Hunt (New York: Putnam, 1900), 23; "Petition of the Inhabitants of the County of Westmoreland, Nov. 2, 1784," in *The Sacred Rights of Conscience,* ed. Daniel Dreisbach and Mark David Hall (Indianapolis: Liberty Fund, 2009), 307–308.

50. William J. Frost, *A Perfect Freedom: Religious Liberty in Pennsylvania* (University Park: Pennsylvania State University Press, 1993), 1–2.

51. Ibid., 1.

52. Ibid.

53. Robert Kavenagh and W. Keith Morris, *Middle Atlantic Colonies: Foundations of Colonial America. A Documentary History,* vol. 2 (New York: Chelsea House, 1983), 1340–1341.

54. Jane E. Calvert, *Quaker Constitutionalism and the Political Thought of John Dickinson* (Cambridge: Cambridge University Press, 2008), 147 n. 52; Bonomi, *Under the Cope of Heaven,* 36.

55. Andrew R. Murphy, *Conscience and Community: Revisiting Toleration and Dissent in Early Modern England* (University Park: Pennsylvania State University Press, 2001), 176. Penn's arguments for civil morality extended to laws against swearing, cursing, and blasphemy, as well as laws against Sunday labor; 176, 183. Most civil libertarians of the time viewed cursing and blasphemy as akin to a breach of the peace, and thus regulable by civil law. In addition, Penn did not view laws against Sunday labor as requiring worship, but only as allowing for worship for those who so desired. Interestingly, Quakers were divided on this latter question, as Benjamin Furley, the prominent Quaker merchant and thinker who played host to John Locke in Holland, viewed Sunday laws as a "vile snare to the conscience of many, who do not look upon that day as of any other than human institution." See "Benjamin Furley's Criticism of *The Frame of Government,*" post May 1682, quoted in Murphy, *Conscience and Community,* 183. In many states, even after disestablishment had happened, and the state was forbidden from supporting or promoting religion, blasphemy laws and Sunday laws continued on the books. It was not until a second round of disestablishment in the late nineteenth century, as the Protestant cultural hegemony began to break up, that these laws as well came into question as being religiously sectarian rather than civil in nature. See Steven

K. Green, *The Second American Disestablishment* (New York: Oxford University Press, 2010), 205–247.

56. Kavenagh and Morris, *Middle Atlantic Colonies,* 1340.

57. Alan P. F. Sell, *John Locke and the Eighteenth Century Divines* (Cardiff: University of Wales Press, 1997), 151; Andrew Murphy also acknowledges a significant shift in Locke's views on toleration, and places the shift as early as "between 1660 and 1667." Murphy, *Conscience and Community,* 221. As developed below, while Locke's views likely began shifting during this period, I believe that the evidence shows that he did not fully embrace his more mature view of toleration until probably sometime into the 1770s.

58. John Dunn, "Measuring Locke's Shadow" (essay), in John Locke, *Two Treatises of Government and a Letter Concerning Toleration,* ed. Ian Shapiro (New Haven: Yale University Press, 2003), 272.

59. Ibid., 151.

60. Ibid., 152, 155.

61. Bourne, *Life of John Locke*, vol. 1, 149.

62. Ibid., 151.

63. John Locke, *Locke: Political Essays,* ed. Mark Goldie (Cambridge: Cambridge University Press, 1997), 10.

64. John Locke, *Two Tracts on Government*, ed. Philip Abrams (Cambridge: Cambridge University Press, 1967), 210.

65. Locke, *Locke: Political Essays*, 15.

66. Locke, *Two Tracts on Government*, 225.

67. Michael P. Zuckert, *Natural Rights and the New Republicanism* (Princeton, N.J.: Princeton University Press, 1998), 191, 193.

68. Locke, *John Locke: Writings on Religion*, 69–72.

69. Ibid., 71.

70. Ibid., 72.

71. Material on Henry Vane, except where otherwise indicated, is from Ruth E. Mayers, "Vane, Sir Henry, the younger (1613–1662)," in *Oxford Dictionary of National Biography* (Oxford: Oxford University Press, 2004), online ed., available at www.oxforddnb.com/view/article/28086, accessed , 01/15/2012.

72. Material on Henry Stubbe, except where otherwise indicated, is from Mordechai Feingold, "Stubbe, Henry (1632–1676)," in *Oxford Dictionary of National Biography*, available at www.oxforddnb.com/view/article/26734 , accessed, 01/15/2012.

73. Marshall, *John Locke: Resistance, Religion and Responsibility*, 6–7.

74. Ibid.

75. A discussion of Vane's contacts and friendship with Roger Williams can be found in James K. Hosmer's dated but quite thorough biography *Young Sir Henry Vane* (Boston and New York: Riverside Press, 1888), 67, 230, 369.

76. Probably the best overview of Vane's years in English politics and administration is Violet A. Rowe, *Sir Henry Vane the Younger: A Study in Political and Administrative History* (London: Athlone Press, 1970).

77. A discussion of Vane's help of Williams with the Rhode Island charter can be found in Rowe, *Sir Henry Vane the Younger*, 198–201.

78. Henry Vane, *Zeal Examined* (London: G. D. Giles Calvert, 1652), 2 (emphasis added).

79. Ibid., 2, 13.

80. Ibid., 9.

81. Ibid., 19–20 (emphasis added).

82. Ibid., 24.

83. Stubbe, Henry, *An Essay in Defence of the Good Old Cause* (London, 1659), 1. For a brief biography of Stubbe, as well as a discussion of the larger context of the ideas in his *Essay*, see James R. Jacob, *Henry Stubb, Radical Protestantism and the Early Enlightenment* (New York: Cambridge University Press, 1983), 9–12, 30–31.

84. Ibid., 28.

85. Ibid., 30.

86. Ibid., 72–73.

87. Marshall, *John Locke: Resistance, Religion and Responsibility*, 6–7.

88. Ibid., 7.

89. Bourne, *Life of John Locke*, vol. 1, 165–174.

90. Woolhouse, *Locke: A Biography*, 60, 63; Sell, *John Locke and the Eighteenth-Century Divines*, 154–155.

91. Bourne, *The Life of John Locke*, vol. 1, 175.

92. Sell, *John Locke and the Eighteenth-Century Divines*, 157.

93. Bourne, *Life of John Locke*, vol. 1, 178.

94. Ibid., 184–185.

95. Locke, *Two Treatises of Government and a Letter Concerning Toleration*, 234–235.

96. Works dealing with Locke's *Essay Concerning Human Understanding* in its treatment of themes related to religious belief, judgment, and toleration include Douglas John Casson, *Liberating Judgment: Fanatics, Skeptics, and John Locke's Politics of Probability* (Princeton, N.J.: Princeton University Press, 2011), 126–158; Gary Fuller, Robert Stecker, John P. Wright, eds., *John Locke: An Essay Concerning Human Understanding in Focus* (New York: Routledge, 2000); Nicholas Jolley, *Locke: His Philosophical Thought* (Oxford: Oxford University Press, 1999); Roger Woolhouse, "Locke's Theory of Knowledge," and Nicholas Wolterstorff, "Locke's Philosophy of Religion," in *The Cambridge Companion to Locke*, ed. Verya Chappell (New York: Cambridge University Press, 1994), 146, 172; Michael Ayers, *Locke Volume I: Epistemology* (New York: Routledge, 1991); John Colman, *John Locke's Moral Philosophy* (Edinburgh: Edinburgh University Press, 1983); Neal Wood, *The Politics of Locke's Philosophy: A Social Study of "An Essay Concerning Human Understanding"* (Los Angeles: University of California Press, 1983). For a discussion of the larger historic background of questions of knowledge, probability, and certainty in the age of Locke in a range of disciplines see Barbara J. Shapiro, *Probability and Certainty in Seventeenth-Century England* (Princeton, N.J.: Princeton University Press, 1983), 74–118.

97. John Locke, *Essays on the Law of Nature*, ed. W. Von Leyden (Oxford: Clarendon Press, 1954), 61.

98. Ibid.

99. Locke scholars have noted a connection between the development of Locke's thought on epistemology and the timing of his changing views on toleration, as well as on the connection between his developed theory of knowledge and his argument concerning toleration. Ayers, *Locke Volume I: Epistemology*, 14–15; Casson, *Liberating Judgment*, 124–25; Jolley, *Locke: His Philosophical Thought*, 191–193.

100. Locke, *Essay Concerning Human Understanding*, 48–53.

101. There are also subdivisions of knowledge into various kinds, such as intuitive, demonstrative, and sensitive, but a discussion of these is beyond the scope of this work. A good overview of these matters can be found at Ayers, *Locke Volume I: Epistemology*, 81–152.

102. Locke, *Essay Concerning Human Understanding*, 652–657; Locke was very much more concerned with practical, useful knowing, rather than theoretical precision. For Locke, "probability, rather than knowledge, must be our guide in most of the affairs of life. … 'Our Business here is not to know all things, but those which concern our conduct.' Therefore it is practical knowledge which is the truly valuable part of knowledge." Colman, *John Locke's Moral Philosophy*, 3, quoting Locke, *Essay Concerning Human Understanding* 1.1.6.

103. Colman, *John Locke's Moral Philosophy*, 3–4.

104. Locke, *Essay Concerning Human Understanding*, 667.

105. Ibid., 619–630.

106. Ibid., 690–694.

107. Ibid., 692–695.

108. Ibid., 689–692.

109. Ibid., 69–71, 706–715.

110. Ibid., 89.

111. Murphy, *Conscience and Community*, 77–78.

112. Ibid., 228.

113. Douglas John Casson, *Liberating Judgment: Fanatics, Skeptics, and John Locke's Politics of Probability* (Princeton, N.J.: Princeton University Press, 2011), 124–125. Casson acknowledges that Locke's views on probable knowledge also drew on a legacy of Protestant thought developed by a number of religious thinkers, including the Dutch lawyer and Arminian remonstrant Hugo Grotius and the English Protestant thinker William Chillingworth; 112–113. For more on Chillingworth's formulation of probable judgment in the context of religious belief, the need to accommodate those beliefs to each individual, and the resultant need for toleration, see Gary Remer, *Humanism and the Rhetoric of Toleration* (University Park: Pennsylvania State University Press, 1996), 141–167.

114. Locke, *John Locke: Writings on Religion*, 41.

115. Locke, *Two Treatises of Government and a Letter Concerning Toleration*, 215.

116. Ibid., 242.

117. Locke, *A Second Letter Concerning Toleration*, in *The Works of John Locke, Vol. VI* (Elibron Classics Replica Edition of London: T. Davison, 1801), *135*.

118. Locke, *Two Treatises of Government and a Letter Concerning Toleration*, 219.

119. Harrison and Laslett, *Library of John Locke*, 102.

120. Richard Ashcraft, *Revolutionary Politics and Locke's Two Treatises of Government* (Princeton, N.J.: Princeton University Press, 1986.)

121. Locke, *Two Treatises of Government and a Letter Concerning Toleration*, 218–220.

122. Locke, *A Third Letter for Toleration*, in *Works* 4:143.

123. As one Locke scholars has put it, Locke's "chief argument [for toleration] derives from his concept of the human understanding itself, and thus the process by which assents must occur, if it is to occur at all. In displaying this argument, we have also discovered a crucial connection between the various letters on toleration and the *Essay Concerning Human Understanding*." J.T. Moore, "Locke on Assent and Toleration," in Richard Ashcraft, ed., *John Locke: Critical Assessments* (London: Routledge, 1991). Moore sees the connection between Locke's views of human understanding and religious toleration, but does not offer a comparison with, or suggest a connection between, those views and that of Protestant dissenters.

124. Murphy, *Conscience and Community*, 149.

125. John Sturgion, "A Plea for Toleration" (London: S. Dover, 1661), reprinted in *Tracts on Liberty of Conscience and Persecution*, ed. Edward B. Underhill (Paris, AR: Baptist Standard Bearer, 2006), 332.

126. Ibid.

127. Ashcraft, *Revolutionary Politics*, 489.

128. Murphy, *Conscience and Community*, 149.

129. Ibid., 229.

130. Sanford Kessler, "John Locke's Legacy of Religious Freedom," in Ashcraft, ed., *John Locke: Critical Assessments*, 191–192, citing to Robert P. Kraynak, "John Locke: From Absolutism to Toleration," *American Political Science Review* 74 (March 1980): 53–68 and George Windstrup, "Freedom and Authority: The Ancient Faith of Locke's *Letter on Toleration*," *The Review of Politics* 44 (April 1982): 242–265.

131. Dworetz, *The Unvarnished Doctrine: Locke, Liberalism, and the American Revolution* (Durham, N.C.: Duke University Press, 1994), 135–136.

132. Ibid., 138.

133. Ibid., 137.

134. Ibid., 175.

135. Ibid., 172–173.

136. Ibid., 137.

137. Michael Zuckert, *The Natural Rights Republic* (Notre Dame, IN: University of Notre Dame Press, 1996), 172.

138. Ibid., 55.

139. Ibid., 175.

140. Ibid., 171.

141. Zuckert, *Natural Rights and the New Republicanism*, 192–193.

142. Harrison and Laslett, *Library of John Locke*, 206, 250.

143. Marshall, *John Locke, Toleration and Early Enlightenment Culture*, 493.

144. Ibid., 494.

145. Jeremy D. Bangs, "Dutch Contributions to Religious Toleration," *Church History* 79, no. 3 (September 2010), 613.

146. Harrison and Laslett, *Library of John Locke*, 102, 189. Locke's library list does not include writings of Martin Luther, but in reading Castellio, whose major works on toleration were in his library, he would have been exposed to Luther's important early works on the two kingdoms and the magistrate's lack of authority in spiritual matters

147. Marshall, *John Locke, Toleration and Early Enlightenment Culture*, 1–2, 9–11.

148. Marshall acknowledges the existence of the Baptists, including Busher, Smyth, and Helwys, and their works, but seems to argue that they were so marginalized as heretics, schismatics and/or libertines, that their arguments had no meaningful effect or impact on society. Marshall, *John Locke, Toleration and Early Enlightenment Culture*, 149–150, 326–334. Marshall is at least partially right as a political matter, but he does not seem to consider the ongoing intellectual and social impact of these ideas on later thinkers who read them and were influenced by them.

149. Ibid., 330–331.

150. This absence in Marshall's works on Locke of a discussion about, or even an acknowledgement of, a major religious thinker on church, state, and toleration, with views very similar to Locke, whose works Locke was clearly familiar with, is puzzling. It casts some measure of doubt on his argument that basically secular, Enlightenment thought served as the impetus to toleration, rather than any strand or version of Protestant, or dissenting Protestant, thought.

151. Marja Smolenaars, "Le Clerc, Jean (1657–1736)," in *Oxford Dictionary of National Biography* available at www.oxforddnb.com/view/article/66368, accessed, 1/15/2012.

152. Bangs, "Dutch Contributions," 608–610.

153. Vivienne Larminie, "Le Cène, Charles (c. 1647–1703)," in *Oxford Dictionary of National Biography,* available at www.oxforddnb.com/view/article/16260, accessed , 1/15/2012. R. W. J. Michaelis, "Papin, Isaac (1657–1709)," in *Oxford Dictionary of National Biography,* available at www.oxforddnb.com/view/article/21250, accessed , 1/15/2012. Martin Greig, "Burnet, Gilbert (1643–1715)," in *Oxford Dictionary of National Biography* >available at www.oxforddnb.com/view/article/4061, accessed, 1/15/2012.

154. James E. Bradley and Dale K. Van Kley, *Religion and Politics in Enlightenment Europe* (South Bend, Ind.: University of Notre Dame Press, 2002), 195.

155. Ibid., 198.

156. James E. Bradley, *Religion, Revolution and English Radicalism: Non-conformity in Eighteenth-Century Politics and Society* (Cambridge: Cambridge University Press, 2002), 134.

157. Sell, *John Locke and the Eighteenth-Century Divines*, 163.

158. Ibid.

159. Ibid., 164.

160. Clinton Rossiter, *The Political Thought of the American Revolution* (New York: Harcourt, 1963), 8.

161. Dworetz, *Unvarnished Doctrine*, 135.

162. Ibid., 177.

163. Ibid., 178–179.

164. Dworetz tries to explain the resonance more generally with appeals to "a foundation of shared 'religious preoccupations' and 'theological commitments,'" which has been neither "explored nor (as far as I can tell) even recognized by students of clerical thought." Ibid., 135–136.

165. David Armitage, "John Locke, Carolina, and the *Two Treatises of Government*," *Political Theory* 32, no. 5 (October 2004), 605.

166. Bourne, *Life of John Locke*, vol. 1, 235–236.

167. As one Locke scholar recently put it, "the Fundamental Constitutions were drafted initially in 1669 during the period of Locke's secretaryship to the Lords Proprietors of Carolina. The secretaryship was an executive as well as administrative position; this fact, combined with Locke's closeness to Anthony Ashley Cooper, the Proprietor most intimately associated with the Fundamental Constitutions, makes it inconceivable that he would not have played at the very least a major supervisory role in their drafting." Armitage, "John Locke, Carolina," 607.

168. Bourne, *Life of John Locke*, vol. 1, 240–241.

169. Ibid.

170. Frederick Robin Ward provides a very useful overview of the unfolding of this historiographical battle in the first chapter to his dissertation, "The Early Influence of John Locke's Political Thought in England, 1689–1720" (Ph.D. diss., University of California, Riverside, 1995).

171. Ibid., 27.

172. Bernard Bailyn, *The Ideological Origins of the American Revolution* (Cambridge, Mass.: Harvard University Press, 1967), 23–24.

173. Ibid., 27.

174. J. G. A. Pocock, *The Machiavellian Moment: Florentine Political Thought and the Atlantic Republican Tradition* (Princeton, N.J.: Princeton University Press, 1975).

175. That there was some humanist influence on Luther in his appreciation for the use of original sources and his skepticism of the deliverances of tradition, as well as his use of certain renaissance-based epistemological challenges to scholastic realism, does not change the fact that Luther's affirmative thought was primarily founded on biblical thought rather than Renaissance thought or philosophy.

CHAPTER 3

1. Chris Beneke, *Beyond Toleration: The Religious Origins of American Pluralism* (Oxford: Oxford University Press, 2006), 52–53.

2. Beneke proposes that it was a pragmatic response to religious pluralism that political liberals expanded, and that Protestants then embraced. Ibid., 32.

3. A good overview of the scholarship representing these competing positions can be found in Thomas S. Engeman and Michael P. Zuckert, *Protestantism and the American Founding* (South Bend, Ind.: University of Notre Dame Press, 2004), especially the chapters by Mark Noll ("The Contingencies of Christian Republicanism") and Michael Zuckert ("Natural Rights and Protestant Politics: A Restatement").

4. Again, both these positions can be found well summarized in *Protestantism and the American Founding*, with Zuckert, "Natural Rights and Protestant Politics," taking the position that it was basically a fundamental change of Puritan Protestant thought, and Thomas West, "The Transformation of Protestant Theology as a Condition of the American Revolution," arguing for organic evolution. Both Zuckert and West do not address the possibility of a dissenting Protestant pedigree for Locke's thought, and thus have Locke helping Puritans to move into new channels, rather than being a popularizer of a long-standing, if minority, Protestant position, as argued in this project.

5. Josiah Smith, *The Divine Right of Private Judgment Vindicated* (Boston, 1730), 29.

6. Thomas J. Little, "The Origins of Southern Evangelicalism: Revivalism in South Carolina, 1700–1740," *Church History* 75, no. 4 (December 2006), 792–794.

7. Ibid., 792–793, n. 79.

8. Smith, *The Divine Right of Private Judgment Vindicated*, 29.

9. Ibid., 19.

10. Ibid., 26.

11. Ibid., 13, 18, 19, 26–27.

12. Cotton Mather, *The True Basis for an Union Among the People of God* (Boston: S. Gerrish, 1718). William Penn can fairly be considered an American, though he spent most of his life in England. The publishing of his church/state works, however, occurred in England.

13. Ibid., 26 (emphasis in original).

14. In *The English Libertarian Heritage: From the Writings of John Trenchard and Thomas Gordon in the Independent Whig and Cato's Letters*, ed. David L. Jacobson (San Francisco: Fox and Wilkes, 1994), 35 (emphasis in original).

15. Ibid., 14.

16. Ibid., 10, 15, 19.

17. Ibid., 14, 17, 20.

18. Martin E. Marty, *Religion, Awakening and Revolution* (New York: Consortium, 1977), 147.

19. Jonathon Mayhew, *Seven Sermons* (Boston: Rogers & Fowle, 1749), 41–64.

20. Ibid., 42–45.

21. Ibid., 43.

22. Luke 12:56.

23. The factual background for this summary of Elisha Williams's life is based on Kevin Michael Sweeney, "River Gods and Related Minor Deities: The Williams Family and the Connecticut River Valley, 1637–1790" (Ph.D. diss., Yale University, 1986).

24. Due to the number of other prominent Williamses in his family, the other well-known religious liberty advocate, Roger Williams, and the fact that Penn's first name was William, I refer to Elisha Williams as "Elisha" throughout this discussion.

25. Sweeney, "River Gods," 316.

26. Elisha Williams, *A Seasonable Plea for the Liberty of Conscience and the Right of Private Judgment in Matters of Religion* (Boston: S. Kneeland and T. Green, 1744), Early American Imprints, ser. 1, no. 5520, 1 (emphasis in original).

27. Ibid., 5.

28. Ibid., 6.

29. Ibid., 7, 8 (emphasis in original).

30. Ibid., 8 (emphasis in original).

31. Ibid., 9–11.

32. Ibid., 9, 12.

33. Ibid., 12, 13.

34. Ibid., 13, 17–18.

35. Ibid., 22, 20, 21.

36. Williams, *Seasonable Plea*, 19–20.

37. Ibid., 19, 54.

38. Ibid., 14.

39. Ibid., 16, 48–49.

40. Ibid., 28, 30.

41. Ibid., 58, 64–65.

42. Details of the life of Isaac Backus found in this section were taken from the introduction to William Gerald McLoughlin, ed., *Isaac Backus on Church, State, and Calvinism* (Cambridge, Mass.: Harvard University Press, 1968) (hereafter Mcloughlin I), and from William Gerald McLoughlin, *Isaac Backus and the American Pietistic Tradition* (Boston: Little, Brown, 1967) (hereafter McLoughlin II).

43. Backus, Isaac, *A seasonable plea for liberty of conscience, against some late oppressive proceedings; particularly in the town of Berwick, in the county of York* (Boston: Printed for, and sold by Philip Freeman, in Union-Street., 1770), Early American Imprints, ser. 1, no. 11556 (filmed).

44. Ibid., 12.

45. Stanley Grenz, *Isaac Backus, Puritan and Baptist: His Place in History, His Thought and Their Implications for Modern Baptist Theology* (Macon, Ga.: Mercer University Press, 1983), 86–87.

46. McLoughlin I, 310–311.

47. Ibid., 312.

48. Probably the best discussion of Backus's use of Locke, and citations of the particular instances of use, can be found in McLoughlin I, 223–226.

49. Ibid., 223–226.

50. William R. Estep, *The Revolution Within the Revolution: The First Amendment in Historical Context, 1612–1789* (Grand Rapids, Mich.: Eerdmans, 1990), 113.

51. McLoughlin II, 122.

52. McLoughlin I, 332; 335; 332–333.

53. Ibid., 333.

54. Edwin Gaustad, *Liberty of Conscience: Roger Williams in America* (Grand Rapids, Mich.: Eerdmans, 1991), 203.

55. Isaac Backus, *A History of New England with Particular Reference to the Baptists,* ed. Edwin Gaustad (New York: Arno Press, 1969), 536–537.

56. Isaac Backus, *The Diary of Isaac Backus*, ed. William G. McLoughlin (Providence: Brown University Press, 1979), 1605 (emphasis added).

57. William G. McLoughlin, *New England Dissent, 1630–1833: The Baptists and the Separation of Church and State,* vol. 2 (Cambridge, Mass.: Harvard University Press, 1971), 753.

58. Grenz, *Isaac Backus, Puritan and Baptist*, 175. McLoughlin overstates, at times, his case regarding Baptists and morals legislation in at least implying that Backus was willing to support certain types of morals legislation that was more explicitly religious or biblical, such as "blue laws," otherwise known as Sunday laws. McLoughlin, *New England Dissent,* 753. Grenz makes a good case that McLoughlin somewhat routinely overstated Backus's conservative nature and outlook, and made him more of a Puritan on issues of church and state than he really was. *Isaac Backus, Puritan and Baptist*, 4–5, n. 9. Still, the fundamental point McLoughlin makes about Backus's and the Baptists' acceptance of certain kinds of civil morality, especially those dealing with intemperance and sexual vices, as the responsibility of the state seems historically sound.

59. McLoughlin, *New England Dissent*, 781.

60. Grenz, *Isaac Backus, Puritan and Baptist*, 87, 150–154.

61. Martin E. Marty, "The Virginia Statute Two Hundred Years Later," in Merrill D. Peterson and Robert C. Vaughan, eds., *The Virginia Statute for Religious Freedom: Its Evolution and Consequences in American History* (Cambridge: Cambridge University Press, 988), 1.

62. Lance Banning, "Madison, the Statute, and Republican Convictions," in *The Virginia Statute for Religious Freedom Its Evolution and Consequences in American History,* 118.

63. John A. Ragosta, *Wellspring of Liberty: How Virginia's Religious Dissenters Helped Win the American Revolution and Secured Religious Liberty* (New York: Oxford University Press, 2010), 131.

64. Ibid., 131; Rhys Isaac, "'The Rage of Malice of the Old Serpent Devil': The Dissenters and the Making and Remaking of the Virginia Statute for Religious Freedom," in Peterson and Vaughan, *Virginia Statute*, 150–151.

65. Ibid., 151.

66. "Petition of the Inhabitants of the County of Westmoreland, Nov. 2, 1784," in Daniel Dreisbach and Mark David Hall, eds., *The Sacred Rights of Conscience* (Indianapolis: Liberty Fund, 2009), 307–308.

67. Ibid., 308.

68. Ragosta, *Wellspring of Liberty*, 3–13, 161–170.

69. Anson Phelps Stokes and Leo Pfeffer, *Church and State in the United States* (New York: Harper and Row, 1964), 19–20.

70. "Memorial of the Presbytery of Hanover Virginia (October 24, 1776)," in Dreisbach and Hall, *Sacred Rights of Conscience*, 269 (emphasis added).

71. Ibid.

72. "Memorial of the Presbytery of Hanover, Virginia (June 3, 1777)," in Dreisbach and Hall, *Sacred Rights of Conscience*, 272.

73. Ibid. (emphasis added).

74. Isaac, "'Rage of Malice of the Old Serpent Devil,'" 149.

75. Ibid., 150.

76. "Memorial of the Presbytery of Hanover, Virginia (August 13, 1785)," in Dreisbach and Hall, *Sacred Rights of Conscience*, 305–306 (emphasis added).

77. Ragosta, *Wellspring of Liberty*, 170.

78. McLoughlin, *New England Dissent*, 803–812.

79. Ibid., 804, 809–811.

80. Ibid., 897–909.

81. Ibid., 1050.

82. Ibid., 1051, 1052, 1060.

CHAPTER 4

1. William Livingston et al., *The Independent Reflector or Weekly Essay on Sundry Important Subjects More particularly adapted to the Province of New-York,* ed. Milton M. Klein (Cambridge, Mass.: Harvard University Press, 1963), 32–33. Others have noted Livingston's use of the free-market model in his *Reflector* argument. Ned. C. Landsman, *From Colonials to Provincials: American Thought and Culture 1680–1760* (Ithaca, N.Y.: Cornell University Press, 1997), 161–162.

2. Livingston et al., *Independent Reflector,* 315, 171–207.

3. Ibid., 44–45.

4. Frank Lambert, *The Founding Fathers and the Place of Religion in America* (Princeton, N.J.: Princeton University Press, 2003), 8–10, 253.

5. The most famous twentieth-century formulation of this idea was that by Justice Oliver Wendell Holmes in the U.S. Supreme Court case *Abrams v. U.S.*, 250 U.S. 616 (1919). In his famous dissent, Holmes wrote: "But when men have realized that time has upset many fighting faiths, they may come to believe even more than they believe the very foundations of their own conduct that the ultimate good desired is

better reached by free trade in ideas—that the best test of truth is the power of the thought to get itself accepted in the competition of the market, and that truth is the only ground upon which their wishes safely can be carried out. That at any rate is the theory of our Constitution."

6. Oliver Wendell Holmes, who coined the modern version of the metaphor on which current legal theory is based, was a committed moral relativist who viewed truth as the view of the strongest contestant. Liva Baker, *The Justice from Beacon Hill* (New York: HarperCollins, 1991), 76–77, 249–251, 607–608. As it is popularly understood, "Holmes' moral relativism influenced his strong advocacy of First Amendment speech rights on the bench. … Holmes believed that there is no absolute truth, and thus 'free speech' stood as essential to the free dissemination of ideas."

7. Arthur Herman, *The Scottish Enlightenment* (London: Fourth Estate, 2001), 181–216.

8. Ibid., 9.

9. In his *Virginia Statute for Religious Freedom*, drafted in 1779, Jefferson stated that "truth is great and will prevail if left to herself; that she is the proper and sufficient antagonist to error, and has nothing to fear from the conflict unless by human interposition disarmed of her natural weapons, free argument and debate; errors ceasing to be dangerous when it is permitted freely to contradict them." In *A Documentary History of Religion in America,* ed. Edwin S. Gaustad (Grand Rapids, Mich.: Eerdmans, 1982), pp. 259–261. Madison used the diversity of religious views in Virginia as one of his main arguments against tax assessments for religious teachers. As he put it, a tax to support certain religious teachers "will destroy that moderation and harmony which the forbearance of our laws to intermeddle with Religion has produced among its several sects. Torrents of blood have been spilt in the old world, by vain attempts of the secular arm, to extinguish Religious discord, by proscribing all difference in Religious opinion." *Memorial and Remonstrance against Religious Establishments* (1785), available at http://religiousfreedom.lib.virginia.edu/sacred/madison_m&r_1785.html.

10. Gordon S. Wood, *The Radicalism of the American Revolution* (New York: Knopf, 1992), 331.

11. Philip Hamburger, *Separation of Church and State* (Cambridge, Mass.: Harvard University Press, 2002), 480.

12. Lambert, *Founding Fathers*, 8, 10, 145.

13. Bernard Bailyn, *The Ideological Origins of the American Revolution* (Cambridge, Mass.: Harvard University Press, 1967), 248, 250.

14. Theodore Sedgwick, *A Memoir of the Life of William Livingston* (New York: Harper, 1833), 79, 168–69, 204–210, 418–420.

15. Madison and Jefferson wrote a great deal on the topic, but over a much greater period of time, with usually less focus on a particular issue and less systematically at one point in time.

16. Henry F. May, *The Enlightenment in America* (New York: Oxford University Press, 1976), xiv–xvi. Historian Daniel Howe goes so far as to call the American

implementation or version of the Enlightenment the "Christian Enlightenment" and the "Protestant Enlightenment." Howe, "John Witherspoon and the Transatlantic Enlightenment," in *The Atlantic Enlightenment*, ed. Susan Manning and Francis Cogliano (Burlington, Vt.: Ashgate, 2008), 61–62.

17. Howe comments that "America also nurtured a Christian Enlightenment ... durable and pervasive in its influence. ... [It] drew strength from the cultural tradition of the Protestant Reformation and synthesized rational empiricism with Christian piety. In America, this Protestant Enlightenment affected a reconciliation between religion and republicanism that Europeans found astonishing." Ibid., 61.

18. Sedgwick, *Memoir of the Life of William Livingston*, 45; a helpful overview of Livingston's life and career can be found at Carl Bridenbaugh, *Mitre and Sceptre: Transatlantic Faiths, Ideas, Personalities, and Politics 1689–1775* (New York: Oxford University Press, 1962), 138–151.

19. Sedgwick, *Memoir of the Life of William Livingston*, 41–43.

20. Ibid., 19–20.

21. Livingston et al., *Independent Reflector*, 6–7.

22. Sedgwick, *Memoir of the Life of William Livingston*, 47, 47.

23. Franklin B. Dexter, *Biographical Sketches of the Graduates of Yale College (October, 1701—May, 1745)* (New York: Henry Holt and Co., 1885), 620.

24. Sedgwick, *A Memoir of the Life of William Livingston*, 48.

25. Ibid., 54.

26. Ibid., 78.

27. Livingston et al., *Independent Reflector*, 246, 412–418.

28. Sedgwick, *Memoir of the Life of William Livingston*, 63, 66, 74. While all three contributed essays to the *Reflector*, it was Livingston who was the primary editor, and who reviewed, edited, and approved all the essays. It is clear that he was the author of those dealing with the College controversy, and he certainly took responsibility for the content of the rest, even if he was not the initial penman. Milton M. Klein, editor's introduction to Livingston et al., *Independent Reflector*, 6. The consistency of thought in those essays dealing with religion and religious freedom would suggest that Livingston was the initial author of these essays as well.

29. For a description of Trenchard's and Gordon's lives and writings, see Caroline Robbins, *The Eighteenth Century Commonwealthman* (Cambridge, Mass.: Harvard University Press, 1959), 115–125.

30. Livingston et al., *Independent Reflector*, 21.

31. Ronald Hamowy, editor's introduction to John Trenchard and Thomas Gordon, *Cato's Letters, or Essays on Liberty, Civil and Religious, and Other Important Subjects*, vol. 1 (Indianapolis: Liberty Fund, 1995), xxii–xxiii.

32. Livingston et al., *Independent Reflector*, 21–22, 49.

33. Bailyn, *Ideological Origins of the American Revolution*, 34–35.

34. Ibid., 34–35, 49.

35. Bridenbaugh, *Mitre and Sceptre*, 147.

36. Ibid., 177, n. 3.
37. Entitled *Some Serious Thoughts on the Design of Erecting a College in the Province of New-York*, it had been published in 1749 by John Zenger, and was, given the author, an unusually uncontroversial discussion of the value and importance of a college to the colony. Livingston et al., *Independent Reflector*, 11.
38. Sedgwick, *Memoir of the Life of William Livingston*, 79.
39. Oddly enough, the Anglicans numbered only about 10 percent of the colonies' population, but they were particularly interested in education, and had long been jealous of the Presbyterian colleges in Massachusetts, Connecticut, and New Jersey. They offered to donate land for the new college, and viewed themselves as having a special right to influence and even control it. Livingston et al., *Independent Reflector,* 34–35.
40. Ibid., 13.
41. Anglican hegemony in New York certainly was a concern of Livingston. In *Reflector* issue 44 he wrote against the idea that the Anglican church was the official or established church of the New York colony. Ibid., 367–375.
42. Ibid., 336–344.
43. Ibid., 172.
44. Ibid., 173.
45. Ibid., 174.
46. John Trenchard and Thomas Gordon, *The Independent Whig* (1720), Early American Imprints, ser. 1, no. 2537, 18–19. There is a certain irony to this criticism, as all three of those so elegantly and articulately criticizing sectarian education had been recipients of it: Livingston at Yale; Trenchard at Trinity in Dublin; and Gordon in his Scottish homeland.
47. Livingston et al., *Independent Reflector,* 175, 176.
48. Ibid.
49. Ibid., 178–179.
50. Ibid., 180, 181.
51. Ibid., 182.
52. Ibid., 392.
53. Ibid., 183.
54. Livingston's observations regarding Pennsylvania match certain predictions William Penn had made almost seventy-five years earlier. In 1675, Penn argued in *England's Present Interest Considered* that a broad-based religious tolerance would lead to national prosperity. Pennsylvania was Penn's experiment based on this hypothesis, and according to onlookers like Livingston, it was a success. *The Political Writings of William Penn,* ed. Andrew R. Murphy (Indianapolis: Liberty Fund, 2002), 33, 50, 58–60.
55. Livingston et al., *Independent Reflector,* 183.
56. Ibid., 207 (emphasis in original).
57. Ibid., 209–214.
58. Ibid., 43.
59. Ibid, 30–31.

60. Ibid., 89–95; 95, n. 1; 90.

61. Ibid., 90, n 1.

62. Ibid., 92.

63. Ibid., 270–277.

64. Ibid., 271.

65. Ibid.

66. *The Papers of William Livingston,* ed. Robert Weiss (New Brunswick, N.J.: Rutgers University Press, 1988), 126–127.

67. Bridenbaugh, *Mitre and Sceptre,* 113.

68. Livingston et al., *Independent Reflector,* 387–397.

69. He frames his arguments against creeds sarcastically, so they appear as a series of argument in defense of creeds. The arguments are a sort of mirror image of the arguments opposing creeds found in article 6 of the *Independent Whig.*

70. Livingston et al., *Independent Reflector,* 389.

71. Ibid., 388.

72. Ibid., 390–395, 392.

73. Ibid., 394, 393.

74. Trenchard and Gordon, *Independent Whig* 6–12.

75. Livingston et al., *Independent Reflector,* 292–298; 292; 294.

76. Sedgwick, *Memoir of the Life of William Livingston,* 113.

77. William Livingston, *A Funeral Elogium on The Reverend Aaron Burr, Late President of the College of New-Jersey* (New York: Printed and sold by H. Gaine, at the Bible and Crown in Hanover-Square, 1757), 11–12.

78. Livingston, *Papers of William Livingston,* 459–464; 460; 460–461.

79. Livingston et al., *Independent Reflector,* 414, 418.

80. Ibid., 306–318.

81. Ibid., 307.

82. Ibid., 308.

83. Ibid., 312–313, 315; 308–310.

84. Ibid., 308 (emphasis added).

85. Ibid., 309 (emphasis in original).

86. Ibid., 314.

87. Ibid., 315, 316.

88. John Milton, *Areopagitica,* vol. 3, pt. 3, Harvard Classics (New York: Collier, 1909–14).

89. John Witte, Jr., *The Reformation of Rights* (Cambridge: Cambridge University Press, 2007), 224–225.

90. Ibid.

91. *Letters and Other Writings of James Madison* (Philadelphia, 1867), IV, 161, 163, quoted in Bridenbaugh, *Mitre and Sceptre,* 157.

92. Edward James Cody, "Church and State in the Middle Colonies, 1689–1763" (Ph.D. diss., Lehigh University, 1970), 3–4.

CHAPTER 5

1. Catherine Drinker Bowen, *Miracle at Philadelphia* (Boston: Little Brown, 1986), 3.
2. A discussion of Witherspoon's impressive career in outline and his activities in the summer of 1787 can be found in Jeffrey H. Morrison, *John Witherspoon and the Founding of the American Republic* (South Bend, Ind.: University of Notre Dame Press, 2005), 2–4, 15–16.
3. George Eugene Rich, *John Witherspoon: His Scottish Intellectual Background* (Ann Arbor: University Microfilms, 1964), 14–16.
4. L. H. Butterfield, *John Witherspoon Comes to America: A Documentary Account Based Largely on New Materials* (Princeton, N.J.: Princeton University Press, 1953), 11.
5. Ibid., 1–7.
6. Morrison, *John Witherspoon and the Founding*, 4.
7. As one historian of Witherspoon put it: "For one reason or another, with the exception of Witherspoon, the presidents of American colleges were not distinguished in the history of the Revolution." Varnum Lansing Collins, *President Witherspoon*, vols. 1 and 2 (New York: Arno Press, 1969), 155.
8. L. Gordon Tait, *The Piety of John Witherspoon: Pew, Pulpit, and Public Forum* (Louisville, Ky.: Geneva Press, 2000), 155.
9. Ibid.
10. John Witherspoon, *The Selected Writings of John Witherspoon*, ed. Thomas P. Miller (Carbondale, IL: Southern Illinois University Press, 1990), 126.
11. Ibid., 128–133.
12. Ibid., 136–138.
13. Ibid., 140.
14. Ibid., 141.
15. Collins, *President Witherspoon*, 55.
16. Carl Bridenbaugh, *Mitre and Sceptre: Transatlantic Faiths, Ideas, Personalities, and Politics 1689–1775* (New York: Oxford University Press, 1962), 281–282, 328–329.
17. Arthur Lyon Cross, *The Anglican Episcopate and the American Colonies* (New York, NY: Longmans, 1902), 213.
18. Cross considered the bishop controversy an important and integral part of the pathway leading to revolution. "Certainly, if the question of the establishment of bishops did not contribute the lion's share in causing that enmity to the mother country, which was manifested mainly in political direction, it was involved in the struggle and deserves to be regarded as an important part of it." Ibid., 214.
19. Bridenbaugh, *Mitre and Sceptre*, xi.
20. As seen in chapter 4, lawyer and controversialist extraordinaire William Livingston had battled against Anglican control of the college, as well as against the idea of an American bishop. His writings, it is considered, helped ignite the more formal opposition to the American bishop movement. Ibid., 156–157.

21. William Livingston, "The American Whig XV," in John Wilson and Donald Drakeman, eds., *Church and State in American History: The Burden of Religious Pluralism*, 2nd ed. (Cambridge, MA: Westview Press, 2003), 57, 61–63.

22. Ibid., 3–8.

23. Ezra Stiles, *A Discourse on the Christian Union* (Boston, 1761), 37, 43. (emphasis in original).

24. Ibid., 28, 30 (italics added; capitalization in original).

25. Bridenbaugh, *Mitre and Sceptre*, 184.

26. Rich, *John Witherspoon*, 71–75.

27. Ibid., 89–90.

28. Ibid., 89 (emphasis added.)

29. Ibid.

30. Ibid.

31. Cross, *Anglican Episcopate*, 224–225.

32. *Selected Writings of John Witherspoon*, 189.

33. Henry May, *The Enlightenment in America* (Oxford: Oxford University Press, 1976), xvi, 342–343. May points out the generally religiously orthodox nature of the Scottish or Didactic Enlightenment.

34. Mark Noll, "James Madison: From Evangelical Princeton to the Constitutional Convention," *Pro Rege* 16 (December 1987), 7–9.

35. Edmund Morgan, *The Gentle Puritan: A Life of Ezra Stiles, 1727–1795* (New York: Norton, 1962), 167–170.

36. A typical entry of his satirical "Maxims" of the moderates claimed that the marks of a superior preacher were "1. His subjects must be confined to social duties. 2. He must recommend them only form rational considerations, viz. the beauty and comely proportions of virtue and its advantages in the present life. 3. His authorities must be drawn from heathen writers, one, or as few as possible, from Scripture. 4. He must be very unacceptable to the common people." John Witherspoon, "Ecclesiastical Characteristics," in *Selected Writings of John Witherspoon*, 71.

37. Daniel W. Howe, "John Witherspoon and the Transatlantic Enlightenment," in *The Atlantic Enlightenment*, ed. Susan Manning and Francis Cogliano (Burlington, Vt.: Ashgate, 2008), 69.

38. Irving Brant, *James Madison, the Virginia Revolutionist* (Indianapolis, IN: Bobbs-Merrill, 1941), 69.

39. Ibid., 67–69; Ralph Ketcham, *James Madison: A Biography* (New York: Macmillan, 1971), 23–24.

40. Brant, *James Madison*, 69.

41. Cross, *Anglican Episcopate*, 231.

42. Brant, *James Madison*, 85.

43. Ibid., 85.

44. Ibid., 79.

45. James Madison to William Bradford, April 1, 1774, in *The Writings of James Madison, 1769–1783,* ed. Gaillard Hunt (New York: Putnam, 1900), 23.

46. Madison to Bradford, January 24, 1774, in *The Papers of James Madison,* vol. 1, *1751–1779,* ed. William T. Hutchinson and William M. E. Rachal (Chicago: University of Chicago Pres, 1962), 19.

47. Thomas Lindsay, "James Madison on Religion and Politics: Rhetoric and Reality," *American Political Science Review* 85 (December 1991), 1321–1337.

48. James Hutson, *Forgotten Features of the Founding: The Recovery of Religious Themes in the Early American Republic* (Lanham, Md.: Lexington Books, 2003), 177.

49. Madison to Bradford, Sept. 25, 1773, in *Papers of James Madison,* 1:96.

50. Hutson, *Forgotten Features of the Founding,* 176–178.

51. Madison to Bradford, January 24, 1774, in *Writings of James Madison,* 1:21.

52. Ibid.

53. Brant, *James Madison,* 244 (emphasis added).

54. Lance Banning, "James Madison, the Statute for Religious Freedom, and the Crisis of Republican Convications," in Merrill D. Peterson and Robert C. Vaughan, eds., *The Virginia Statute for Religious Freedom: Its Evolution and Consequences in American History* (Cambridge: Cambridge University Press, 1988), 112; Ketcham, *James Madison,* 73; Brant, *James Madison,* 247–249.

55. Brant, *James Madison,* 245.

56. Ibid., 343.

57. Banning, "James Madison, the Statute for Religious Freedom," 116.

58. In *Writings of James Madison,* 2:88–89.

59. Ibid., 89.

60. Ibid., 184.

61. Ibid., 184.

62. Ibid., 184–185.

63. Ibid., 187.

64. Ibid., 186.

65. Westlaw searches on April 30, 2007, in the Allfeds database (Memorial w/3 Remonstrance and Madison); (Wall w/3 separation and Jefferson).

66. Probably the best and most complete resource for exploring both Madison's religious ideas as well as his views on church, state and religious freedom is Robert S. Alley, ed., *James Madison on Religious Liberty* (Buffalo, NY: Prometheus Books, 1985). This volume collects the important primary documents on Madison, religion, and freedom, as well as presenting a number of essays by the most important scholars and both Madison and church and state, including Robert Alley, John Wilson, E.A. Dick Howard, Daniel J. Boorstin, and Donald Drakeman.

67. John Ragosta has documented the strong relationship between Madison and the Virginia Baptists, who were a strongly influential part of his political constituency in Virginia, both at the time of the passage of Jefferson's statute and the framing of

the First Amendment. It is not surprising that Madison would draw on religious language and ideas in framing his public statements on church, state, and religious liberty. John A. Ragosta, *Wellspring of Liberty: How Virginia's Religious Dissenters Helped Win the American Revolution & Secured Religious Liberty* (New York: Oxford University Press, 2010), 166–167.

68. Despite arguments that the Virginia Statute and the First Amendment were radically different documents, Madison seems to have believed that they contained essentially the same principles, guarding against the same kinds of encroachments. Irving Brant, "Madison: On the Separation of Church and State," *William and Mary Quarterly* 18 (January 1951), 23. One of the more thoughtful recent works on Madison's views in relation to religion and the constitution, and a comparison of his views with those of Jefferson and Washington, is Vincent Phillip Munoz, *God and the Founders: Madison, Washington, and Jefferson* (Cambridge, Cambridge University Press: 2009). Munoz does a helpful job in showing that the "founders," even those viewed as closely allied, such as Jefferson and Madison, did not have a single or shared view on church and state.

69. "If a religious establishment is measured by the legal authority to assess taxes for church support, then disestablishment occurred in the remaining states in the following order: North Carolina (1776), New York (1777), Virginia (1776–1779), Maryland (1785), South Carolina (1790), Georgia (1798), Vermont (1807), Connecticut (1818), New Hampshire (1819), Maine (1820), and Massachusetts (1833)." Carl H. Esbeck, "Dissent and Disestablishment: The Church-State Settlement in the Early American Republic," *Brigham Young University Law Review* 4 (2005): 1590.

70. Collins, *President Witherspoon*, 162.

71. Martha Lou Lemmon Stohlman, *John Witherspoon: Parson, Politician, Patriot* (Louisville, KY: Westminster John Knox Press, 1989), 158.

72. Collins, *President Witherspoon*, 161; Stohlman, *Parson, Politician, Patriot*, 159.

73. Morrison, *John Witherspoon and the Founding*, 109.

74. Philip Schaff, *Bibliotheca Symbolica Ecclesiæ Universalis: The Creeds of Christendom, with a History and Critical Notes* (New York and London: Harper & Brothers, 1887), 807–808.

75. Ibid.

76. Morrison, *John Witherspoon and the Founding*, 109 (emphasis added).

77. Ibid.

78. Schaff, *Bibliotheca Symbolica Ecclesiæ Universalis*, 808–809.

79. *Selected Writings of John Witherspoon*, 213.

80. Ibid.

81. Philip Hamburger, *Separation of Church and State* (Cambridge, Mass.: Harvard University Press, 2002); Daniel Dreisbach, *Thomas Jefferson and the Wall of Separation between Church and State* (New York: New York University Press, 2002). For a brief discussion of these books and others like them, see the appendix.

82. Supreme Court justice Clarence Thomas expressed such a view in a recent case involving the display of the Ten Commandments on government property. *Van Orden v. Perry*, 545 U.S. 677, 692–693 (2005).

83. This is a good part of Philip Hamburger's thesis in his *Separation of Church and State*, 479–481.

84. Schaff, *Bibliotheca Symbolica Ecclesiæ Universalis*, 653, 809.

85. Ibid., 807.

86. David Sehat, *The Myth of American Religious Freedom* (New York, NY: Oxford University Press, 2011), 5–8. Ironically, just two or three years before Sehat's book was published, another book with an almost identical name was published by theologian Kenneth R. Craycraft, Jr., making the completely opposite argument. Craycraft argued, in *The American Myth of Religious Freedom* (New York, NY: Spence Publishing Company, 2008), that Jefferson and Madison used Lockean ideas to set up a coercive liberal state that undermined religious freedom in the name of secularism. These two starkly different interpretations of the same facet of American history begin to become explicable when one understands the paradigms they are written from, one from a neo-puritian perspective, the other from basically a secular liberal view. For more on these interpretive paradigms and the literature that corresponds to them, see the epilogue and appendix to this book at p. 175–176.

87. Steve Green documents this changing shift in the enforcement of Sunday laws in American courts through the early to mid-nineteenth century in *The Second Disestablishment: Church and State in Nineteenth-Century America*, 231–247.

88. An overview of this history and the present conflict over religion and morality in the public schools is in Kent Greenawalt's *Does God Belong in Public Schools?* (Princeton, NJ: Princeton University Press, 2005). Also, see Steven K. Green, The Bible, the School, and the Constitution (New York, NY: Oxford University Press, 2012).

EPILOGUE

1. For an excellent overview of this continuing evolution of disestablishment in the 19th century, see Steven Green, *The Second Disestablishment: Church and State in Nineteenth-Century America* (New York: Oxford University Press, 2010).

2. This chapter will include a sketch summary of a more detailed reading of these three writers set out in Nicholas P. Miller, "The Dawn of the Age of Toleration: Samuel Pufendorf and the Road Not Taken," *Journal of Church and State* 50 (spring 2008), 255–275.

3. Samuel Pufendorf, *Of the Nature and Qualification of Religion in Reference to Civil Society* (Indianapolis, IN: Liberty Fund, 2002), xii–xiii. A discussion of Pufendorf and his views on toleration can be found at Simone Zurbuchen, "From Denominationalism to Enlightenment: Pufendorf, Le Clerc, and Thomasius on Toleration," in *Religious Toleration: "The Variety of Rites" from Cyrus to Defoe*, ed. John Christian Laursen (New York: St. Martin's Press, 1999), 191–204.

4. J. B. Schneewind, *The Invention of Autonomy* (Cambridge: Cambridge University Press, 1998), 118.

5. Pufendorf, *Religion in Reference to Civil Society*, xi.

6. Ibid., xiii.

7. Perez Zagorin, *How the Idea of Religious Toleration Came to the West* (Princeton, N.J.: Princeton University Press, 2003), 285. For an extended discussion of the opposition to Bayle within French Protestant circles see Guy H. Dodge, *The Political Theory of the Huguenots of the Dispersion* (New York: Columbia University Press, 1947).

8. Pierre Bayle, *Political Writings*, ed. Sally L. Jenkinson (Cambridge: Cambridge University Press, 2000), back cover; for a helpful overview of Bayle's thought in relation to toleration see Sally Jenkinson, "Bayle and Leibniz: Two Paradigms of Tolerance and Some Reflections on Goodness without God," in Laursen, *Religious Toleration*, 173–186.

9. Zagorin, *How the Idea of Religious Toleration Came to the West*, 270.

10. Ibid., 282–283.

11. Ibid., 280–281; Pierre Bayle, *A Philosophical Commentary on These Words of the Gospel, Luke 14.23, 'Compel Them to Come In, That My House May Be Full'* (1686), edited by John Kilcullen and Chandran Kukathas (Indianapolis: Liberty Fund, 2005), 219–233.

12. Bayle, *A Philosophical Commentary*, 145–149.

13. Alan M. Dershowitz, "Want to torture? Get a warrant," *The San Francisco Chronicle* A-19, January 22, 2002

14. Vincent Phillip Muñoz, *God and the Founders: Madison, Washington, and Jefferson* (Cambridge, Cambridge University Press: 2009). While Munoz's categories are not precisely the same as I set forth, there is significant overlap in our analysis. His view of Washington's Anglican establishment would basically correspond with my Puffendorf/medieval category, Madison with my Locke/dissenting protestant category, and Jefferson with my Baylean/liberal category.

15. Schneewind, *Invention of Autonomy*, 118.

16. Gordon Wood, *The Radicalism of the American Revolution* (New York: Knopf, 1992).

17. Ibid., 191.

18. Ibid., 330–331.

19. Ibid. 331.

20. Edmund Burke, *The Portable Edmund Burke*, ed. Isaac Kramnick (New York: Penguin Books), 263 (emphasis added).

21. A good overview is provided by Christian Smith, *The Secular Revolution: Power, Interests, and Conflict in the Secularization of American Public Life* (Berkeley: University of California Press, 2003). Helpful works dealing more generally with secularization in the West include Callum G. Brown and Michael Snape, eds.,

Secularization in the Christian World: Essays in Honor of Hugh McLeod (Burlington, Vt.: Ashgate, 2010); Hugh McLeod and Werner Urstorf, eds., *The Decline of Christendom in Western Europe, 1750–2000* (Cambridge: Cambridge University Press, 2003); Steve Bruce, ed., *Religion and Modernization: Sociologists and Historians Debate the Secularization Thesis* (Oxford: Oxford University Press, 1992).

22. Steven Green documents the rise of the substitution of secular theories for natural law foundations occurring as early as the mid-nineteenth century in a wide range of legal areas, from oaths to probate law, to church property disputes, to Sunday closing laws. Green, *Second Disestablishment*, 204–247.

23. The process and causes of secularization in American higher education have been ably and persuasively documented by George Marsden, *The Soul of the American University: From Protestant Establishment to Established Nonbelief* (New York: Oxford University Press, 1996).

24. David L. Chappell, *A Stone of Hope: Prophetic Religion and the Death of Jim Crow* (Chapel Hill, NC: University of North Carolina Press, 2007); Mark Noll, *God and Race in American Politics: A Short History* (Princeton, NJ: Princeton University Press, 2010).

25. Scholars who would largely reject the stricter separation between church and state and would be sympathetic to a model of greater church-state cooperation include Robert N. Bellah, *The Broken Covenant: American Civil Religion in Time of Trial* (Chicago: University Of Chicago Press, 1992); Daniel Dreisbach, *Thomas Jefferson and the Wall of Separation Between Church and State* (New York: New York University Press, 2002), Philip Hamburger, *Separation of Church and State* (Cambridge, Mass.: Harvard University Press, 2002); Richard John Neuhaus, *The Public Square: Religion and Democracy in America* (Grand Rapids, Mich.: Eerdmans, 1986); Harold J. Berman, *Law and Revolution,* Vol. 2, *The Impact of the Protestant Reformations on the Western Legal Tradition* (Cambridge, Mass: Harvard University Press, 2006).

26. A number of books have chronicled the rise of executive power over the last several decades, including Gary Wills, *Bomb Power: The Modern Presidency and the National Security State* (New York: Penguin Press, 2010); Arthur Schlesinger, Jr., *The Imperial Presidency* (New York: Mariner Books, 2004).

27. Ibid.

28. ABC News, "Court Backs Vouchers for Religious Schools," June 27, 2002, available at http://abcnews.go.com/US/story?id=91506#.TxiB_kof_8A, accessed on 1/19/2012.

29. Stephanie Condon, "Republican candidates decry 'war on religion,' available at http://www.cbsnews.com/8301-503544_162-57354594-503544/republican-candidates-decry-war-on-religion/, accessed on 1/19/2012.

30. Republican presidential candidate Mitt Romney's speech, where he attempted to persuade the evangelical wing of the Republican Party that his Mormon beliefs

were in the pale of their orthodoxy, can be found in *New York Observer*, December
6, 2007, available at www.observer.com/2007/romneys-religion-speech, accessed
on 1/19/2012.

31. David D. Kirkpatrick, "Bush Sought Vatican Official's Help on Issues, Report
Says," *The New York Times*, June 13, 2004, available at http://www.nytimes.
com/2004/06/13/us/bush-sought-vatican-official-s-help-on-issues-report-says.
html, accessed on 1/18/2012.

32. *McCreary County v. ACLU*, 125 S. Ct. 2722, 2753; 162 L. Ed. 2d 729, 768 (2005),
(Scalia, J., dissenting); *Van Orden v. Perry Thomas*, 125 S. Ct. 2854, 2864; 162 L. Ed.
2d 607, 620 (2005) (Scalia, J., concurring).

33. Virginia Declaration of Rights, article 16, in *The Federal and State Constitutions,
Colonial Charters*, ed. F. N. Thorpe (Washington, D.C., 1909), vol. 7, 3812–3814;
James Madison, *Memorial and Remonstrance against Religious Assessments* (1785),
para. 1.

34. Steven Green acknowledges the multiple sources of higher law, including nature
and revelation, but he seems to conflate natural law and revealed, or scriptural law,
when he says "natural law came to be seen as arising primarily from the scriptures
and God's will, though reason remained a tool for perceiving its commands." *Second
Disestablishment*, 151. This is, in my view, to get it somewhat backward, as natural
law, while in places overlapping with scripture, was seen primarily in contrast to
scriptural law. Natural law was God's revelation to all humanity, through the deliverances of reason in reflection on the natural world and human nature, whereas
scriptural law was understood only through written scriptures by the faithful.
This is an important point, as a belief in a higher law does not equate to a belief
in Christianity being part of the common law, as Green appears to argue; 154–155.
A line of Protestant natural law theorists and thinkers from Hugo Grotius to Samuel
Pufendorf, to John Locke, to John Witherspoon would, while accepting that both
illuminated each other, made a clear distinction between natural law and morality and that of scriptural revelation. The natural rights thinkers of the American
founding who drew on this tradition, such as Madison and Jefferson, relied on conceptions of a higher, natural law, yet opposed either scripture or Christianity being
considered part of the legal founding of the nation. See Michael Zuckert's chapters "Natural Rights and Protestant Politics" and "Natural Rights and Protestant
Politics: A Restatement," in Thomas S. Engeman and Michael P. Zuckert, eds.,
Protestantism and the American Founding (South Bend, Ind.: University of Notre
Dame Press, 2004), 26–27, 272–273.

35. Mark Noll, *America's God: From Jonathan Edwards to Abraham Lincoln* (Oxford:
Oxford University Press, 2002).

36. This has been quite thoroughly documented in a number of credible journalistic
works, including Jane Mayer, *The Dark Side: The Inside Story on How the War
on Terror Turned into a War on American Ideals* (New York: Anchor Books,
2008); Stephen Grey, *Ghost Plane: The True Story of the CIA Rendition and*

Torture Program (New York: St. Martin's Press, 2007); Seymour Hersh, *Chain of Command: The Road from 9/11 to Abu Ghraib* (New York: HarperCollins, 2004). Indeed, the government itself has released documents that support many of the claims regarding coercive interrogation techniques. U.S. Department of Justice, *The Secret Torture Memos: Bush Administration Memos on Torture as Released by the United States Department of Justice, April 16, 2009* (Rockville, Md.: Arc Manor, 2009).

37. Jonathon Turley, "10 reasons the U.S. is no longer the land of the free," The Washington Post, January 13, 2012, available at http://www.washingtonpost.com/opinions/is-the-united-states-still-the-land-of-the-free/2012/01/04/gIQAvcD1wP_story.html?tid=sm_twitter_washingtonpost, accessed on 1/19/2012.

38. Yunji de Nies, "With Reservations, Obama Signs Act to Allow Detention of Citizens," ABC News, December 31, 2011, available at http://abcnews.go.com/blogs/politics/2011/12/with-reservations-obama-signs-act-to-allow-detention-of-citizens/, accessed on 1/19/2012.

39. A similar observation has been made about our present dilemma by Peter Berger, director of the Institute on Culture, Religion and World Affairs, in two articles in the *American Interest*: "Between Relativism and Fundamentalism," September/October 2006, and "Moral Certainty, Theological Doubt," May/June 2008.

40. Casson, *Liberating Judgment: Fanatics, Skeptics, and John Locke's Politics of Probability* (Princeton, N.J.: Princeton University Press, 2011), 261.

APPENDIX

1. Lecler, Joseph, *Toleration and the Reformation*, 2 Vols (New York, NY: Longmans Green, 1960); W.K. Jordan, *The Development of Religious Toleration in England*, 4 Vols, (Gloucestor, MA: Peter Smith, 1965), first pub. in 1932 by George Allen & Unwin Ltd.

2. Perez Zagorin, *How the Idea of Religious Toleration Came to the West* (Princeton, NJ: Princeton University Press, 2005); Benjamin J. Kaplan, *Divided by Faith: Religious Conflict and the Practice of Toleration in Early Modern Europe* (Cambridge, Mass.: Harvard University Press, 2007); John Coffey, *Persecution and Toleration in Protestant England, 1558–1689* (New York: Longman, 2000).

3. John Marshall, *John Locke, Toleration and Early Enlightenment Culture* (Cambridge: Cambridge University Press, 2006); John Marshall, *John Locke: Resistance, Religion and Responsibility* (Cambridge: Cambridge University Press, 1994).

4. Anson Phelps Stokes and Leo Pfeffer, *Church and State in the United States*, Vol I-III (New York, NY: Harper & Row Publishers, 1950).

5. Leo Pfeffer, *Church, State and Freedom* (Boston, MA: Beacon Press, 1953).

6. Mark A. Noll and Luke E. Harlow, eds., *Religion and American Politics: From the Colonial Period to the Present* (New York, NY: Oxford University Press, 1990, 2007).

7. Thomas J. Curry, *The First Freedoms: Church and State in America to the Passage of the First Amendment* (New York, NY: Oxford University Press, 1986).

8. Leonard Levy, *The Establishment Clause* (New York: McMillan, 1986).

9. Frank Lambert, *The Founding Fathers and the Place of Religion in America* (Princeton, NJ: Princeton University Press, 2003); John Witte, Jr., *Religion and the American Constitutional Experiment: Essential Rights and Liberties* (Boulder, Colo.: Westview Press, 2000).

10. John Witte, Jr., *The Reformation of Rights* (Cambridge: Cambridge University Press, 2007), 319.

11. Bernard Bailyn, *The Ideological Origins of the American Revolution* (Cambridge, Mass.: Harvard University Press, 1967) xi–xii; Gordon S. Wood, *The Radicalism of the American Revolution* (New York: Vintage Books, 1993), 4–5.

12. Winnifred F. Sullivan, *The Impossibility of Religious Freedom* (Princeton, NJ: Princeton University Press, 2005); David Sehat, *The Myth of American Religious Freedom* (New York, NY: Oxford University Press, 2011).

13. Sehat, *The Myth of American Religious Freedom*, 5–8.

14. Martha C. Nussbaum, *Liberty of Conscience: In Defense of America's Tradition of Equal Equality* (New York, NY: Perseus Books), 67–68.

15. Ibid., 68.

16. Jon Meacham, *American Gospel: God, the Founding Fathers, and the Making of a Nation* (New York, NY: Random House, 2006).

17. Philip Hamburger, *Separation of Church and State* (Cambridge, Mass.: Harvard University Press, 2002); Daniel Dreisbach, *Thomas Jefferson and the Wall of Separation between Church and State* (New York: New York University Press, 2002); James Hutson, *Church and State in America: The First Two Centuries* (Cambridge: Cambridge University Press, 2007).

18. Dreisbach, *Thomas Jefferson and the Wall of Separation between Church and State*, 68–69.

19. Other works by Hutson in this project include *Forgotten Features of the Founding: The Recovery of Religious Themes in the Early American Republic* (Lanham, MD: Lexington Books, 2003) and *The Founders on Religion: A Book of Quotations* (Princeton: Princeton University Press, 2005). Hutson provides a somewhat more sophisticated and scholarly version of the "Christian America" arguments popularized by the indefatigable and voluble David Barton, such as those found in Barton's *Original Intent: The Courts, the Constitution, & Religion* (Aledo, TX: Wallbuilder Press).

20. Donald L. Drakeman, *Church, State, and Original Intent* (Cambridge: Cambridge University Press, 2009). Drakeman also argues that the Establishment Clause was only meant to prevent a single national church.

21. Chris Beneke, *Beyond Toleration: The Religious Origins of American Pluralism* (Oxford: Oxford University Press, 2006).

22. Ibid., 32–33.

23. William R. Estep, *The Revolution within the Revolution: The First Amendment in Historical Context, 1612–1789* (Grand Rapids, MI: Eerdmans, 1990).

24. John Ragosta, *Wellspring of Liberty: How Virginia's Religious Dissenters Helped Win the American Revolution and Secured Religious Liberty* (New York, NY: Oxford University Press, 2010).

Bibliography

PRIMARY SOURCES

Backus, Isaac. *The Diary of Isaac Backus.* 3 vols. Edited by William G. McLoughlin III. Providence: Brown University Press, 1979.

Backus, Isaac. *A History of New-England, With Particular Reference to the Denomination of Christians Called Baptists.* Boston: Edward Draper, 1777.

Backus, Isaac. *A History of New England With Particular Reference to the Baptists. Edited by* Edwin Gaustad. New York: Arno Press, 1969.

Backus, Isaac. *Isaac Backus on Church State, and Calvinism.* Edited by William G. McLoughlin. Cambridge, Mass.: Harvard University Press, 1968.

Backus, Isaac. *A seasonable plea for liberty of conscience, against some late oppressive proceedings; particularly in the town of Berwick, in the county of York.* Boston: Printed for, and sold by Philip Freeman, in Union-Street., 1770.

Backus, Isaac. *Soul Liberty: The Baptists' Struggle in New England, 1630–1833.* Hanover, N.H.: University Press of New England, 1991.

Bayle, Pierre. *A Philosophical Commentary on These Words of the Gospel, Luke 14.23, 'Compel Them to Come In, That My House May Be Full'* (1686), edited, with an Introduction by John Kilcullen and Chandran Kukathas (Indianapolis: Liberty Fund, 2005).

Bayle, Pierre. *Political Writings.* Edited by Sally L. Jenkinson. Cambridge: Cambridge University Press, 2000.

Castellio, Sebastian. *Concerning Heretics; Whether They Are to be Persecuted and How They Are to be Treated. A Collection of the Opinion of Learned Men Both Ancient and Modern.* Edited by Roland Bainton. New York: Columbia University Press, 1935.

Douglass, William. *A Summary, Historical and Political, of the First Planting, Progressive Improvements, and Present State of the British Settlements in North America.* Boston, Mass.: Rogers and Fowle, 1749–52.

Dreisbach, Daniel, and Mark David Hall, eds. *The Sacred Rights of Conscience.* Indianapolis: Liberty Fund, 2009.

Jacobson, David L., ed. *The English Libertarian Heritage: From the Writings of John Trenchard and Thomas Gordon in the Independent Whig and Cato's Letters.* San Francisco: Fox and Wilkes, 1994.

Klaassen, Walter, ed. *Anabaptism in Outline: Selected Primary Sources, Classics of the Radical Reformation*. Scottdale, Pa.: Herald Press, 1981.

Livingston, William. *A Funeral Elogium on The Reverend Aaron Burr*. New York: Gaine, Hanover Square, 1757.

Livingston, William. *The Independent Reflector or Weekly Essay on Sundry Important Subjects More particularly adapted to the Province of New-York*. Edited by Milton M. Klein. Cambridge, Mass.: Harvard University Press, 1963.

Livingston, William. *The Papers of William Livingston*. Edited by Robert Weiss, New Brunswick, N.J.: Rutgers University Press, 1988.

Locke, John. *An Essay Concerning Human Understanding*. Edited by P. H. Nidditch. Oxford: Oxford University Press, 1975.

Locke, John. *Essays on the Law of Nature*. Oxford: Clarendon Press, 1954.

Locke, John. *John Locke: Writings on Religion*. Edited by Victor Nuovo. Oxford: Oxford University Press, 2002.

Locke, John. *Locke: Political Essays*. Cambridge: Cambridge University Press, 1997.

Locke, John. *Two Tracts on Government*. Edited by Abrams. Cambridge: Cambridge University Press, 1967.

Locke, John. *Two Treatises of Government and a Letter Concerning Toleration*. New Haven, Conn.: Yale University Press, 2003.

Locke, John. *The Works of John Locke, vol. VI*. Elibron Classics Replica Edition, 2005 of the edition of London, T. Davison, 1801.

Luther, Martin. "The First Sermon, March 9, 1522, Invocavit Sunday." In *Selected Writings of Martin Luther 1520–1523*. Vol. 2. Edited by Theodore G. Tappert. Minneapolis: Fortress Press, 2007.

Luther, Martin. *Martin Luther: Selections from His Writings*. Edited by John Dillenberger. New York: Anchor Books, 1961.

Luther, Martin. "The Second Sermon, March 10, 1522, Monday after Invocavit." In *Selected Writings of Martin Luther 1520–1523*. Vol. 2. Edited by Theodore G. Tappert. Minneapolis: Fortress Press, 2007.

James Madison. *Memorial and Remonstrance against Religious Assessments*. 1785.

Madison, James. *The Papers of James Madison*. Vol. 1. *1751–1779*. Edited by William T. Hutchinson and William M. E. Rachal. Chicago, 1962.

Madison, James. *The Writings of James Madison*. Edited by Gaillord Hunt. New York: Putnam, 1900.

Mather, Cotton. *The True Basis for an Union Among the People of God*. Boston: S. Gerrish, 1718.

Mayhew, Jonathon. *Seven Sermons*. Boston: Rogers & Fowle, 1749.

McBeth, H. Leon, ed. *A Sourcebook for Baptist Heritage*. Nashville: Broadman Press, 1990.

Milton, John. *Areopagitica*, vol. 3, pt. 3, Harvard Classics, New York: Collier, 1909–14.

Milton, John. *John Milton: Complete Poems and Major Prose*. Edited by Merritt Hughes. Indianapolis: Hackett, 2003.

Milton, John. *The Student's Milton: Being the Complete Poems of John Milton, With the Greater Part of His Prose Works.* Edited by Frank Allen Patterson. New York: Appleton-Century-Crofts, 1957.

Morton, Nathaniel. *New-Englands Memoriall: Or, a Brief Relation of the Most Memorable and Remarkable Passages of the Providence of God, Manifested to the Planters of New-England in America.* Cambridge: S.G. and M.J. for John Usher of Boston, 1669.

Penn, William. *The Political Writings of William Penn.* Edited by Andrew R. Murphy. Indianapolis: Liberty Fund, 2002.

Pufendorf, Samuel. *Of the Nature and Qualification of Religion in Reference to Civil Society.* Indianapolis: Liberty Fund, 2002.

Smith, Josiah. *The Divine Right of Private Judgment Vindicated.* Boston, N.E., 1730.

Stiles, Ezra. *A discourse on the Christian Union.* Boston, 1761.

Stubbe, Henry. *An Essay in Defence of the Good Old Cause.* London, 1659.

Sturgion, John. "A Plea for Toleration." London: S. Dover, 1661. Reprinted in *Tracts on Liberty of Conscience and Persecution*, edited by Edward B. Underhill. Paris, Ark: Baptist Standard Bearer, 2006.

Trenchard, John and Gordon, Thomas. *The Independent Whig.* Early American Imprints, ser. 1, no. 2537 (1720).

Underhill, E. B., ed. *Tracts on Liberty of Conscience and Persecution.* London: J. Haddon, Finsbury, 1846. Reprint, Paris, Ark: Baptist Standard Bearer, 2006.

Vane, Henry. *Zeal Examined.* London: G. D. Giles Calvert, 1652.

Williams, Elisha. *A Seasonable Plea for the Liberty of Conscience and the Right of Private Judgment in Matters of Religion.* Boston: S. Kneeland and T. Green, 1744.

Witherspoon, John. *The Selected Writings of John Witherspoon.* Edited by Thomas P. Miller. Carbondale: Southern Illinois University Press, 1990.

SECONDARY SOURCES

Achinstein, Sharon, and Elizabeth Sauer, eds. *Milton and Toleration.* Oxford: Oxford University Press, 2007.

Alley, Robert S., ed. *James Madison on Religious Liberty.* Buffalo, NY: Prometheus Books, 1985.

Armitage, David. "John Locke, Carolina, and the *Two Treatises of Government.*" *Political Theory* 32, no. 5 (October 2004).

Armstrong, Brian. *Calvinism and the Amyraut Heresy: Protestant Scholasticism and Humanism in Seventeenth-Century France.* Eugene, OR: Wipf and Stock, 2004.

Ashcraft, Richard. *John Locke: Critical Assessments, Vol. II.* London & New York: Routledge, 1991.

Ashcraft, Richard. *Revolutionary Politics and Locke's Two Treatises of Government.* Princeton, N.J.: Princeton University Press, 1986.

Ayers, Michael. *Locke Volume I: Epistemology.* New York: Routledge, 1991.

Bailyn, Bernard. *The Ideological Origins of the American Revolution.* Cambridge, Mass.: Harvard University Press, 1967.

Baker, Liva. *The Justice from Beacon Hill.* New York: HarperCollins, 1991.

Bangs, Jeremy D. "Dutch Contributions to Religious Toleration." *Church History* 79, no. 3 (September 2010), 595–600.

Barry, John M. *The Creation of the American Soul.* New York, NY: Viking Adult, 2012.

Bellah, Robert N. *The Broken Covenant: American Civil Religion in Time of Trial.* Chicago: University of Chicago Press, 1992.

Benedict, Philip. *Christ's Churches Purely Reformed: A Social History of Calvinism.* New Haven, Conn.: Yale University Press, 2004.

Beneke, Chris. *Beyond Toleration: The Religious Origins of American Pluralism.* Oxford: Oxford University Press, 2006.

Berger, Peter. "Between Relativism and Fundamentalism." *American Interest,* September/October 2006 (Part 1), May/June 2008 (Part 2).

Berger, Peter. *Between Relativism and Fundamentalism.* Grand Rapids, MI: Eerdmans, 2009.

Bergsten, Torsten. *Balthasar Hubmaier: Anabaptist Theologian and Martyr.* Valley Forge, Pa.: Judson Press, 1978.

Berman, Harold J. *Law and Revolution, II, The Impact of the Protestant Reformations on the Western Legal Tradition.* Cambridge, Mass.: Harvard University Press, 2006.

Bonomi, Patricia U. *Under the Cope of Heaven: Religion, Society, and Politics in Colonial America.* Oxford: Oxford University Press: 1986.

Bourne, H. R. Fox. *The Life of John Locke.* New York: Harper & Brothers, 1876.

Bowen, Catherine Drinker. *Miracle at Philadelphia.* Boston, Mass.: Little, Brown, 1986.

Bradley, James E. *Religion, Revolution and English Radicalism: Non-conformity in Eighteenth-Century Politics and Society.* Cambridge: Cambridge University Press, 2002.

Bradley, James E., and Dale K. Van Kley. *Religion and Politics in Enlightenment Europe.* South Bend, Ind.: University of Notre Dame Press, 2002.

Brant, Irving. *James Madison, the Virginia Revolutionist.* Indianapolis: Bobbs-Merrill, 1941.

Brant, Irving. "Madison: On the Separation of Church and State." *William and Mary Quarterly* 18 (January 1951), .

Brecht, Martin. *Martin Luther 1521–1532: Shaping and Defining the Reformation.* Minneapolis: Augsburg Fortress, 1990.

Bridenbaugh, Carl. *Mitre and Sceptre : Transatlantic Faiths, Ideas, Personalities, and Politics 1689–1775.* New York: Oxford University Press, 1962.

Brown, Callum G., and Michael Snape, eds. *Secularization in the Christian World: Essays in Honor of Hugh McLeod.* Burlington, Vt.: Ashgate, 2010.

Bruce, Steve, ed. *Religion and Modernization: Sociologists and Historians Debate the Secularization Thesis.* Oxford: Oxford University Press, 1992.

Burns, J. H. *The Cambridge History of Political Thought 1450–1700.* Cambridge: Cambridge University Press, 1995.

Burrage, Champlin, ed. *The Early English Dissenters in the Light of Recent Research (1550–1641).* Vol. 1. Cambridge: Cambridge University Press, 1912. Reprint, Paris, Ark: Baptist Standard Bearer, 2001.

Butler, Jon. *The Huguenots in America: A Refugee People in New World Society.* Cambridge, Mass.: Harvard University Press, 1992.

Butterfield, L. H. *John Witherspoon Comes to America: A Documentary Account Based Largely on New Materials.* Princeton, N.J.: Princeton University Press, 1953.

Byrd, James P., Jr. *The Challenges of Roger Williams.* Macon, Ga.: Mercer University Press, 2002.

Calvert, Jane E. *Quaker Constitutionalism and the Political Thought of John Dickinson.* Cambridge: Cambridge University Press, 2008.

Casson, Douglas John. *Liberating Judgment: Fanatics, Skeptics, and John Locke's Politics of Probability.* Princeton, N.J.: Princeton University Press, 2011.

Chapman, Alister, John Coffy, and Brad Gregory, eds. *Seeing Things Their Way: Intellectual History and the Return of Religion.* South Bend, Ind.: University of Notre Dame Press, 2009.

Chappell, David L. *A Stone of Hope: Prophetic Religion and the Death of Jim Crow.* Chapel Hill, NC: University of North Carolina Press, 2007.

Cody, James Edward. "Church and State in the Middle Colonies, 1689–1763." Ph.D. diss., Lehigh University, 1970.

Coffey, John. *Persecution and Toleration in Protestant England, 1558–1689.* New York: Longman, 2000.

Collins, Varnum Lansing. *President Witherspoon.* Vols. 1 and 2. New York: Arno Press, 1969.

Colman, John. *John Locke's Moral Philosophy.* Edinburgh: Edinburgh University Press, 1983.

Conklin, George Newton. *Biblical Criticism and Heresy in Milton.* New York: King's Crown Press, 1949.

Craycraft, Jr., Kenneth R. *The American Myth of Religious Freedom.* New York, NY: Spence Publishing Company, 2008.

Cross, Arthur Lyon. *The Anglican Episcopate and the American Colonies.* New York: Longmans, Green, 1902.

Curry, Thomas J. *The First Freedoms: Church and State in America to the Passage of the First Amendment.* Oxford: Oxford University Press, 1986.

D'Aubigne, J.H. Merle. *History of the Reformation of the Sixteenth Century.* Edinburgh: Oliver & Boyd, 1846.

Dexter, Franklin B. *Biographical Sketches of the Graduates of Yale College (October, 1701—May, 1745).* New York: Henry Holt and Co., 1885.

Dickens, A. G., John Tonkin, and Kenneth Powell. *The Reformation in Historical Thought.* Cambridge, Mass.: Harvard University Press, 1985.

Dodge, Guy H. *The Political Theory of the Huguenots of the Dispersion.* New York: Columbia University Press, 1947.

Drakeman, Donald L. *Church, State, and Original Intent.* Cambridge: Cambridge University Press, 2009.

Dreisbach, Daniel. *Thomas Jefferson and the Wall of Separation between Church and State.* New York: New York University Press, 2002.

Dreisbach, Daniel, and Mark David Hall, eds. *The Sacred Rights of Conscience.* Indianapolis: Liberty Fund, 2009.

Duke, Alastair. *The Reformation and Revolt in the Low Countries.* London: Hambledon and London, 2003.

Dunn, John. "Measuring Locke's Shadow" (essay). In John Locke, *Two Treatises of Government and a Letter Concerning Toleration,* edited by Ian Shapiro. New Haven: Yale University Press, 2003),

Dunn, Mary Maples. *William Penn: Politics and Conscience.* Princeton, N.J.: Princeton University Press, 1967.

Dworetz, Steven M. *The Unvarnished Doctrine: Locke, Liberalism, and the American Revolution.* Durham, N.C.: Duke University Press, 1994.

Engeman, Thomas S., and Michael P. Zuckert. *Protestantism and the American Founding.* South Bend, Ind.: University of Notre Dame Press, 2004.

Esbeck, Carl H. "Dissent and Disestablishment: The Church-State Settlement in the Early American Republic." *Brigham Young University Law Review* 4 (2005), 1590.

Estep, William R. *The Revolution within the Revolution: The First Amendment in Historical Context, 1612–1789.* Grand Rapids, Mich.: Eerdmans, 1990.

Frost, William J. *A Perfect Freedom: Religious Liberty in Pennsylvania.* University Park: Pennsylvania State University Press, 1993.

Fuller, Gary, Robert Stecker, and John Wright, eds. *John Locke: An Essay Concerning Human Understanding in Focus.* New York: Routledge, 2000.

Gaustad, Edwin S., ed. *A Documentary History of Religion in America.* Grand Rapids, Mich.: Eerdmans, 1982.

Gaustad, Edwin S. *Liberty of Conscience: Roger Williams in America.* Grand Rapids, Mich.: Eerdmans, 1991.

Gaustad, Edwin, and Leigh Schmidt. *The Religious History of America: The Heart of the American Story from Colonial Times to Today.* San Francisco: HarperSanFrancisco, 2002.

Geiter, Mary K. *Profiles in Power: William Penn.* Singapore: Pearson Education Asia, 2000.

Gill, Anthony. *The Political Origins of Religious Liberty.* Cambridge: Cambridge University Press, 2008.

Goldie, Mark, ed. *The Reception of Locke's Politics.* Vol. 5. *The Church, Dissent and Religious Toleration, 1689–1773.* London: Pickering and Chatto, 1999.

Green, Steven K. *The Second American Disestablishment.* New York: Oxford University Press, 2010.

Greenawalt, Kent. *Does God Belong in Public Schools?* Princeton, NJ: Princeton University Press, 2005.

Greengrass, Mark. *The Longman Companion to the European Reformation, c. 1500–1618*. London: Longman, 1998.

Gregory, Brad. *Salvation at Stake*. Cambridge, Mass.: Harvard University Press, 1999.

Grenz, Stanley. *Isaac Backus, Puritan and Baptist: His Place in History, His Thought and Their Implications for Modern Baptist Theology*. Macon, Ga.: Mercer University Press, 1983.

Grey, Stephen. *Ghost Plane: The True Story of the CIA Rendition and Torture Program*. New York: St. Martin's Press, 2007.

Guggisberg, Hans R. *Sebastian Castellio, 1515–1563: Humanist and Defender of Religious Toleration*. Surrey, England: Ashgate, 2003.

Hall, David D. *Worlds of Wonder, Days of Judgment*. Cambridge, Mass.: Harvard University Press, 1989.

Hall, Timothy. *Separating Church and State: Roger Williams and Religious Liberty*. Urbana and Chicago, IL: University of Illinois Press, 1998.

Hamburger, Philip. *Separation of Church and State*. Cambridge, Mass.: Harvard University Press, 2002.

Hamilton, Marci A. "The Religious Origins of Disestablishment Principles." Vol. 81 Notre Dame Law Review, No. 5, pp 1755–1791, 2006.

Harrison, John R., and Peter Laslett. *The Library of John Locke*. Oxford: Oxford University Press, 1965.

Haskins, George Lee. *Law and Authority in Early Massachusetts*. Lanham, Md.: University Press of America, 1960.

Herman, Arthur. *The Scottish Enlightenment*. London: Fourth Estate, 2001.

Hersh, Seymour. *Chain of Command: The Road from 9/11 to Abu Ghraib*. New York: HarperCollins, 2004.

Hershberger, Guy F., ed. *The Recovery of the Anabaptist Vision. A Sixtieth Anniversary Tribute to Harold Bender*. Scottdale, PA, Herald Press, 1957.

Hillerbrand, Hans J., ed. *The Protestant Reformation*. New York: Harper and Row, 1968.

Hobson, Theo. *Milton's Vision: The Birth of Christian Liberty*. New York, NY: Continuum International Publishing Group, 2008.

Holifield, E. Brooks. "Let the Children Come: The Religion of the Protestant Child in Early America." *Church History* 76, no. 4 (December 2007), 750–777.

Holt, Mack P. "Putting Religion Back into the Wars of Religion." *French Historical Studies* 18 (fall 1993).

Holt, Mack P. "Religion, Historical Method, and Historical Forces: A Rejoinder." *French Historical Studies* 19 (spring 1996).

Howe, Daniel W. "John Witherspoon and the Transatlantic Enlightenment." In *The Atlantic Enlightenment*, ed. Susan Manning and Francis Cogliano. Burlington, Vt.: Ashgate, 2008.

Hutson, James. *Church and State in America: The First Two Centuries.* Cambridge: Cambridge University Press, 2007.

Hutson, James. *Forgotten Features of the Founding: The Recovery of Religious Themes in the Early American Republic.* Lanham, Md.: Lexington Books, 2003.

Hutson, James. The Founders on Religion: A Book of Quotations. Princeton: Princeton University Press, 2005.

Illick, Joseph E. *Colonial Pennsylvania: A History.* New York: Scribner's, 1976.

Isaac, Rhys. *The Transformation of Virginia 1740–1790.* Chapel Hill: University of North Carolina Press, 1982.

Jacob, James R. *Henry Stubb, Radical Protestantism and the Early Enlightenment.* New York: Cambridge University Press, 1983.

Jolley, Nicholas. *Locke: His Philosophical Thought.* Oxford: Oxford University Press, 1999.

Kaplan, Benjamin J. *Divided by Faith: Religious Conflict and the Practice of Toleration in Early Modern Europe.* Cambridge, Mass.: Harvard University Press, 2007.

Kavenagh and Morris, eds. *Middle Atlantic Colonies: Foundations of Colonial America. A Documentary History.* Vol. 2. New York: Chelsea House, 1983.

Ketcham, Ralph. *James Madison: A Biography.* New York: Macmillan, 1971.

King, John. *Foxe's "Book of Martyrs" and Early Modern Print Culture.* Cambridge: Cambridge University Press, 2006.

Lambert, Frank. *The Founding Fathers and the Place of Religion in America.* Princeton, N.J.: Princeton University Press, 2003.

Landsman, Ned. C. *From Colonials to Provincials: American Thought and Culture 1680–1760.* Ithaca, N.Y.: Cornell University Press, 1997.

Laursen, John C. *Religious Toleration: "The Variety of Rites" from Cyrus to Defoe.* New York: St. Martin's Press, 1999.

Laursen, John C., and Cary J. Nederman, eds. *Beyond the Persecuting Society.* Philadelphia: University of Pennsylvania Press, 1998.

Lecler, Joseph. *Toleration and the Reformation.* Vol 1. New York: Longmans Green, 1960.

Levy, Leonard. *The Establishment Clause.* New York: McMillan, 1986.

Lindsay, Thomas. "James Madison on Religion and Politics: Rhetoric and Reality." *American Political Science Review* 85 (December 1991).

Little, Thomas J. "The Origins of Southern Evangelicalism: Revivalism in South Carolina, 1700–1740." *Church History* 75, no. 4 (December 2006).

MacCulloch, Diarmaid. *The Reformation: A History.* New York: Viking, 2003.

Marsden, George. *The Soul of the American University: From Protestant Establishment to Established Nonbelief.* New York: Oxford University Press, 1996.

Marshall, John. *John Locke: Resistance, Religion and Responsibility.* Cambridge: Cambridge University Press, 1994.

Marshall, John. *John Locke, Toleration and Early Enlightenment Culture.* Cambridge: Cambridge University Press, 2006.

Marty, Martin E. *Religion, Awakening and Revolution*. New York: Consortium, 1977.

May, Henry F. *The Enlightenment in America*. New York: Oxford University Press, 1976.

Mayer, Jane. *The Dark Side: The Inside Story on How the War on Terror Turned into a War on American Ideals*. New York: Anchor Books, 2008.

McGrath, Alister. *Christianity's Dangerous Idea: The Protestant Revolution—A History from the Sixteenth Century to the Twenty-First*. New York: HarperCollins, 2007.

McLeod, Hugh, and Werner Urstorf, eds. *The Decline of Christendom in Western Europe, 1750–2000*. Cambridge: Cambridge University Press, 2003.

McLoughlin, William G. *Isaac Backus and the American Pietistic Tradition*. Boston: Little, Brown, 1967. (McLoughlin II)

McLoughlin, William G., *Isaac Backus on Church, State, and Calvinism*. Cambridge, MA: Harvard University Press, 1968. (McLoughlin I).

McLoughlin, William G. *New England Dissent, 1630–1833: The Baptists and the Separation of Church and State*, Vol. 2. Cambridge, MA: Harvard University Press, 1971.

Meacham, Jon. *American Gospel: God, the Founding Fathers, and the Making of a Nation*. New York, NY: Random House, 2006.

Miller, Nicholas P. "The Dawn of the Age of Toleration: Samuel Pufendorf and the Road Not Taken." *Journal of Church and State* 50 (spring 2008), 255–275.

Miller, Perry. *Roger Williams: His Contribution to the American Tradition*. New York: Atheneum, 1953.

Miller, William Lee. *The First Liberty: Religion and the American Republic*. New York: Paragon House, 1988.

Moore, J.T. "Locke on Assent and Toleration," in Richard Ashcraft, ed. *John Locke: Critical Assessments*. London: Routledge, 1991.

Morgan, Edmund. *The Gentle Puritan: A Life of Ezra Stiles, 1727–1795*. New York: Norton, 1962.

Morgan, Edmund S., ed. *Puritan Political Ideas*. Indianapolis: Bobbs-Merrill, 1965.

Morrison, Jeffrey H. *John Witherspoon and the Founding of the American Republic*. South Bend, IN: University of Notre Dame Press, 2005.

Muñoz, Vincent Phillip, *God and the Founders: Madison, Washington, and Jefferson*. Cambridge, Cambridge University Press: 2009.

Murphy, Andrew R. *Conscience and Community: Revisiting Toleration and Religious Dissent in Early Modern America*. University Park: Pennsylvania State University Press, 2001.

Nash, Gary B. *First City: Philadelphia and the Forging of Historical Memory*. Philadelphia, PA: University of Pennsylvania Press, 2002.

Neuhaus, Richard John. *The Public Square: Religion and Democracy in America*. Grand Rapids, MI: Eerdmans, 1986.

Nicole, Roger. *Moyse Amyraut: A Bibliography*. New York: Garland, 1981.

Noll, Mark A. *America's God: From Jonathon Edwards to Abraham Lincoln*. New York: Oxford University Press, 2002.

Noll, Mark A. *God and Race in American Politics: A Short History.* Princeton, NJ: Princeton University Press, 2010.

Noll, Mark A. "James Madison: From Evangelical Princeton to the Constitutional Convention." *Pro Rege* (December 1987), 7–9.

Noll, Mark A. and Harlow, Luke E., eds. *Religion and American Politics: From the Colonial Period to the Present.* New York, NY: Oxford University Press, 1990, 2007.

Nussbaum, Martha C. *Liberty of Conscience: In Defense of America's Tradition of Religious Equality.* New York, NY: Basic Books, 2008.

Oakley, Francis. "Christian Obedience and Authority, 1520–1550." In *The Cambridge History of Political Thought 1450–1700.* Cambridge: Cambridge University Press, 1991.

Oberman, Heiko A. *Luther: Man between God and the Devil.* New York: Image Books, 1992.

Oyer, John S. *Lutheran Reformers against Anabaptists.* The Hague: Baptist Standard Bearer, 2000.

Oxford Dictionary of National Biography. Oxford: Oxford University Press, 2004.

Parker, William Riley. *Milton: A Biography.* Oxford: Oxford University Press, 1996.

Peare, Catherine Owens. *William Penn: A Biography.* Ann Arbor: University of Michigan Press, 1966.

Perry, Ralph Barton. *Puritanism and Democracy.* New York: Harper Torchbooks, 1944.

Peterson, Merrill D., and Robert C. Vaughan, eds. *The Virginia Statute for Religious Freedom: Its Evolution and Consequences in American History.* Cambridge: Cambridge University Press,

Pfeffer, Leo. *Church, State and Freedom.* Boston: Beacon Press, 1953.

Pocock, J. G. A. *The Machiavellian Moment: Florentine Political Thought and the Atlantic Republican Tradition.* Princeton, N.J.: Princeton University Press, 1975.

Pointer, Richard W. *Protestant Pluralism and the New York Experience.* Bloomington: Indiana University Press, 1988.

Ragosta, John A. *Wellspring of Liberty: How Virginia's Religious Dissenters Helped Win the American Revolution and Secured Religious Liberty.* New York: Oxford University Press, 2010.

Remer, Gary. *Humanism and the Rhetoric of Toleration.* University Park: Pennsylvania State University Press, 1996.

Rich, George Eugene. *John Witherspoon: His Scottish Intellectual Background.* Ann Arbor: University Microfilms, 1964.

Robbins, Caroline. *The Eighteenth Century Commonwealthman.* Cambridge, Mass.: Harvard University Press, 1959.

Rossiter, Clinton. *The Political Thought of the American Revolution.* New York: Harcourt, Brace and World, 1963.

Rowe, Violet A. *Sir Henry Vane the Younger: A Study in Political and Administrative History.* London: Athlone Press, University of London, 1970.

Schaff, Philip. *Bibliotheca Symbolica Ecclesiæ Universalis: The Creeds of Christendom, with a History and Critical Notes.* New York: Harper & Brothers, 1887.

Schlesinger, Arthur, Jr. *The Imperial Presidency.* New York: Mariner Books, 2004.

Schneewind, J. B. *The Invention of Autonomy.* Cambridge: Cambridge University Press, 1998.

Scott, Jonathan. *England's Troubles: Seventeenth-Century English Political Instability in European Context.* Cambridge: Cambridge University Press, 2000.

Sedgwick, Theodore. *A Memoir of the Life of William Livingston.* New York: J. J. Harper, 1833.

Sell, Alan P. F. *John Locke and the Eighteenth Century Divines.* Cardiff: University of Wales Press, 1997.

Sehat, David. *The Myth of American Religious Freedom.* New York, NY: Oxford University Press, 2011.

Sensabugh, George F. *Milton in Early America.* Princeton, N.J.: Princeton University Press, 1964.

Shapiro, Barbara J. *Probability and Certainty in Seventeenth-Century England.* Princeton, N.J.: Princeton University Press, 1983.

Skinner, Quentin. *The Foundations of Modern Political Thought.* Vol. 2. *The Age of the Reformation.* Cambridge: Cambridge University Press, 1978.

Smith, Christian. *The Secular Revolution: Power, Interests, and Conflict in the Secularization of American Public Life.* Berkeley: University of California Press, 2003.

Southern, R. W. *Western Society and the Church in the Middle Ages.* New York: Penguin, 1990.

Stohlman, Martha Lou Lemmon. *John Witherspoon: Parson, Politician, Patriot.* Louisville, Ky.: Westminster John Knox Press, 1989.

Stokes, Anson Phelps, and Leo Pfeffer. *Church and State in the United States.* New York, NY: Harper and Row, 1950, 1954.

Sweeney, Kevin Michael. "River Gods and Related Minor Deities: The Williams Family and the Connecticut River Valley, 1637–1790." Ph.D. diss.,Yale University, 1986.

Tait, L. Gordon. *The Piety of John Witherspoon: Pew, Pulpit, and Public Forum.* Louisville, KY: Geneva Press, 2000.

U.S. Department of Justice. *The Secret Torture Memos: Bush Administration Memos on Torture as Released by the United States Department of Justice, April 16, 2009.* Rockville, MD: Arc Manor, 2009.

Vedder, Henry C. *Balthasar Hubmaier: The Leader of the Anabaptists.* New York: AMS Press, 1971.

Volkmar, Lloyd B. *Luther's Response to Violence.* New York: Vantage Press, 1974.

Waddington, George. *A History of the Reformation on the Continent.* London: Duncan and Malcom, 1841.

Ward, Frederick Robin. "The Early Influence of John Locke's Political Thought in England, 1689–1720." Ph.D. diss., University of California, Riverside, 1995.

Williams, George. *The Radical Reformation*. Kirksville, MO: Truman State University Press, 2000.

Wills, Gary. *Bomb Power: The Modern Presidency and the National Security State*. New York: Penguin Press, 2010.

Wilson, John, and Donald Drakeman, eds. *Church and State in American History: The Burden of Religious Pluralism*. 2nd ed. Boston, MA: Beacon Press, 1987.

Witte, John, Jr. *The Reformation of Rights: Law, Religion, and Human Rights in Early Modern Calvinism*. New York: Cambridge University Press, 2007.

Witte, John, Jr. *Religion and the American Constitutional Experiment: Essential Rights and Liberties*. Boulder, CO: Westview Press, 2000.

Wolterstorff, Nicholas. "Locke's Philosophy of Religion." In *The Cambridge Companion to Locke*, edited by Verya Chappell. New York: Cambridge University Press, 1994.

Wood, Gordon S. *The Radicalism of the American Revolution*. New York: Knopf, 1992.

Wood, Neal. *The Politics of Locke's Philosophy: A Social Study of "An Essay Concerning Human Understanding*. Los Angeles: University of California Press, 1983.

Woolhouse, Roger. *Locke: A Biography*. Cambridge: Cambridge University Press, 2007.

Woolhouse, Roger. "Locke's Theory of Knowledge." In *The Cambridge Companion to Locke*, edited by Verya Chappell. New York: Cambridge University Press, 1994.

Wright, William J. *Martin Luther's Understanding of God's Two Kingdoms: A Response to the Challenge of the Skeptics*. Grand Rapids, MI: Baker Academic, 2010.

Young, B. W. *Religion and Enlightenment in Eighteenth-Century England: Theological Debate from Locke to Burke*. Oxford: Clarendon Press, 1998.

Zagorin, Perez. *How the Idea of Religious Toleration Came to the West*. Princeton, NJ: Princeton University Press, 2005.

Zuckert, Michael P. *Natural Rights and the New Republicanism*. Princeton, NJ: Princeton University Press, 1998.

Zuckert, Michael P. *The Natural Rights Republic*. Notre Dame, IN: University of Notre Dame, 1996.

Index

American Revolution, xv, 117, 139, 162, 169, 184
   Baptist attitudes toward, 105–106, 109
   religious influences on, 80, 85–86, 137, 163–164
Amyraut, Moise, Huguenot theologian, 55–56
Anabaptists, xvii, 12, 17, 23, 25, 83, 116, 123, 181, 187–188
   English Baptists, influence on, 32–33, 44
   Influence of generally, 81
   Luther, connection with, 27–28, 30
   Netherlands, 28–29
   Peasant's Revolt, 25–26
   persecution of, 17–18, 25–27, 29–30
Anglican/s, 113, 126, 141, 143, 152, 174, 178, 183, 207, 214
   in American, 87–88, 102, 108–110
   as the established church, xvi, xviii, 5–6, 40, 79
   American Bishop dispute, 137–139, 141
   King's College dispute, 13, *112–114, 117, 120–124,* 209
   and the Puritans, 33
Arminian/s, 83–84, 95, 197
Ashcraft, Richard, 77, 198
Ashley/Shaftsbury, Lord, Lockes's employer, 87, 200

Backus, Isaac, American Baptist leader, 8, 13, 61, 86–87, 94–95, *101–113,* 175, 202–203
Bainton, Roland, 30
Baptist/s, xiii, xvi, xvii, 3, 6, 12, 152, 178, 193, 199
   American, xvi–xvii, 61, 62, 91–92, 95, 101–103, 106–108, 111–113, 116, 152, 174, 203
   church/state views, 34–36, 77, 83, 85–86, 130, 152
   Danbury Baptists, 147
   English Baptists' origins, 32–34, 189
   jailing of, in Virginia, xvi–xvii, 143
   Locke, John, influence on, 67, 70–71, 75–76, 78, 81, attitude towards, 87, 105–106
   Luther, use of, 38–39
   Milton, John, influence on, 40–42, 44, 46–47, 83
   pleas to King and parliament for religious liberty, 35–40
   soul liberty, 78
   Virginia Assessment Bill, opposition to, 109–111, 148, 178, 182, 211–212
   Vane, Henry, influence on, 68–69
   Williams, Roger, influence on, 68
baptism, xiv, 18, 21, 29, 33–34, 41, 102, 188
Barrow, Henry & the Barrowists, 33
Barry, John M., 193
Barton, David, 218

Bayle, Pierre, Huguenot theologian, 32, 84, 157, *159–162*, 164, 178, 214

Bailyn, Bernard, 89, 115, 120, 175

Beneke, Chris, 3, 178, 201

Bible/Scripture, 2, 5, 15, 17, 20, 30, 53, 159, 183
  authority of, 40, 42, 44, 64
  Holy Spirit, role in interpreting, 31, 66–67, 99
  Locke, John, use of, 66–67
  Madison, James, on interpreting, 145–147
  Penn, William, use of, 56–57
  obscurity of, 31, 38
  perspicuity of, 31, 38
  reading in public schools, 153, 156
  right to use and study, *see* right of private judgment
  translation of, 30–31
  Williams, Elisha, use of, 97–100

biblical interpretation, 2, 17, 20, 37–38, 99, 145, 148

Bishop, American, dispute, 137–139, 141

blasphemy, 150, 153, 156, 194

Boston, xiii, xv, xvii, 62, 92, 108, 180

Bradley, James, 85

Burke, Edmund, 163–164

Bush, President George W., 165, 166–167, 173

Bush, President George H.W., 165

Busher, Leonard, Baptist writer, *35–36*, 38–40, 44, 199

Calvin, John, xiv, 27, 159
  Castellio, dispute with, 29–30, 32, 188
  teachings, 95, 189

Calvinist/ism, 55, 81, 84, 96, 108, 118, 159, 174–175

Carolina Colony, 5, 87–91, 113, 162, 200

Casson, Douglas, 75, 197

Castellio, Sebastion, 12, *29–32*, 35–38, 44, 77, 82, 181, 188, 199

Catholic/s, xvii, 18, 27, 33, 45, 52, 70–72, 78, 88, 184, 192

Chapman, Alistar, 184

Charlemagne, Emperor, 158, 161

Charles I, King of England, 40, 50, 71

Charles II, King of England, 47, 49–51, 78, 118

Charles V, Emperor, 15, 16, 19–20, 185

Chauncy, Charles, leader of Reformed Dutch Church in America, 85

Chillingworth, William, author of *The Religion of Protestants*, 40–42, 44, 197

Clinton, President William, 165–166

Coffey, John, 6, 172

College of New Jersey, 135–136, 141, *see also*, Princeton University

Columbia University, 114

Congregationalist, xiv (defined), 85, 94, 101, 103

conscience, 1, 119, 138, 154, 160, 163, 168, 174, 179, 182, 194
  Backus, Isaac, on, 102, 106–107, 113
  Baptist view of, 34–35, 37, 110–113
  Diet of Speyer, assertion at, 16–18, 27, 40
  erring, xiv, 74, 160
  Livingston, William, on, 128–129
  Locke, John, on, 66, *74–79*, 81, 83, 85
  Luther, Martin, on, 19–20, 186
  Madison, James, on, 142–144, 146, 151
  medieval conception of, 20
  Mather, Cotton, on, 92
  Milton, John, on, 40, 42, 45, 47, 70, 76, 191
  Penn, William, on, 56–57, 60, 62–63, 65
  Vane, Henry, on, 68–70
  Williams, Elisha, on, 97, 113
  Williams, Roger, on, 176, 193
  Witherspoon, John, on, 137,
  rights, liberty, or freedom of, xiv, xv, 1, 5, 13, 17, 18

Constitution of Carolina, 5, 87–88

Constitution of Connecticut, 111–112

Constitution of Massachusetts, 107

Constitution of Pennsylvania, 87

Constitution of the American
    Prebyterian church, 134–135,
    149–151, 154

Constitution of the United States, 61–62,
    94, 108, 117, 134–136, 147–148, 154,
    170

Constitution of Virginia, 143–144, 167

Constitutional Convention, federal, 62,
    108, 117, 134, 178

Craycraft, Kenneth R., 213

Curry, Thomas, 5, 173–174, 183

Darwinism, 164

deist/ism, 14, 94, 112, 119, 124, 126, 140,
    142, 176

democracy/democratic, xiv, xv, 40, 161, 163

disestablishment, xv, xvii-xviii, 1, 63,
    89–90
    baptist advocacy of, 86–87, 111–113
    in Connecticut, 111–112
    definitions of, 100, 152–153, 174, 176,
        182, 194, 212
    Enlightenment connections, 113, 115,
        116–117, 131
    First Amendment connection, 13
    explanations for, 1–5, 89–90, 152–154,
        156, 173, 174–179
    Milton, John, advocacy of, 47, 83
    in New Hampshire, 111
    religious causes of, 6–7, 12–14, 53–54,
        80, 116, 131–132, 143, 154, 159, 181
    religious liberty, connection with,
        143–144, 147
    in Vermont, 111
    in Virginia, 62, 109–111, 113, 148
    also see, establishment

Democrat/ic, 165, 169

Department of Justice, 166, 217

Dickens, A.G., 45

dissenting Protestants/ism, 1, 23, 48,
    159, 162–164, 165, 180–181
    (defined)
    in America, xviii, 48, 53, 101, 111–113,
        130–132, 152, 154, 156–157
    church/state views of, 7, 13, 29, 44,
        87–90, 125, 128
    Enlightenment, relationship with,
        14, 116
    Locke, John, influence on, 54, 60,
        66–71, 75, 78–79, 81–85
    Penn, William, influence on, 56, 60

Dreisbach, Daniel, 176–177

Dworetz, Steven, 79–80, 86, 200

Edict of Nantes, 47, 50, 157–158, 169

Edwards, Jonathan, American Calvinist
    preacher, xiv, 13, 95

Elizabeth I, Queen, 33

England, xv, xviii, 68, 99, 105, 181, 201
    Anglican establishment in, 35–36, 41,
        44, 122, 125, 142
    Enlightenment in, 14
    colonial religious policy, 11
    reformation in, 28
    religious liberty advocacy in, 39, 78, 93,
        118–119
    the Restoration, 47, 49
    toleration in, 6, 8, 32–33, 50–52, 172

Enlightenment, the, xvii, 1–4, 14, 46,
    92, 109
    disestablishment, role in, 2–4, 12,
        53–54, 82, 89, 91, 174–175
    elite thought, 5, 7, 109–110, 113, 183
    relationship to religious thought, 13,
        81, 98, 116–117, 120, 128, 131, 140,
        142, 146,
    religiously skeptical version, 82–84,
        91, 93–94, 115, 124, 142, 163–164,
        172–173, 175, 199
    Scottish, 136, 210

episcopacy, 39, 40, 138–139, 141
epistemology, 58, 60, 64, 73, 79, 82, 98,
    104–105, 197
establishment of religion,
    in Connecticut, 111–112
    at King's College, 114–117, 122
    in Massachusetts, xiii-xv
    in New Hampshire, 111
    in Virginia, xvi-xvii, 109–111, 113
    Williams', Elisha, definition of, 100
    See also disestablishment
Estep, William, 3, 178

First Amendment, 4, 13, 134, 142, 144,
    152–154, 156, 173–175, 177–178
Fisher, Hugh, Presbyterian Minister in
    South Carolina, 91
Fox, George, Quaker founder, 53, 56
Fox, John, martyrologist, 5, 183
Furley, Benjamin, Quaker friend of
    Locke, 52–53, 84, 194

German higher idealism, 164
Gill, Anthony, 9–12
Gordon, Thomas, co-author of the
    Independent Whig, 93, 119–120, 141,
    206–207
Great Awakening, First, 5, 13, 90, 94–96,
    102, 115, 154
Great Awakening, Second, 90
Green, Steven K., 194, 213, 215–216
Greenawalt, Kent, 213,
Grotius, Hugo, Dutch Protestant legal
    writer, 84, 89, 197, 216

Hall, Timothy L., 193
Hamburger, Philip, 115, 176–177, 213
Helwys, Thomas, Baptist writer, *35–38*,
    40, 69, 199
Henry, Patrick, xv, 109, 147
    Virginia religious assessments bill, 109,
    135, 144–145, 182

heretic/heresy, 19, 20, 22–23, 26–30, 46,
    60, 70–71
    seditious heresy, 25–27, 72
Hobbes, Thomas, 59, 65–66, 75
Hollywood, 164
Holmes, Oliver Wendell, 204–205
Holt, Mark, 184
Hubmaier, Balthasar, Anabaptist writer,
    27–28
Huguenots, xvii, 49, 158
Hutchinson, Anne, 68
Hutson, James, 176–177, 217–218

James II, King of England, 49–51
Jefferson, Thomas, xv, 4, 84, 113, 144, 148,
    167–168, 174, 177
    Danbury letter re Wall of Separation,
    147–148
Jesus Christ, 58, 62, 85, 98, 110, 150, 166
Jew/s xvii, 28, 77, 78, 88, 129
Jewish, 167
Jordan, W.K., 172
Justinian Code, 161

Kaplan, Benjamin, 172, 181
Karlstadt, Andreas, Wittenberg radical,
    23
Kerry, John, 167

Lambert, Frank, 174
Laud, Archbishop William, 40–41
law of nature. *See* natural law/law of
    nature
Lecler, Joseph, 172, 186
Levy, Leonard, 174, 183
Limborch, Philip van, Dutch theologian,
    82, 84
Livingston, John Henry, American
    church leader, 85
Livingston, William, New York lawyer,
    xvii, 8, 13, 132
    background, 118–120, 206–207

American Whig, 139

Bishop dispute, 139

Independent Reflector, 114, 117,
   119–120, 121–129, 131

King's College dispute, 13, 114–116,
   120–124, 138, 204, 206–207, 209

religious views, 125–128

religious liberty views, 128–131, 207

Locke, John, xii, 3, 61, *63–90,* 157–165,
   171–172, 214, 216

and the Carolina constitution, 5,
   87–88

contacts with Protestant dissenters, 29,
   32, 67–72, 199, 201

early church/state views, 63–72, 195

*Essay Concerning Human
   Understanding,* 72–75, 104, 192,
   197–198

In Holland, 49–54, 194

influence in America, 79–90, 91,
   95–99, 101, 118–120, 129–132, 140,
   176

Letter on Toleration, 75–79

Penn, William, contacts with, 12–13,
   51–56, 58–59

*Reflections upon the Roman
   Commonwealth,* 64–65

Two Tracts of Government, 64–66, 71

use by Protestant dissenters, 102,
   104–113, 203

Louis XIV, King of France, 49

Luther, Martin, 15–16, 20, 181, 185, 200

*Address to the Christian Nobility of the
   German Nation, 20–22*

early views on church and state, 20–25,
   186–187

influence of, 12, 18, 27–31, 35–38, 89,
   105, 116, 158, 182

influence on Locke, John, 77, 81–82,
   199

influence on Milton, John, 43–44, 46

Invocavit Sermons, 23–24

on the Peasant's War, the Anabaptists,
   and seditious heresy, 25–27

on the Priesthood of all Believers, 2, 8

*Secular Authority: To What Extent
   Should it be Obeyed,* 22–23

on the Two Kingdoms, 22, 27, 35–36,
   43, 77, 81, 105, 186

Lutheran/ism, 157

in America, 123

church/state positions, 23, 27, 31

princes, 15, 17–18

states, 17

worship or rituals, 16–17

Machiavellian moment, 89

Madison, James, xv- xvii, 8, 13, 61–62, 116,
   135, 156, 168, 178

church/state views, 134, *141–148,* 205,
   211–214, 216

Creator, philosophical use of,
   167–168

Federal Constitutional convention,
   134–135, 154–155, 156

early religious fervency, 142–143

Federalist 51, 123

Livingstone, William, connections
   with, 123, 131,

Memorial and Remonstrance, 109–111,
   146–148, 150, 167

opposition to Patrick Henry's religious
   assessments bill, 135, 144–146, 153,
   182, 205

at Princeton, 141–142

Virginia Statute of Religious Freedom,
   109

Virginia constitution, passage of,
   143–144

Marsden, George, xi, 173, 215

Marshall, John, 82–85, 172–173, 199

Maryland, xiii, xv

Mason, George, Virginian politician,
   143, 167

Massachusetts, xiii, xiv, 4, 10, 11, 35, 61, 68, 94, 95, 103, 107–108, 153, 156

Mather, Cotton, American Puritan divine, 92–93

McLoughlin, William, 107, 193, 203

Mayhew, Jonathon, American minister, 94

McGrath, Alister, E. 2–3

Meacham, Jon, 176

Mennonites, 28, 34–36, 82, 152, 181, 189

Methodists, xvi, xviii, 112

Melanchthon, Philipp, Lutheran theologian, 16–18, 26–27

Middle Colonies, xiii, xviii, 4, 5, 113, 132, 173, 177

Mill, John Stuart, 19th century British philosopher, 164

Miller, Perry, 61

Milton, John, ix, 3, 8, 12, 54, 60, 76–77, 181
    Areopagitica, 39–40
    Christian Doctrine, 46, 190–191
    contacts with Protestant dissenters, 41–42, 44, 61
    Considerations Touching the Likeliest Means to Remove Hirelings Out of the Church, 47
    influence of, 47–48, 76–77, 83–84, 130–131
    Paradise Lost, 39, 48
    A Treatise of Civil Power in Ecclesiastical Causes, 40, 42–46

Moore, J.T., 198

moral philosophy, 142

Mormon, 166, 215

Munoz, Phil, 162, 178, 212, 214

Muntzer, Thomas, radical reformer, 25, 181

Murphy, Andrew, 75, 77, 194–195

Murton, John, Baptist author, 37–39, 42, 44–45, 48, 60, 68–69, 78, 83

Muslims/Turks, 15–16, 28, 30, 77–78

natural law/law of nature, 54, 58, 63, 78, 80–81, 86, 153, 157, 164, 177, 216

Napoleon, Emperor, 161

Native Americans, 88

Netherlands/Holland, 28–29, 32–34, 36–37, 49, 51, 82, 90, 118, 125, 194, 189

new light/old light controversy, 13, 94–96, 102, 119

New England, 13, 173, 176–178
    colonial church/state arrangements, xiii–xvi, 60, 89, 101–103, 107, 123, 162
    disestablishment in, 5, 111, 113, 148, 153, 162

New Netherlands, 5

New York, xiii, xvii, 5, 8, 62, 113, 114, 142

Noll, Mark, ix–xi, 173, 201

Nussbaum, Martha, 176, 193

Obama, President Barak, 165–166, 169

Owen, John, Puritan theologian, 55–56, 64

Paine, Thomas, 5, 156

Peasant's War/Revolt, 23, 25–26

Penn, William, ix, xvii, 3, 8, 12, 29, 76, 96–97, 103–106
    background of, 54–56, 192
    The Great Case of Liberty of Conscience, 52, 54, *56–60,* 81–82
    Locke, connections with, 51–53, 64, 75, 78, 87, 89–90
    influence in America, 5, 53, *60–63,* 113, 135, 194, 201, 207
    influence in England, 51, 52, 54, 78, 84, 192
    Pennsylvania, founder of, 5, 51, 63

Pennsylvania, xvii-xviii, 5, 51, 53–54, 60, 62, 133
    constitution of, 62–63, 87–88, 162
    example of religious freedom to other colonies, 62–63, 78, 89–90, 109, 123, 142, 207

petition/s, 7, 35, 109–111, 148
  Great Baptist, 109–110
  Presbyterian, 109–110
Pfeffer, Leo, 173
Philadelphia, xiii, xvii, 4, 54, 62, 133,
  134–136, 142, 148, 155
Pocock, J.G.A., 89
Presbyterian/s, 39, 91, 92, 109–111, 113,
  119, 122–123, 135–136, 141, 207
  New National Constitution, 134,
    148–152, 154
  Virginian, xvii, 145, 178
  See also Puritans, Presbyterian
Priesthood of all Believers, 1–2, 8, 20,
  77, 159
  Luther, Martin, on, 21–22, 29, 31, 31, 77
Princeton University, 119, 131, 135–136,
  140–142, *also see,* College of New
  Jersey
private judgment. *See* right of private
  judgment
Protest of the Princes, 16–18
Protestant/s/ism, xviii, 1, 14, 28, 33, 45,
  48, 55, 100, 131, 148
  Bible, attitude towards, 37, 40–43, 86,
    96, 98, 191
  church/state views, 158–159, 162–165,
    167–170, 172, 174, 176–178, 183, 201
  definitions of, 1, 17, 180–181
  divines or ministers, 79, 84, 93
  dissenting. *See* dissenting Protestants/
    ism
  Enlightenment, attitude towards, 98,
    104, 113, 116–117, 124, 131, 198, 201,
    205, 214
  history and historians of, 5, 15, 17,
    39–46, 48
  king/ruler, 51, 122
  magisterial, 23, 29, 48, 74, 125, 146,
    154, 157, 163
  morality, civil, 153, 164, 194, 216
  persecution by, 18, 37, 74

princes, 27, 44
radical, 51, 154, 181
religious liberty, 106, 108, 122
  See also Locke, John, dissenting
    Protestant influences
Protestant Episcopal Church, 152
Protestant Reformation, 1–3, 14, 15, 16,
  18, 32, 45–46, 110, 131, 154, 172, 181,
  186, 206
Pufendorf, Samuel, Lutheran legal
  thinker, 81, *157–158,* 159–162,
  165–166, 168, 213, 216
  The Law of Nature and Nations, 157
  *Of the Nature and Qualifications of
    Religion in Reference to Civil Society,*
  157–158
Puritans, xiv, 3, 107, 130, 180–181
  American, xiv, xv, 35, 68, 74, 80, 87,
    92, 107, 113, 159, 162, 174–175, 178,
    180, 203
  and the Bible, 92
  Church order and democracy, xiv
  Church/state views, 54, 107, 157, 162,
    174, 177, 181
  Congregational/ist, xiv, 94, 101–103,
    138
  English, 33, 35, 54, 55
  Independents, xiv, 3, 41, 64, 68
  Locke, influence, 64, 80–81, 87, 107, 201
  Presbyterian, xiv, xvii, xviii, 39, 45,
    55, 85
  Right of Private Judgment, 92–93, 95

Quakers, xiii, xvi, xvii, 43, 45, 51–52, 53,
  55–57, 60, 64, 78, 83, 102, 192
  American influence, 5–6, 61, 78, 88,
    102, 110, 123, 147, 152, 174
  civil morality views, 194
  Lantern discussion group, 82
  Locke, John, relation to, 64, 72, 75,
    82, 84
  Penn, William, 3, 12, 51, 52–56, 178

Radical Reformation, 181

Ragosta, John, 109, 111, 178–179, 211–212

Reagan, President Ronald, 165, 174

reformation. *See* Protestant Reformation

religion/s, 13–14, 112 (defined), 167–168
(defined), 175–176, 181, 184
 in early America, 13, 61, 163–164, 183
 in writing history, 1–6, 9–12, 184
 internal nature of true religion, 76–78,
  97, 107, 110, 130, 145–147
 plurality of, 71, 115, 175
 things indifferent, 64, 72
 use of force in, 34–37, 42, 44, 59
 wars of, 50, 166, 215

religious freedom/liberty, xv–xvii, 1, 5, 7,
 10, 50, 162, 169, 173, 193
 as American myth, 153, 175, 176, 179, 213
 Anabaptists on, 28, 34
 Backus, Isaac, on, 89, 102–103,
  105–108, 113
 Baptists on, 34–37, 41, 110–113,
  178–179
 Castellio, Sebastian, on, 29
 Livingstone, William, on, 118, 120,
  124, *128–130*, 206
 Locke, John, on, 49, 52–54, 64, 70, 73,
  75–76, 78, 82, 85, 88–89
 Luther, Martin, on, 20–27, 186–187
 Madison, James, on, 13, 109, 135,
  141–144, 146, 151, 211–212
 Milton, John, on, 41, 45, 47–48, 50,
  83, 191
 Penn, William, on, *52–56*, 59, 60, 63, 78
 pragmatic arguments for, 10–12, 62, 158
 Protestant concepts of, 15, 18, 32, 154,
  163, 170, 172, 181
 religious arguments for, 12–14, 28, 32
 Williams, Elisha, on, 96–101
 Williams, Roger, on, 41, 61–62, 193
 Witherspoon, John, on, 135, 137–141

republic of letters, 82–85

republicanism, 88, 163, 176–177, 206

Rhode Island, xiv, 5, 10, 41, *60–62*, 68, 88,
 138, 139, 162, 168, 193, 196

right of private judgment, xviii, 1–3, 4,
 95, 132, 157, 171, 178, 182
 as theological principle, 45, 50, 57, 68,
  70, 76, 85, 91–94, 95, 98, 100, 106,
  129, 138–140
 as Enlightenment principle, 50, 54,
  76–77, 91–93, 94
 meld of religious and Enlightenment
  ideas, 76, 80, 86, 91, 95, 113, 116,
  124–130, 145, 148
 as a national American principle, 135,
  149–151

right/s, 58–59
 animal, 161
 civil, 170, 62, 88, 163, 165, 170
 of conscience, 13, 18, 27, 77, 107, 128,
  138, 154
 of Englishman, 101, 105, 123
 fundamental, 143
 human, 57, 120, 147, 161, 170
 inalienable, 112, 167–169
 individual, xiv, 50, 65, 89, 97, 104–105,
  116, 144, 158–159, 161, 168
 of God, 56–57, 96, 99, 103
 natural, 78, 81, 86–87, 98, 105–106,
  110–111, 140, 157, 164, 170, 216
 religious, 18

Robinson, John, Pilgrim leader, 35

Romney, Mitt, 166

Rousseau, J., 5, 159

Sattler, Michael, Anabaptist writer, 27–28

Schleitheim confession, 28

Scotland, 14, 32, 137, 139, 157, 162

secular, 167, 169, 178, 215
 authorities, 26, 28, 205
 arguments for religious freedom, 39,
  72, 84, 94, 156–157, 159–161
 arguments for marketplace of ideas,
  113, 115, 117

Enlightenment, 3, 172–173, 175, 199
jurisdiction, 21, 72
thinkers, 93, 129, 152, 170, 175–176
secularism, 4, 152, 170, 177, 213
secularist, 14, 152, 167
secularization/izing, 2, 54, 164, 167, 181, 214, 215
seditious heresy, 25–27, 72
Sehat, David, 175, 213
separation of church and state, xiv, 47, 63, 109, 115, 160, 163, 167, 169–170, 176
Servetus, Michael, anti-trinitarian physician, 29
Simons, Menno, founder of Mennonites, 28–29
Skinner, Quentin, 6, 196
slaves/slavery, xvi, 58, 90, 124, 142, 153
Smith, Christian, 214
Smith, Josiah, Presbyterian minister in South Carolina, 92–93
Smyth, John, Baptist leader/writer, 33–34, 35, 37, 69, 199
South/Southern Colonies, xiii, xv, 5, 89, 113, 132, 173
Spain, 11, 99
Speyer, Diets of, *15–18*, 22, 24, 40, 42, 44, 46, 48, 92
Stiles, Ezra, Congregational minister and President of Yale, 126, 138–140
Stokes, Anson Phelps, 173, 182
Stubbe, Henry, Locke friend, 67, 70–71, 77, 83, 196
Sturgion, John, Baptist writer, 78
Sullivan, Winnifred F., 175
Sunday/Sabbath laws, 108, 153, 156, 194, 203, 213, 215
Supreme Court of the United States, 61, 136, 167, 173, 177, 194, 204, 213

Ten Commandments, 167–168, 213
terror/terrorists, 161, 169
Thomas, Clarence, 213

torture, 9, 161, 170
Trenchard, John, co-author of *Independent Whig,* 93, 119–120, 141, 206–207
Twisck, Pieter, Anabaptist writer, 34–37
Two Kingdoms Doctrine, 22, 27, 35–36, 43, 77, 81, 105, 186, 199

University of Virginia, 113, 117

Valla, Lorenzo, Italian humanist, 186
Vane, Henry, Protestant political leader, 61, 67–71, 82, 83, 195–196
Vane, Walter, brother of Henry, 67, 71
Virginia, 173, 205
colonial church/state arrangement, xv–xvii, 10–11, 141–143
constitution and religious freedom provision, 143–144, 167–168
disestablishment, 5, 113, 153, 178–179, 212
dispute over Patrick Henry's Religious Assessments bill, 108–111, 135, 144–146, 148, 182
Voltaire, 5, 159
vouchers, school, 166

War Powers Act, 165
Ward, Frederick Robin, 200
Washington, George, xv, 134, 145, 149, 162, 178, 212, 214
Westminster Confession of Faith, 92, 149, 151
Westphalia, Peace of, 50
Williams, Elisha, 3, 8, 13, 108, 112–113, 116, 130, 175, 178, 202
background of, 94–95
influence of, 102, 105–106
Seasonable Plea for the Liberty of Conscience, 96–101, 102–105, 107, 118

Williams, Roger, 5, 105, 108, 175, 193, 202
  Bloudy Tenet, 39
  church/state views, 53, 60, 74, 78, 160,
    174, 176, 193
  influence of, 60–61, 68, 83, 105, 108,
    174, 176, 193
  Milton, contacts with, 41–42, 45
  Rhode Island founder, 48, 68, 196
William and Mary, College of, 51, 136, 141
Williamsburg, xiii, xv, xvi, xvii
Winthrop, John, American Puritan
  leader, 68
Witherspoon, John, 8, 13, 142, 154–155,
  156, 162, 181, 206, 209–210, 216
  background, 135–136

American Revolution, 136–138
Anglican Bishop dispute, 138–141
drafting of the Presbyterian constitu-
  tion, 133–135, 149–151
Lectures on Moral Philosophy, 140, 151
Witte, John, 174–175
Wood, Gordon, 115, 163, 175
Worms, Diet of, 15, 17, *18–20,* 185

Yale College, 13, 95, 118–119, 122, 126, 136,
  138, 207

Zagorin, Perez, 172, 188
Zuckert, Michael, xii, 80–81, 201, 216
Zwickau prophets, Wittenberg radicals, 26